1001 Freundschaft
Von Menschen im Oman und in Deutschland

1001 Friendships
Stories about People in Oman and Germany

1001 صداقة
لأناس من عُمان والمانيا

Verlag Donata Kinzelbach
www.kinzelbach-verlag.de

Herausgeberinnen und Copyright: Gabriele Brähler und Natascha Plankermann
Vervielfältigung auch auszugsweise, nur mit schriftlicher Genehmigung der Herausgeberinnen.

Druckerei Theissen Medien Gruppe

ISBN 978-3-942490-45-0

Sultan Qaboos ibn Said, 1974

Inhalt Contents

Wirtschaft /
Economy

Kultur und Medien /
Culture and Media

Religion und Erziehung / Religion and Education

Wissenschaft und Gesundheit /
Science and Health

Gesellschaft und friedlicher Austausch /
Society and Friendly Exchange

Über dieses Buch

Wir erzählen in drei Sprachen Geschichten besonderer Beziehungen zwischen den Menschen in Oman und Deutschland – 1001 Freundschaften sind es sicher, wenn nicht mehr …

Ein Freundespaar zeigt unser Titel: Khalid Alfahdi und Steffen Sauer, den er bei seinem Studium in Deutschland kennengelernt hat.

Wir haben uns entschieden, die Artikel in voller Länge in Englisch und Deutsch zu veröffentlichen, damit dieses Buch handlich bleibt. Mit der jeweils vorangestellten Kurzfassung möchten wir der arabischen Sprache einen besonderen Stellenwert einräumen.

About this book

We tell stories in three languages of special relationships between the people of Oman and Germany – 1001 Friendships at least, if not more …

Our cover shows a pair of friends: Khalid Alfahdi and Steffen Sauer, whom he met during his studies in Germany.

We have decided to publish the stories in full length in English and German for convenience. The abstracts preceding each story reflect the importance we place on Arabic.

Mit großer Freude präsentiere ich dieses Buch, von dem ich mit Gewissheit sagen kann, dass es den Leser mit neuen Fakten über den Oman bereichern sowie sein Verständnis über die exzellenten Beziehungen zwischen dem Oman und Deutschland erweitern wird.

Die Beziehungen zwischen dem Sultanat von Oman und der Bundesrepublik Deutschland blicken auf eine lange Geschichte zurück. Diese begannen im siebzehnten Jahrhundert, als erste deutsche Reisende das Land besuchten. Seit diesem Zeitpunkt wurden die bilateralen Beziehungen auf politischer und sozialer Ebene intensiviert und vertieft.

Dieses außergewöhnliche Buch wirft das Licht auf genau diese Beziehung, zwischen den Menschen aus dem Sultanat von Oman und Deutschland, in den verschiedensten Bereichen der Wirtschaft, der Bildung, der Gesundheit, der Kultur, des Tourismus, der Filmproduktion, der Kunst und nicht zuletzt einer Lebensfreundschaft.

Anhand von Berichten aus der Sicht von unterschiedlichen omanischen und deutschen Erzählern konnte ich erleben, wie reale Modelle der Zusammenarbeit, Konzepte der Freundschaft, des Friedens, des Respekts und der Toleranz entstanden sind.

Im Jahr 2020 wird das Sultanat von Oman sein goldenes Jubiläum, die fünfzigjährige Thronbesteigung Seiner Majestät zelebrieren und die Bundesrepublik Deutschland 31 Jahre der Wiedervereinigung feiern. Darum glaube ich fest daran, dass dieses Buch neue Brücken der Kooperation aufbauen wird. Es ist ein Beispiel dafür, wie soziale und kulturelle Kommunikation zwischen den Menschen im 21. Jahrhundert aussehen könnte.

I.E. Frau Lyutha Sultan Al-Mughairy
Botschafterin des Sultanats von Oman
In der Bundesrepublik Deutschland

I am greatly pleased to present this book, which I am confident will both contribute to the reader's knowledge and enhance understanding of the excellent relations between Oman and Germany.

The contacts between the Sultanate of Oman and the Federal Republic of Germany have a long and rich history. It began as long ago as the seventeenth century when several German travelers visited Oman. Since that time, the relationship between the two countries has strengthened and deepened not just or solely on a government-to-government basis but on a people-to-people basis.

This extraordinary book reveals tellingly the varied nature of the relationship, which encompasses dialogue and cooperation between the Omani and German peoples in fields such as business, education, health, culture, tourism, film-making, religious tolerance, arts and, not least, friendships for life.

Through the tales told by many Oman and German storytellers, I have learnt about lives lived and ideas advanced to create models of cooperation among peoples in which the concepts of friendship, peace, respect and tolerance are paramount.

As the Sultanate looks forward to celebrating its golden jubilee in the year 2020, while in the same year Germany will celebrate the 30th anniversary of German reunification, I trust that this book will open additional opportunities to enhance the contact and cooperation between Oman and Germany. This book demonstrates how a relationship like that between the Omani and German peoples can offer a model for cultural and social communication between nations and peoples in the 21st century.

H.E. Lyutha Sultan Al-Mughairy
Ambassador of the Sultanate of Oman
to the Federal Republic of Germany

Seit einigen Jahren erfreut sich das Sultanat wachsender Beliebtheit bei Reisenden aus Deutschland. Dass die Internationale Tourismus-Börse (ITB) in Berlin das Sultanat Oman als Partnerland für das Jahr 2020 auserkoren hat, unterstreicht die Bedeutung des Landes für die weltweite Reisebranche. So verwundert es nicht, dass inzwischen eine stattliche Anzahl deutschsprachiger Reiseführer vorliegt.

Mit dem vorliegenden Werk erweitern Natascha Plankermann und Gabriele Brähler die Literatur zu Oman um ein wichtiges und neuartiges Element. Das Buch spannt thematisch einen weiten Bogen und beleuchtet dabei die Vielfalt und Tiefe der deutsch-omanischen Beziehungen weit jenseits touristischer Aspekte. Dabei stehen in erster Linie zeitgenössische Akteure im Mittelpunkt, Menschen aus Deutschland und Oman. Ihre persönlichen Erlebnisse und Erfahrungen, ihre individuelle Geschichte der Begegnung beider Länder, vermitteln anschauliche Einblicke in das moderne Sultanat Oman, und lassen dadurch seine Geschichte, Kultur, Wirtschaft und Gesellschaft lebendig werden.

Dieses Buch beschreibt beispielhaft, wie Menschen aus verschiedenen Kulturkreisen in gegenseitigem Respekt zueinander finden und Brücken bauen, dabei das Fundament für Frieden und Freundschaft zwischen Völkern und Staaten legen. Mehr denn je stehen die hervorragenden deutsch-omanischen Beziehungen modellhaft für eine Welt der Zusammenarbeit und Verständigung. In Zeiten wie der unseren macht ein solches Buch Mut.

S.E. Thomas F. Schneider
Botschafter der Bundesrepublik Deutschland
im Sultanat Oman

The Sultanate has been enjoying great popularity with travellers from Germany for a few years now. The choice by the International Tourism Fair in Berlin to select Oman as partner country for 2020 underlines the importance of the country for the global tourism sector.

With this book Natascha Plankermann and Gabriele Brähler have added an important and novel element to literature about Oman. The book covers a wide spectrum of topics and sheds light on the diversity and depth of German-Omani relationships beyond aspects of tourism. It mainly focusses on contemporary players, people from Germany and Oman. Their personal experiences and their individual stories of encounters in both countries give a vivid insight into the modern Sultanate of Oman, and bring to life its history, culture, economy and society.

The book demonstrates in an exemplary manner how people from different cultural backgrounds can come together with mutual respect for one another and build bridges, thereby laying the basis for peace and friendship between peoples and states. More than ever the excellent German-Omani relationship stands as a model for a world of cooperation and understanding. In times like ours such a book gives hope.

H.E. Thomas F. Schneider
Ambassador of the Federal Republic of Germany
To the Sultanate of Oman

Kaffeetisch neben einem Lagerfeuer in der Wüste.
Coffee table next to a campfire in the desert.

Auf eine Tasse Kaffee (tasa qahwa)

Just a Cup of Coffee (tasa qahwa)

Wie Omaner und Deutsche einander näher kamen – ein Blick in die Geschichte

How Omanis and Germans became close – a look at the history

دعوة على فنجان قهوة
كيف اقترب العُمانيون والألمان من بعضهم البعض ـ نظرة على التاريخ

يرتبط العُمانيون والألمان بأشياء أكثر مما يعرفه معظم الناس في كلا البلدين. يعطي برونو كايزر، رئيس الجمعية الألمانية العُمانية منذ فترة طويلة، رؤية عن تاريخ هذه الصداقة بين البلدين. يتعلم الناس في العديد من المجالات من بعضهم البعض ويتبادلون المعرفة والخبرة. وقد قدمت الشركات الألمانية منذ الستينات مساهمتها الفعالة في تطوير البنية التحتية العُمانية. الجامعة الالمانية للتكنولوجيا في عُمان هي الجامعة الألمانية الوحيدة في شبه الجزيرة العربية وتقوم بتدريب الطلاب منذ عام 2007م.

Kaffeekannen schmücken ein Tor in Maskat. Eine Tasse Kaffee zu reichen ist eine Willkommensgeste – im Oman ebenso wie in Deutschland.
Coffee pots decorate a gate in Maskat. Serving a cup of coffee is a welcome gesture – in Oman as well as in Germany.

Omaner und Deutsche verbindet mehr als die meisten Menschen beider Länder wissen. Bruno Kaiser, langjähriger Präsident der Deutsch-Omanischen Gesellschaft, gibt einen Einblick in die Geschichte dieser Völkerfreundschaft.

Deutsche und Omaner nutzen unbewusst die gleichen Wörter, jeden Tag, etwa wenn sie eine Tasse Kaffee (tasa qahwa) trinken... So nah wie die Sprachen, sind sich auch viele Menschen dieser beiden Völker, die rund 7000 Kilometer voneinander entfernt leben. Eine Entfernung, die heute auch mithilfe sozialer Medien und Apps für die Übertragung von Sprache in Sekundenbruchteilen überbrückt wird – täglich irgendwo zwischen Maskat und München.

Das hat viele Gründe, vor allem aber diesen: Deutschland genießt im Oman hohes Ansehen. Nicht allein, weil Herrscher Sultan Qaboos ibn Said seit den 1970er Jahren einen Wohnsitz in Garmisch-Partenkirchen hat (siehe dazu auch Seiten 194 bis 201). Bruno Kaiser, langjähriger Präsident der Deutsch-Omanischen Gesellschaft, gibt einen Einblick in die jüngste Geschichte der Verbindung beider Länder: „Als Sultan Qaboos 1970 die Regierungsgewalt im

There is more that connects Omanis and Germans than most people from either country know. Bruno Kaiser, who has been President of the German-Omani Association for many years, presents a short history of the friendship between these two nations.

Germans and Omanis unknowingly use the same words every day; for example, when they drink a cup of coffee (Tasse Kaffee – tasa qahwa). It's not just the languages that are similar, so too are many members of both peoples, which live around 7,000 kilometres apart. It is a distance that is bridged today by social media and apps that allow communication to happen in a split second, every day somewhere between Muscat and Munich.

There are several reasons for the close connection, the main one being that Germany is held in high esteem in Oman. Even Oman's ruler, Sultan Qabus ibn Said, has maintained a residence in Garmisch-Partenkirchen since the 1970s (for more, see Page 194 to 201). Bruno Kaiser, who has been President of the German-Omani Association for many years, provides a look at the history of the relationship between the two countries: "When Sultan Qabus succeeded his father as the ruler of the Sultanate, he had

Festlich geschmückt für den Tag der Deutschen Einheit: die deutsche Botschaft in Maskat, eröffnet 2017.
Festively decorated for the German Reunification Day: the German Embassy in Muscat, opened in 2017.

Sultanat von seinem Vater übernahm, hatte er ein Land zu modernisieren, in dem die Menschen jahrzehntelang abgeschottet gelebt hatten. Dennoch war es nicht frei von äußeren Einflüssen geblieben, die auch für Unruhe sorgten. So benötigte der junge Sultan etwa noch fünf Jahre, bis er einen Aufstand in der Provinz Dhofar durch ein Friedensabkommen beenden konnte. Konsequent erneuerte er Oman schon in den ersten Jahren seiner Regentschaft nach innen und öffnete das Sultanat nach außen. In solchem Kontext ist die Aufnahme diplomatischer Beziehungen mit der Bundesrepublik Deutschland 1972 zu sehen. Interessant ist in diesem Zusammenhang, dass die ersten westdeutschen Diplomaten mit ihrer ‚Botschaft' im Camp Dursait der Firma Hochtief untergebracht waren. Die Firma war seit Ende der 60er Jahre im Zuge des Ausbaus der Infrastruktur im Sultanat mit dem Bau von Häfen beschäftigt."

a land to reform where the people had been isolated for decades. That didn't mean that it wasn't free of external influences, some of which caused unrest. Thus, the young Sultan needed another five years until he could end an uprising in the Dhofar province by means of a peace treaty. Immediately in the first years of his reign, he continuously transformed Oman internally and opened it up to the outside world. This is what led him to open up diplomatic relations with the Federal Republic of Germany in 1972. It's interesting that the first West German diplomats and their 'embassy' were housed at Camp Dursait – owned by German company Hochtief. Since the end of the 1960s, the company had been engaged to construct ports as part of the expansion of Oman's infrastructure."

The German Federal Foreign Office states that political relations between the two countries have always been am-

Auf eine Tasse Kaffee (tasa qahwa)

Das Auswärtige Amt beschreibt die politischen Beziehungen bis auf den heutigen Tag als freundschaftlich und problemlos. Bundespräsident Christian Wulff besuchte Oman im Dezember 2011, es gab viele Treffen auf Ministerebene und die Bundesländer entsenden regelmäßig Delegationen zu Gesprächen in das Sultanat. Im Oktober 2017 eröffnete Bundestagspräsident Norbert Lammert die neue Deutsche Botschaft in Maskat. Dort feiern Omaner und Deutsche gemeinsam jedes Jahr Anfang November den Tag der Deutschen Einheit – weil die Temperaturen erst dann ein Fest im Freien zulassen.

Exportschlager: Autos, Arznei und Kunststoffe

Seit den sechziger Jahren tragen deutsche Firmen dazu bei, dass eine leistungsfähige Infrastruktur im Sultanat entsteht – mit Exportgütern wie Autos und Fahrzeugteilen, Arzneimitteln, Kunststoffen, Industriechemikalien und Maschinen. Die Zahlen bei den Ausfuhren nach Oman steigen stetig: Sie lagen nach letzten Angaben 2017 bei 916,5 Millionen Euro (2016: 834,1 Millionen Euro) – wobei wohl auch über die Vereinigten Arabischen Emirate deutsche Produkte nach Oman gelangen, vermuten die Experten des Auswärtigen Amtes. Importe von Oman nach Deutschland beliefen sich nach letzten Zahlen 2017 auf 38,8 Millionen Euro (2016: 39,4 Millionen Euro). Deutschland nimmt zwar nicht unmittelbar omanisches Öl und Gas ab - liefert aber über die Firma Oxea, die ehemalige Ruhrchemie, Technologie und Know-how an den Golf, damit die fossilen Brennstoffe innerhalb des Landes weiterverarbeitet werden können (siehe dazu Beitrag ab Seite 58).

Viele deutsche Unternehmen investieren direkt im Oman: Siemens versorgte Gaskraftwerke in Sohar und Barka mit Turbinen und die Flughafen München GmbH beriet beim Ausbau der Flughäfen in Maskat und Salalah, die in den letzten Jahren eröffneten. Deutschland wird im Gegenzug von omanischen Geschäftsleuten als wichtiger Messeplatz wahrgenommen – das zeigt sich schon allein daran, dass Oman Partnerland der Internationalen Tourismus Börse (ITB Berlin) 2020 ist. Der Austausch beider Länder floriert auch im Gesundheitsbereich: Omanische Patienten kommen zur medizinischen Behandlung nach Deutschland, zum Beispiel nach Wiesbaden, München oder an den Rhein. Mediziner stehen in enger Verbindung, omanische Studierende sammeln seit Jahren Erfahrungen in deutschen

icable and without any issues. In December 2011, Federal President Christian Wulff visited Oman and took part in many meetings at ministerial level. The German Federal States regularly dispatch delegations to the Sultanate. In October 2017, German President Norbert Lammert opened the new German embassy in Muscat. It's there that Omanis and Germans annually celebrate German Reunification Day in early November, a month later than in Germany, because only then do temperatures allow an outdoor celebration.

Export winners : cars, medicines and synthetic materials

Since the 1960s, German companies have contributed to the emergence of an efficient infrastructure in the Sultanate – with export goods such as cars and vehicle parts, medicines, synthetic materials, industrial chemicals and machinery. The number of exports to Oman are constantly rising: In 2017, they reached €916.5 million (2016: €834.1 million); however, experts from the Federal Foreign Office believe that German products also reach Oman via the United Arab Emirates. According to the latest figures, imports from Oman to Germany amounted to €38.8 million in 2017 (2016: €39.4 million). Germany may not be a direct buyer of Omani oil and gas, but German company Oxea, formerly known as Ruhrchemie, brings technology and know-how to the Gulf so that fossil fuels can be processed within the country (for more, see Page 58).

Many German companies invest directly in Oman. Siemens provided turbines for gas powerplants in Sohar and Barka, and Munich Airport (Flughafen München GmbH) consulted on the expansion of the airports in Muscat and Salalah, which were opened in recent years. In return,

> „Der Austausch beider Länder
> floriert auch im
> Gesundheitsbereich"

> "Exchange between the two
> countries also flourishes
> in the health sector"

OP-Sälen, zum Beispiel an der Düsseldorfer Heinrich-Heine-Universitätsklinik (siehe Seiten 170 bis 177).

Die Düsseldorfer Hochschule ist nicht die einzige, deren Mediziner und Wissenschaftler sich mit der Sultan-Qaboos-Universität austauschen. Auch der Deutsche Akademische Austauschdienst (DAAD) und die Alexander von Humboldt-Stiftung sind daran beteiligt, die 2014 unterzeichnete gemeinsame Absichtserklärung beider Länder zur Zusammenarbeit in Kultur, Bildung, Wissenschaft und Forschung in die Praxis umzusetzen. Schwerpunkt der bilateralen Kultur- und Bildungsbeziehungen ist die wissenschaftlich-technische Zusammenarbeit. Seit 2005 betreut der DAAD omanische Studierende, die mit einem Stipendium der Regierung ein Bachelor-Studium in Deutschland absolvieren – einer von ihnen ist Khalid Alfahdi (siehe Seiten 202 bis 209).

Wenn Gäste von Rhein, Main oder Isar an den omanischen Golf fliegen, kommen sie immer häufiger, um Urlaub zu machen: Touristen aus Deutschland stellen laut dem Auswärtigen Amt nach Großbritannien die zweitgrößte Gruppe unter den Touristen aus Europa. Und rund 750 deutsche Staatsangehörige haben Oman zu ihrem Wohnsitz erkoren (Stand: 2018). Sie treffen sich auch schon mal in Maskats schönem Royal Opera House, der ersten Oper auf der arabischen Halbinsel, wenn dort zum Beispiel Carl Orffs „Carmina Burana" mit omanisch-musikalischem Begleitprogramm erklingt.

Eine Gesellschaft für die Freundschaft

Anfang der 1990er Jahre war es an der Zeit, zivilgesellschaftlich die Beziehungen der beiden Staaten zu flankieren, nachdem bisher die wirtschaftlichen und die politischen Kontakte den Ton bestimmten. „So wurde 1992, rund zwanzig Jahre nach den ersten diplomatischen Beziehungen zwischen der Bundesrepublik Deutschland und dem Sultanat Oman, in Bonn die Deutsch-Omanische Gesellschaft (DOG) als eingetragener Verein gegründet", berichtet der langjährige Präsident Bruno Kaiser. Im Gründungsprotokoll ist von dem Wunsch die Rede, einen Beitrag zur Festigung der Freundschaft zwischen den Menschen in Oman und Deutschland zu leisten, das gegenseitige Verständnis füreinander in Deutschland und Oman zu stärken und die Zusammenarbeit auf kulturellem, wirtschaftlichem, wissenschaftlichem und sportlichem Gebiet zu fördern. Außerdem sollte ein Forum der

Omani businesspeople consider Germany an important trade-fair country. You don't have to look any further for evidence of that than the fact that Oman will be the partner country of the International Tourism Trade Fair (ITB Berlin) in 2020. Exchange between the two countries also thrives in the healthcare sector: Omani patients come to Germany for medical care, for example to Wiesbaden, Munich or the Rhine area. Physicians are in close contact, Omani students gain experience in German operating theatres; for example, at the Düsseldorf Heinrich Heine University Hospital (for more, see Page 170 to 177).

Düsseldorf University is not the only university whose physicians and scientists exchange information with the Sultan-Qabus-University. The German Academic Exchange Service (DAAD) and the Alexander von Humboldt Foundation are also involved in implementing the Declaration of Intent, signed by both countries in 2014, to cooperate in the areas of culture, education, science and research. The focus of these bilateral cultural and educational relations is cooperation in the fields of science and technology. Since 2005, the DAAD has also been responsible for coordinating Omani students who do a Bachelor's

An der GUTech, der einzigen deutschen Universität auf der arabischen Halbinsel, studieren überwiegend Frauen.
At GUTech, the only German university on the Arabian Peninsula, most of the students are women.

Begegnung und des Austauschs zwischen Deutschland und Oman geschaffen werden.

Bruno Kaiser: „Initiativen zur Etablierung eines solchen zivilgesellschaftlichen Engagements gab es mehrere und es ist ein Glücksfall, dass sie schließlich alle in der Gründung der Deutsch-Omanischen Gesellschaft mündeten. Diese fußte zudem auf den engen Kontakten zwischen dem Wissenschaftler und heutigen DOG-Ehrenmitglied Prof. Fred Scholz mit dem damals in Hamburg lebenden Onkel von Sultan Qaboos, Seyyed Tarik Al Said. Es war der ausdrückliche Wunsch von Seyyed Tarik, eine solche Gesellschaft ins Leben zu rufen. Unterstützt wurde dieser von dem damaligen omanischen Botschafter in Bonn, Sheikh Saud Al Nabhani, und seinem deutschen Freund Otfried Hennig. Beide waren familiär eng verbunden durch ihre Frauen, die gemeinsam eine Arztpraxis in Bonn führten."

Hennig, seinerzeit Parlamentarischer Staatssekretär beim Bundesminister der Verteidigung, danach Spitzenkandidat der CDU in Schleswig-Holstein und später Abgeordneter in Kiel, brachte die notwendige politische

degree in Germany on a government scholarship – one of these students is Khalid Alfahdi (for more, see Page 202 to 207).

When people from Rhine, Main or Isar fly to the Gulf of Oman, it's increasingly because they want to spend their holiday there. According to the Federal Foreign Office, Germans make up the second largest tourist group from Europe behind the UK. And around 750 German citizens have chosen Oman as their residence (as of 2018). They may to choose to meet at Muscat's beautiful Royal Opera House, the first opera house on the Arabian Peninsula, when Carl Orff's Carmina Burana plays, accompanied by a selection of Omani music.

A society for friendship

At the beginning of the 1990s, after years of focusing on economic and political contacts, it was time to start focusing on the civil-society relations between the two countries. "In 1992, around twenty years after the first diplomatic relations had been taken up between the Federal Republic of Germany and the Oman Sultanate, the German-Omani Association (DOG) was founded," reports Kai-

Just a Cup of Coffee (tasa qahwa)

Bruno Kaiser, langjähriger Präsident der Deutsch-Omanischen Gesellschaft, mit Seyyed Tarik, der sich für die omanisch-deutschen Beziehungen einsetzt.
Bruno Kaiser, long-time president of the German-Omani Association, with Seyyed Tarik, who is committed to Omani-German relations.

ser. The minutes of the founding session record the wish to strengthen the friendship between the peoples of Oman and Germany, to increase mutual understanding in Germany and Oman and to promote cooperation in the areas of culture, economics, the sciences and sports. In addition, a forum for getting together and exchanging ideas and experiences between Germany and Oman was to be created. Bruno Kaiser: "There were several initiatives to establish such a civil society, and it was a stroke of luck that they all led to the foundation of the German-Omani Association. It was also based on the close contact between scientist (and honorary DOG member) Professor Fred Scholz and Seyyed Tarik Al Said, Sultan Qabus's uncle, who was then living in Hamburg. It was Seyyed Tarik's express wish to bring such a society into being. He was supported by the then Omani ambassador in Bonn, Sheikh Saud Al Nabhani, and his German friend Otfried Hennig. The two men had close ties because their wives had a medical practice together in Bonn."

Unterstützung des Vorhabens von deutscher Seite mit. Sheikh Saud genoss und genießt bei Sultan Qaboos großes Vertrauen wegen seines vermittelnden Einsatzes bei dem Versöhnungsprozess zwischen dem Stamm der Al Nabhani und der Al Busaidi Dynastie. Also war auch von omanischer Seite die entsprechende Protektion auf höchster Stelle gesichert.

Bruno Kaiser erinnert sich an die Gründungsversammlung, zu der er von Sheikh Saud eingeladen wurde: „Als Koordinator der Deutsch-Arabischen Parlamentariergruppe hatte ich öfter mit ihm zu tun und lernte ihn näher kennen im Verlauf von gemeinsamen Reisen in meine Heimat, den Schwarzwald. So habe ich das Glück, mich auch heute noch für die Gesellschaft engagieren zu können." Er selbst bekleidete den Präsidenten-Posten zwischen 2012 und 2018 und zählt die Ausstellung „Greetings from Oman" zur landeseigenen Post- und Briefmarkengeschichte im Museum für Kommunikation Berlin im Jahr 2015 und die Oman-Konferenz im Deutschen Bundestag 2017 zu den herausragenden Ereignissen dieser Zeit. Aktueller Präsident der DOG (Stand: 2019) ist Dr. Wolfgang Zimmermann.

Wenn Omaner Deutsch lernen, dann tun sie es meist mithilfe des Goethe-Instituts. Es hat seinen Hauptsitz in Abu Dhabi, betreibt aber seit 2007 eine Dependance in

Hennig, then Parliamentary State Secretary for the Federal Minister of Defence, and later top candidate of the CDU in Schleswig-Holstein and member of the Kiel Parliament, provided the necessary political support for the project from the German side. Sheikh Saud has long enjoyed Sultan Qabus's trust because of his efforts mediating the reconciliation between the Al Nabhani Tribe and the Al Busaidi Dynasty. This meant that the project also received the highest level of support from the Omani side.

Bruno Kaiser recalls the founding session, which he was invited to by Sheikh Saud: "As the coordinator of the German-Arab group of parliamentarians, I dealt with him several times, and we got to know each other better whenever we travelled to my home in the Black Forest. I feel very fortunate to still be involved with the Association today." Kaiser held the office of President between 2012 and 2018 and counts the 2015 exhibition "Greetings from Oman", highlighting the country's post and stamp history at the Museum for Communication in Berlin and the Oman Conference at the German Federal Parliament among the outstanding events of this period. The current DOG President is Dr Wolfgang Zimmermann.

Omanis who learn German usually do this with the help of the Goethe Institute. Its central office is in Abu Dhabi, but there has also been a branch in Muscat since 2007, which

Auf eine Tasse Kaffee (tasa qahwa)

Maskat in Kooperation mit dem omanischen Bildungsministerium. Darüber hinaus wird an vier omanischen Universitäten Deutsch gelehrt, seit 2012 auch als zweite Fremdsprache an fünf staatlichen und einigen privaten omanischen Sekundarschulen. Zwei der Schulen wurden in die Partnerschulinitiative PASCH (www.pasch-net.de) aufgenommen. Zurzeit lernen 1500 Omani Deutsch (laut dem Auswärtigen Amt) und jedes Jahr beantragen viele von ihnen ein Visum, um einmal die Alpen oder den Rhein zu sehen. Dann wird die Tasse Kaffee (tasa qahwa) nicht nur virtuell beim Gespräch über die Smartphone-App, sondern auch in der Wirklichkeit miteinander getrunken - mal in München, mal in Maskat.

Informationen zur Deutsch-Omanischen Gesellschaft gibt es unter www.deutschoman.de.

is run in cooperation with the Omani Ministry of Education. In addition, German is taught at four Omani Universities, and has been available as a second foreign language at five state and several Omani secondary schools since 2012. Two of these schools have been accepted into the PASCH exchange-school programme (www.pasch-net.de). According to the Federal Foreign Office, there are currently 1,500 Omanis who are learning German, and every year many among them apply for a visa in order to see the Alps or the Rhine. Then that cup of coffee (Tasse Kaffee – tasa qahwa) doesn't just have to be sipped while chatting via a smartphone but can be enjoyed in real life – be it in Munich or in Muscat.

Information on the German-Omani Association can be found at www.deutschoman.de.

GUTech – Arabiens einzige deutsche Universität

Friedhelm Jost, Honorargeneralkonsul des Sultanats Oman, pflegte bis zu seinem Tod 2010 enge Kontakte nach Oman, vor allem zur Nationalbank. Dadurch wurden Projekte möglich und es gab finanzielle Unterstützung vor allem im wissenschaftlichen Bereich. Jost, damals Präsident der Deutsch-Omanischen Gesellschaft, engagierte sich gemeinsam mit Professor Michael Jansen für die Gründung der deutsch-omanischen Universität GUTech (German University of Technology) in Maskat. Im Dezember 2006 wurde ein Vertrag zur Errichtung dieser Privatuniversität mit der Rheinisch-Westfälischen Technischen Hochschule (RWTH) Aachen als deutschem Partner unterzeichnet. Sie nahm im Herbst 2007 ihren Betrieb auf. Mit 60 Studierenden fing alles an. Jedes Jahr stiegen die Zahlen. Im Jubiläumsjahr zum zehnten Geburtstag besuchten rund 2000 Studierende die GUTech, 80 Prozent von ihnen waren Frauen. Die GUTech umfasst vier Fakultäten: Computerwissenschaft und Ingenieurwesen, Wirtschaft und Ökonomie, Angewandte Geowissenschaft sowie Städtebau und Architektur. Das Studium schließen die jungen Omaner und Studierende aus anderen Golfstaaten in sieben Studiengängen mit dem Bachelor ab. Seit 2017 hat die Universität zudem die Zulassung für den ersten Master-Studiengang in Geologie.

Weitere Auskünfte gibt es unter www.gutech.edu.om.

GUTech – the only German university in the Arab world

Friedhelm Jost, Honorary Consul General of the Sultanate of Oman, cultivated close contacts in Oman until his death in 2010, particularly with the National Bank of Oman. That made several projects possible and resulted in financial support, especially in the sciences. Jost, then President of the German-Omani Association, was a driving force for the foundation of the German-Omani University GUTech (German University of Technology) in Muscat in cooperation with Professor Michael Jansen. In December 2006, a contract was signed to establish this private university with the Rheinisch-Westfälische Technische Hochschule (RWTH) in Aachen as its German partner. It opened its doors in autumn 2007 with 60 students. Every year, the numbers have grown. When it celebrated its tenth anniversary, approximately 2,000 students were in attendance at GUTech, with women making up 80 percent. GUTech comprises four faculties: Computer Science and Engineering, Economics, Applied Geoscience, and Urban Planning and Architecture. Bachelor's degrees are available to young Omanis in seven study programmes. In 2017, the university's first master programme in Geology was also approved.

More information: www.gutech.edu.om.

Just a Cup of Coffee (tasa qahwa)

Malerische Wadis (hier Wadi Shab) und kilometerlange Strände locken immer mehr Touristen nach Oman.
Picturesque wadis (here Wadi Shab) and miles of beaches attract more and more tourists to Oman.

Reisen im Oman – Aufbruch im Morgenland

Exploring Oman – Dawn of the Orient

Unterwegs in einem Land,
das Tradition und Trend vereinen will

Travelling in a country
that wants to embrace the old and the new

الرحلة إلى عُمان – رحلة إلى الشرق
زيارة في بلد يريد دمج العادات والتقاليد والحياة العصرية

من نصيحة خاصة إلى هدف عصري: إن عُمان قد أفلحت في الوصول إلى أن تكون هدف سياحي وأيضاً كشريك في السياحة العالمية في عام 2020م في برلين. وهنا نتحدث عن الشرق الأسطوري وبلد الأحلام وبلد الألف ليلة وليلة. لكن توجد هناك بعض النظرات القليلة الحيلة والأسئلة كمثل: ماذا ينتظرني في عُمان؟ هل يمكن أن تكون الرحلة إلى عُمان خطيرة؟ هل يجب على النساء أن يغطين أجسادهن في عباءة سوداء؟ إلا أن التجارب تبين أن: من يريد زيارة عُمان يجب أن يكون لديه بعض الانفتاح والقدرة على تقبل الأشياء الغير مألوفة وأيضاً يقوم بمراعاة بعض الأمور. بالرغم من أن السياحة تتطور بشكل سريع، إلا أن العادات والتقاليد مازالت تلعب دوراً كبيراً في المجتمع. وهذا هو رأي وزارة السياحة العُمانية وبنفس الوقت تريد أن يكون هذا فرصة واستمرارية لتحقيق الهدف والذي هو هام للوزارة.

هذا الاهتمام بالسياحة الاقتصادية سوف يكون له في المستقبل فرصة في استمرارية الحياة لكثير من القرى المبنية من الطين على مدار مئات السنين.

Die mächtigen Forts (hier in Nizwa) gehören zu den kulturellen Sehenswürdigkeiten Omans.
Mighty fortresses (here in Nizwa) belong to the cultural sights of Oman.

Vom Geheimtipp zum Trendziel: Oman macht als Reiseland von sich reden, auch als Partner der Internationalen Tourismus-Börse in Berlin 2020. Oft wird vom märchenhaften Orient erzählt, dem Traum aus 1001 Nacht. Dennoch blicken viele Deutsche ratlos und fragen: „Was erwartet mich? Sind Reisen dorthin gefährlich, müssen Frauen die körperverdeckende schwarze Abaya tragen?" Die Erfahrung zeigt: Wer im Oman reist, sollte offen sein für Außergewöhnliches und zugleich Rücksicht nehmen. Denn der Tourismus entwickelt sich zwar rasant, doch Traditionen spielen weiter eine große Rolle. Das sieht das omanische Ministerium für Tourismus aber auch als Chance und hat Nachhaltigkeit zu einem wichtigen Ziel erklärt. Das neue Interesse am Ökotourismus bedeutet unter anderem eine wirtschaftliche Überlebens-Chance für jahrhundertealte Lehmdörfer. Eine kleine Geschichte über das Reisen im Oman.

Wer von Salalah, der Hauptstadt der Provinz Dhofar, in das Fischerdörfchen Mirbat fährt, hat ungefähr eine Stunde Zeit. Das reicht, damit sich die typisch europäischen Erwartungen entfalten können: ein romantischer Hafen mit lauschigen Cafés und Restaurants; eine Fla-

From insider tip to trendy destination: Oman is making a name for itself as a tourist destination. It's also partner of the 2020 International Tourism Trade Fair in Berlin. People talk about it as the fairy tale Orient, the dream out of 1001 Arabian Nights. Nevertheless, many people don't have a clue about Oman and ask questions such as: What should I expect? Is it dangerous to travel there? Do women have to wear a black abaya that covers their entire body? Experience shows that anyone who visits Oman should be open to experiencing the extraordinary, but they also need to be respectful of the Omani culture. Although tourism is growing quickly, tradition still plays a huge role. This is actually something that the Omani Ministry of Tourism sees as an opportunity, and it has set sustainability as an important goal. The growing interest in ecological tourism means that century-old villages with mud-brick houses have a chance of economic survival. A short history of travel in Oman.

It's about a one-hour drive from Salalah, the capital of the Dhofar province, to the fishing village of Mirbat. That's normally enough time for Europeans to think they have a picture of Oman: a romantic port with quaint

Exploring Oman – Dawn of the Orient

niermeile, auf der sich abends buntes Volk tummelt. Daran denken auch wir unwillkürlich – und müssen zum wiederholten Male über uns selbst lächeln, kaum sind wir in Mirbat angekommen. Denn dort gibt es natürlich nichts von alledem.

In der Mittagshitze liegt der Ortskern verlassen, arabische Fensteraugen lugen braun aus blanken Wänden hinaus auf den leeren Platz. Ab und zu radelt ein Inder vorbei oder ein Kind lugt durch eine Tür. Immerhin erreicht der Gast diesen Ort durch einen schmückenden Holzbogen hindurch, der links und rechts in zwei stilisierten Weihrauch-Räuchergefäßen fußt – sinnbildlich stehen sie für das ehemals so wertvolle Gut, das von Mirbat aus verschifft wurde und teils vielleicht noch wird. Staubige Straßen mit den üblichen „obstacles" (Bodenschwellen, die Raser bremsen sollen) führen zwischen vereinzelt stehenden Häusern hindurch, von denen manche verlassen wirken, andere waren vielleicht früher Lagergebäude und wurden für die Bewohner umgebaut. Alles atmet Schlichtheit unter der Sonne. Das gilt auch für den Hafen: Die Fischerboote, die vor Anker liegen, tragen Zeichen harter Arbeit auf dem Meer: gebrauchte Netze; über die Planken geworfene, abgetragene Kleidung, Messer, Angelruten. Weiße Mövenexkremente beflecken die Außenhaut der Dhaus. Nebenan ein langgestrecktes Gebäude – der Fischmarkt, in dem ein dicker Riffbarsch mit herausquellenden Augen mit dem Tode ringt, ein paar interessierte Kunden umringen ihn. Einige Schritte von dort: ein Restaurant, spartanisch, immerhin mit Schatten spendendem Terrassendach über den weißen Plastikstühlen. Ein älterer Omaner, in Kumma und Dishdasha gekleidet, saugt entspannt an seiner Shisha, zwei Bangladeshi ruhen sich aus und tun so, als fänden sie es ganz normal, dass Frauen mittleren Alters sich ein paar Tische weiter hinsetzen, um Tee zu bestellen.

cafés and restaurants or a promenade where all sorts of people stroll in the evening. We inevitably think about this too, but when we arrive at Mirbat, we have to smile at ourselves once again because, of course, none of that can be found there.

In the midday heat, the centre of the village is deserted, brown Arabian windows look out from their shining walls over the empty square. Occasionally, an Indian cycles past, or a child peeks through a door. To get here, visitors pass through an ornamental wooden archway, carved in the fashion of two stylised incense burners. These are symbols of a once highly-valued commodity that was shipped from Mirbat and might still be. Dusty streets, that are only partially paved and are covered with the usual obstacles (speedbumps that are supposed to slow down speeding cars), wind their way between solitary houses, some of which seem abandoned while others may have been storage buildings that have been converted into residential housing. It all exudes simplicity under the sun. The same goes for the port. The fishing boats that are anchored there show the signs of working life on the sea: old fishing nets; threadbare clothes thrown over the planks; knives and fishing rods. White seagull droppings stain the outer skin of the Dhows. Next to them is a long building – the fish market, where a fat damselfish with bulging eyes is in the throes of death, a few interested customers look on. A few paces away is a simple restaurant, but at least its terrace roof shades the white plastic chairs. An elderly Omani, dressed in dishdasha robes and a kumma cap, leisurely smokes his shisha, two Bangladeshis rest and pretend that it is absolutely normal for two middle-aged women to sit down a few tables away to order some tea.

Even the most idyllic places in Oman look the same – life takes place behind the protective walls of the hous-

Verlassene Lehmhäuser (rechts im Bild) werden zum Teil als Hotels wiederbelebt – etwa in Al Hamra (etwa 50 Kilometer südwestlich von Nizwa).
Abandoned mud-brick houses (right in photo) have been partly revived as hotels – for example in Al Hamra (about 50 kilometres southwest of Nizwa).

Selbst die idyllischsten Orte in Oman sehen ähnlich aus – das Leben spielt sich hinter den schützenden Wänden der Häuser ab. Tagsüber ziehen sich die Bewohner selbst im arabischen Winter mit seinen um die 25 Grad in klimatisierte Räume zurück. Mit dem Sonnenuntergang tauchen sie dann für ein paar Besorgungen im Foodstuff-Tante-Emma-Laden oder – je nachdem – zum Fußballspielen am Strand wieder auf. Die schroffe Kargheit der Städtchen ist bisher für Besucher nicht verändert worden. Das gefällt uns, selbst wenn uns der geschilderte Anblick allzu deutlich vor Augen führt, wie sehr unser Kulturkreis uns prägt. Wie sind wir doch die zum Teil dick aufgetragene Servilität gegenüber zahlungskräftigen Gästen gewohnt, die in zahlreichen südländischen Küstenorten Europas herrscht – und möchten doch gerade dieser aufgesetzten Art den Rücken kehren. Dennoch können wir uns ein etwas gefälligeres Café für die Fremden, die in Mirbat und anderen Dörfern künftig einkehren werden, vorstellen.

Wie wird sich der Tourismus im Land entwickeln? Werden künftig noch mehr Kreuzfahrtschiff- oder Resortgäste in Bus- und Autokarawanen in die Souks, Wadis und Berge chauffiert, strömen sie in immer größeren Scharen hinter die erhabenen Mauern der Forts? Werden sie daran danken, Knie und Schultern zu bedecken? Die Omaner würden aus Höflichkeit zwar nichts sagen, wenn sie Touristen in Shorts und mit Spaghetti-Trägertops herumspazieren sehen – doch sie empfinden dies als stillos und verstehen nicht, weshalb sich Europäer nicht angemessen kleiden. Dieses kleine Beispiel zeigt: Es wird nicht leicht sein, die Grenze zwischen den Wünschen und Gepflogenheiten der Gäste, die durch die neuen Flughäfen in Maskat und Salalah sowie die vielen ehrgeizigen Hotelprojekte ins Land kommen sollen, und dem eher zurückgezogenen Alltagsleben der Angestammten

es. During the day, the locals retreat to their air-conditioned homes, even in the Arabian winter when its around 25 degrees Celsius. When the sun sets, they reappear to do buy food in the small grocer shops; if it's cool enough, they play soccer on the beach. The harsh barrenness of Oman's small towns hasn't been changed on account of the tourists. We like that, even though the picture just described shows us all too clearly how much we are shaped by our culture. We are so used to the servility shown towards affluent tourists that is widespread in numerous southern locations on the coast, yet it's this very type of insincere behaviour that we're trying to avoid. Nonetheless, we can imagine that in the future there will be more tourist-friendly cafés in Mirbat and other villages.

What's the future for tourism in this country? Will even more cruise-ship or resort guests be chauffeured to the souqs, wadis and mountain in buses and caravans of cars? Will they swarm in ever larger droves behind the imposing walls of the forts? Will they remember to cover their knees and shoulders? Omanis are too polite to say anything when they see tourists walking around in shorts and tops with spaghetti straps – but they do consider it in bad taste and don't understand why Europeans don't dress appropriately. This small example shows that it won't be easy to reconcile the rather secluded everyday life of the locals with the expectations and habits of the very tourists, who are being targeted by the new airports in Muscat and Salalah, and the many ambitious hotel projects.

This can also be seen at Salalah beach, where abandoned villages are soon to make way for new resorts. The area surrounding the entire incense souq will be redeveloped in the future. It's becoming apparent that

Pure, unverstellte menschliche Begegnungen im Oman – hier mit Amur Al Rawahi am gastlich gedeckten Tisch in der Wüste.
Genuine, unadulterated human encounters in Oman – here with Amur Al Rawahi at a table laid out for guests.

zu ziehen. Das lässt sich auch am Strand von Salalah er-ahnen, wo verlassene Dörfer bald Platz für neue Resorts machen sollen. In deren Umfeld wird künftig der gesam-te Weihrauch-Souk umgebaut. Es zeichnet sich ab, dass die Region ein neues Gesicht bekommt, wenn Oman als Partnerland der ITB (Internationale Tourismus-Börse in Berlin) 2020 auftritt.

Der alte Weihrauch-Hafen Al Baleed mit seinem angren-zenden Museum wurde bereits fein hergerichtet. Wie an einer Perlenschnur findet man kleine Caféhäuschen für die Besucher auf einer Mauer aufgereiht, die das antike Ausgrabungsfeld vom Strand abgrenzt. Doch die Häus-chen stehen leer, noch hat kein Pächter zugeschlagen – die Miete ist zu hoch, erfahren wir von den Locals. Die nehmen uns Reisende freundlich im eigenen Wagen mit und zeigen uns stolz ihre Stadt, die wir ansonsten nur durch die Fenster eines Ausflugsbusses oder Leihwa-gens gesehen hätten. Zu Fuß lassen sich die weitläufigen Städte in Oman nur viertelweise erkunden, isoliert lie-gen manche Sehenswürdigkeiten wie die zart sandstein-farbene Sultan Qaboos-Moschee mitten im Verkehrsdi-ckicht.

Die puren, unverstellten menschlichen Begegnungen, die in Oman möglich sind, und der lebhafte Austausch der gegenseitigen Gepflogen- und Gegebenheiten dürfen

the region will have a whole new look when Oman is the partner country of the ITB in Berlin in 2020.

The old incense port of Al Baleed, with its adjacent mu-seum, has already been given a makeover. Like a string of pearls, visitors can find small cafés lined along a wall that separates the ancient excavation site from the beach. But the little buildings are empty; the locals tell us that the rent is too high. They happily take us trav-ellers in their own cars and proudly show us their town, which we would otherwise only have seen through the windows of a tourist bus or rental car. On foot, it's only possible to explore the sprawling towns in Oman quarter by quarter, some of the sights lie isolated in the middle of heavy traffic, such as the delicate sand-stone-coloured Sultan Qabus Mosque.

The genuine, unadulterated personal encounters that are possible in Oman and the lively exchange of views and customs must not, in our view, make way to super-ficial business practices. When we're not there, we miss our candid conversations with the locals. They always show us so much of what connects and, at the same time, what differentiates the Occident from the Orient. Whenever we show an Omani photos of our hometowns of Berlin and Düsseldorf, and answer questions about Germany, we feel like we aren't just Europeans but true

Nachhaltig unterwegs

Die Deutschen sind Weltmeister im Reisen – sie wollen nicht nur am Pool liegen, sondern sportlich unterwegs sein, Land und Leute kennenlernen.

Im Oman trifft man deutsche Touristen dabei, wie sie die trutzigen Forts besichtigen, auf zerklüftete Berge klettern oder die wilde Küste mit kilometerlangen Stränden entlangfahren. Auch die Wadis – Flussläufe, die tiefe Täler graben können – sind beliebte Ziele. Dahinter: die Weite der Wahiba-Wüste und des leeren Viertels Rub Al Khali. Diese Besonderheiten des Sultanats eröffnen viele Möglichkeiten, sie auf umweltfreundliche Weise kennen zu lernen – so dass die Umwelt nicht leidet, sondern die Region und die Menschen vor Ort von den Gästen profitieren.

Trekking und Wandern: Für Kletterer ist der Jebel Shams, mit etwa 3000 Metern der höchste Berg Omans, spannend. Wanderer erkunden den Wadi Tiwi oder den Wadi Shab. Auch durch die Höhlen des Hadschar-Gebirges, zum Beispiel Madschlis al-Dschinn (zweitgrößte Höhlenkammer der Welt laut omanischen Angaben) sind Touren möglich. Mehrtägige Wanderungen planen Reisende am besten zwischen September und Mai. Dann herrschen durchschnittlich angenehme 25 bis 30 Grad.

Klettern und Cruisen: Kaum jemand vermutet, dass es im Oman abgesicherte Sportklettergebiete gibt. Die meisten liegen im Hajar-Gebirge, etwa ein bis drei Stunden von Maskat entfernt. Wadi Mistal, Wadi Daykah, Kubrah Canyon oder Sharaf al Almayn heißen einige der Klettergebiete mit unterschiedlichen Schwierigkeitsstufen. Bergtouren sind auch in Musandam möglich, dem äußersten nördlichen Zipfel Omans an der Straße von Hormuz. Die Gegend wird das Norwegen Arabiens genannt – wegen ihrer Fjorde, die sich in hohe Bergketten hineingraben. Wer dort klettern oder mit einer Dhau (traditionelles hölzernes Schiff) cruisen will, sollte ab Maskat in die Provinzstadt Khasab fliegen.

Canyoning: Beim Canyoning erkunden Reisende eine Schlucht von oben nach unten – gefragte Disziplinen sind dabei Abseilen, Abklettern, Springen, Rutschen, Schwimmen und von Fall zu Fall ist sogar Tauchen angesagt. Manchmal ist die Schlucht so eng, dass gerade ein Mensch hindurchpasst. Mit azurblauem Wasser gefüllte Naturpools, bizarre Felsformationen, steile Felsrutschen, Naturhöhlen und Wasserfälle – all das erhält der sportlich Aktive als Lohn zum Beispiel im Snake Canyon des Wadi Bimmah.

Radfahren / Mountain biking: Wer im Urlaub gern mit dem Rad die Berge erkundet, kann das im Hadschar-Gebirge tun. Im Ort Al Hamra starten Touren mit professionellen Guides, die auch durch traditionelle Dörfer führen.

Wüstenwandern: Rub Al Khali heißt übersetzt „Leeres Viertel". Geführte Wandertouren in der größten Wüste der Welt oder in den Sharqiya Sands – eine rund dreistündige Fahrt von Maskat entfernt - bedeuten Stille, Einsamkeit, Wärme und unendliche Weite. Im Nomadic Desert Camp (www.nomadicdesertcamp.com) genießt man beim nächtlichen Lagerfeuer und beim Licht der Öllampen das originale Nomadenfeeling.

sich aus unserer Sicht nicht in oberflächliche Geschäfts-tüchtigkeit verwandeln. Wenn wir nicht dort sind, ver-missen wir die offenen Gespräche mit den Einheimi-schen, die uns so sehr spüren lassen, was Abend- und Morgenland miteinander verbindet und zugleich unter-scheidet. Zeigen wir einem Omaner auf dem Smartphone Fotos unserer Heimatstädte Berlin und Düsseldorf und beantworten wir seine Fragen dazu, dann fühlen wir uns im besten Sinne als Europäerinnen und Weltbürge-rinnen zugleich. Wir empfinden es als bereichernd, mit den Muslims im Sultanat über Religion zu sprechen – sie finden schöne Gleichnisse und leben im Alltag bewusst eine Wertschätzung der anderen Glaubensrichtungen, so dass wir uns für uns Christenmenschen fast schämen. Wie sollten wir erklären, dass hierzulande Kirchen ver-lassen und säkularisiert werden?

Nicht nur die Rufe der Imame bringen Reisende im Oman unweigerlich zum Nachdenken über das Miteinander der Kulturen und Religionen, das hier fast selbstverständlich erscheint. Der Aufbruch im Morgenland ist deutlich zu spüren, mitreißend und zugleich belebend, befruchtend in seiner besonderen Art für uns Europäer, die wir selbst neue Wege finden müssen – gesellschaftlich, politisch und im Hinblick auf unseren Glauben, der alles andere als fest und unverbrüchlich ist.

global citizens. We enjoy talking about religion with Muslims in the Sultanate and comparing our beliefs. Omanis have a real appreciation of other faiths, which makes us almost ashamed as Christians. How can we ex-plain to them that churches in Germany are being aban-doned and secularised?

The sound of Imams calling to prayer inevitably make travellers in Oman reflect on the coexistence of cultures and religions that seems almost taken for granted here. The dawn of the Orient can be clearly felt, infectious and also inspiring, giving a special spark to us Europeans, who need to find our own new paths – for our society, for our politics and for our faiths, which are far from fixed and inalienable.

Die Oper in Maskat – der Besuch einer Aufführung ist zugleich ein gesellschaftliches Ereignis.
The Royal Opera House in Muscat – taking in a performance is also a chance to socialise.

Sustainable tourism

The Germans are world champions when it comes to travel – they don't just enjoy lying by a pool, they also want to do sports and get to know a country and its people.

In Oman, you'll find German tourists visiting impressive forts, climbing rugged mountains or driving along the wild coast with its beaches that go for miles. The wadis – river courses that can carve out deep valleys – are also popular destinations. Further on is the expanse of the Wahiba Desert and the abandoned Rub al-Khali area. These unique features of the Sultanate offer many opportunities to learn about the country in an eco-friendly way that ensures the region and the local people benefit from tourism without damaging the environment.

Trekking and hiking: Jebel Shams, Oman's highest mountain at roughly 3,000 metres, is an exciting challenge for mountain climbers. Hikers can explore the Wadi Tiwi or the Wadi Shab. You can also take a tour through the caves of the Hajar Mountains, including Madschlis Al Dschinn (the second largest cave chamber in the world, according to Omani data). The best time to go hiking over a period of several days is between September and May. The average temperature then is a pleasant 25-30 degrees Celsius.

Climbing and sailing: Hardly anyone suspects there are safe areas for rock-climbing in Oman. Most of them are located in the Hajar Mountains, around one to three hours from Muscat. Wadi Mistal, Wadi Daykah, Kubrah Canyon or Sharaf al Almayn are some of the most popular climbing areas, with differing levels of difficulty. Mountain tours are also possible in Musandam, the northernmost tip of Oman on the Strait of Hormuz. The area is referred to as the Norway of Arabia, because of its fjords that stretch into the high mountain ranges. If you want to go climbing there or sail on a Dhow (a traditional sailing vessel) you should fly from Muscat to the provincial town of Khasab.

Canyoning: Travellers can explore a canyon from top to bottom – popular activities include abseiling, climbing, jumping, sliding, swimming and occasionally even diving. Sometimes the canyon is so narrow that a human only just fits through. Natural pools filled with azure water, bizarre rock formations, steep rock slides, natural caves and waterfalls reward canyoners who take on the challenge of Snake Canyon in the Wadi Bimmah.

Mountain biking: If you prefer to explore the mountains on bike when you're on vacation, you can do so in the Hajar Moutains. Bike tours with professional guides, that take you through traditional villages, start at Al Hamra.

Desert hiking: The literal translation of Rub Al Khali is "Empty Quarter." Guided hiking tours in the world's largest desert or in the Sharqiya Sands – roughly a three-hour drive from Muscat – offer serenity, solitude, warmth and infinite space. At the Nomadic Desert Camp (www.nomadicdesertcamp.com), you can enjoy a campfire at night and feel like a genuine nomad surrounded by the light of oil lamps.

Vom Lehmdorf den Blick über Palmen schweifen lassen

Wer Oman durchquert, trifft immer wieder auf die Ruinen verfallener Lehmdörfer – aufgegeben für moderne Wohnungen mit fließend Wasser und Elektrizität oder einen Job in der Hauptstadt. Nur mithilfe neuer Einnahmen können diese Dörfer modernisiert werden und bleiben so erhalten. Dabei spielen Gäste aus dem Ausland eine große Rolle, wie sich in Misfah Old House erleben lässt: Es liegt im Dorf Misfat Al Abryeen, etwa 40 Kilometer südwestlich von Nizwa.

Das kleine Hotel ist über ein Gewirr von Gassen mit unebenen Pflastersteinen und dicht an dicht stehenden Häuschen zu erreichen. Der heimische Esel nimmt dabei die unterschiedlich hohen Stufen deutlich trittsicherer als die fremden Gäste. Diese wohnen in charmant einfach eingerichteten Zimmern – mit einem bequemen Bodenlager zum Schlafen, ein paar Sitzkissen in alten Webmustern für eine gemütliche Plauderrunde und einer schlichten Kleiderstange. Auf der Terrasse nehmen die Besucher auf kuriosen Schemeln aus Kokosstämmen Platz, um den grandiosen Blick über Palmengipfel bis zur fernen, rauen Berglandschaft zu genießen. Zum Abendessen werden regionale Köstlichkeiten wie Thymiantee und Lammfilets mit selbst angebautem Gemüse dazu serviert. Nachts wiegt das sanfte Plätschern des Wassers, das durch die schmalen Kanälchen des traditionellen Al-Falaj-Bewässerungssystems rauscht, den Besucher in den Schlaf.

In Dörfern wie Misfat Al Abryeen entstehen Arbeitsplätze und neue Einkunftsquellen durch Übernachtungen oder den Verkauf von Tonwaren, Datteln und aromatischem Honig an die Gäste. Ähnliches gilt auch für das „Bait al Jabal Hospitality Inn", ein Ökohotel in der Region Al Hamra mit zehn Zimmern im etwa 350 Jahre alten Dorf Al Hamra. Hier kann sich der Tourist fühlen wie Einheimische vor Hunderten von Jahren – mit Wandnischen als offene Ablagen, dekorativen Webwaren auf dem Boden und unter der Decke.

Die GUTech (German University of Technology in Oman) unterhält ein Projekt in Al Hamra, um alte regionale Dorfstrukturen zu pflegen und zu erhalten.

Eine Auswahl an Reiseanbietern und Ökohotels

www.arab-adventures.com Ob Camping, Wandern oder Mountain Biking - der einheimische Reiseanbieter bietet ein breites Angebot, vor allem für Sportliche, aber auch für Menschen, die die arabische Kultur kennenlernen möchten.
www.omantrekkingguides.com Aktive finden hier viele Ideen für Abenteuer in der Natur Omans.
www.khasabtours.com Eine Anlaufstelle für Reisende in der Exklave Musandam.
www.misfaholdhouse.com Wer das charmante Ökohotel in der Nähe von Nizwa besuchen möchte, sollte vorab reservieren.
experienceoman.om Hier gibt es Informationen – auch auf Deutsch – zu Unternehmungen für Omanreisende vom omanischen Tourismusministerium.
www.oman.de Die Omanexperten von „Arabia Felix" planen individuelle Reisen.

Abendstimmung im Morgenland – hier am Al Qurm-Strand in Maskat.
Evening atmosphere in the Orient – here at the Al Qurm beach in Muscat.

Reisen im Oman - Aufbruch im Morgenland

Enjoy the view over palm trees from a mud-brick village

Anyone who traverses Oman will keep coming across the ruins of crumbling mud-brick villages – abandoned in favour of modern apartments with running water and electricity, or a job in the capital. The only way these villages can be modernised and survive is to find new sources of revenue. Foreign guests play a huge part in this, as can be seen with the Misfah Old House: It's located in the village of Misfat Al Abryeen, around 40 kilometres to the Southwest of Nizwa.

The small hotel is reached via a labyrinth of laneways with uneven cobblestones and houses packed tightly together. Donkeys are more sure-footed than the foreign guests. Tourists are accommodated in charming, plainly furnished rooms – with comfortable bedding on the floor for sleeping, a few cushions in traditional weave for a pleasant chat and a simple clothes rail. On the terrace, visitors sit down on stools made from coconut-tree trunks in order to enjoy the magnificent view over the tops of palm trees reaching all the way to the distant, rugged mountain landscape. Regional delicacies are served for dinner, such as thyme tea and lamb fillet with locally grown vegetables. At night, the gentle splash of water flowing through the narrow canals of the traditional Al Falaj irrigation system lulls visitors to sleep.

In villages such as Misfat Al Abryeen, new jobs and sources of revenue are being created as a result of travellers staying overnight or from selling pottery, dates and aromatic honey to guests. The same thing is happening at the Bail al Jabal Hospitality Inn, an eco-hotel with ten rooms in the 350-year-old village of Al Hamra. Here, tourists can experience what it was like to be a local hundreds of years ago – with alcoves in the walls as open shelves and ornamental woven textiles on the floor and hanging from the ceiling.

The GUTech (German University of Technology in Oman) runs a project in Al Hamra to maintain old regional village structures.

A selection of tour operators and eco-hotels

www.arab-adventures.com
Whether camping, hiking or mountain biking – this local tour operator offers a broad range of services, especially for sports enthusiasts or those who want to learn more about Arabian culture.
www.omantrekkingguides.com: This company has a lot on offer for active people looking for adventures in Oman.
www.khasabtours.com: A contact point for travellers in the Musandam Governorate.
www.misfaholdhouse.com: Those who want to visit this charming eco-hotel close to Nizwa should book in advance.
experienceoman.om: This website run by the Ministry of Tourism Oman has loads of information for people travelling to Oman.
www.oman.de The experts of „Arabia Felix" plan individual trips

Getöpferte Mitbringsel aus dem Oman – Weihrauchbrenner gehören dazu.
Pottery souvenirs from Oman – incense burners are a staple.

Die Corniche in Matrah ist beliebte Flaniermeile für Einheimische und Gäste
The Corniche in Matrah is a popular promenade for locals and guests.

Trügerische Postkartenidylle

Deceptive Postcard Idyll

Immer mehr Kreuzschifffahrt-Touristen
belasten den Souk von Matrah

The growth in cruise-ship tourism
is leaving its mark on the souq of Matrah

بطاقات بريدية مصورة خادعة
يشكل الكثير من سواح السفن البحرية عبئ على سوق مطرح.

يشكل الكثير من سياح السفن البحرية عبء على سوق مطرح. حيث أن كثيراً من السياح هم ألمان و يحتلون المركز الثالث في جدول السياحة البحرية العالمية الحديثة. عندما ترسي سفينتان أو ثلاثة سفن في مرفأ السلطان قابوس يتزاحم السياح في حارات السوق الضيقة التقليدية. وهذا لا يتناسب مع تطلعات السلطان نحو سياحة نوعية. لذلك يجب أن يكون هناك طرق بناءة لكي تكون هناك رقابة على الازدحام الكبير للسفن الكبيرة في الميناء، وبنفس الوقت تكون هذه الإجراءات وسيلة حتى يستفيد تجار البلد والشركات من هذه السياحة.

Die Deutschen belegen Platz drei auf der internationalen Liste der modernen Kreuzfahrer. Wenn zwei oder drei Schiffe im Sultan Qaboos Hafen liegen, drängen sich Reisende aus aller Welt dicht an dicht in den schmalen Gassen. Das Sultanat strebt Qualitäts-Tourismus an. Konstruktive Maßnahmen sind gefragt, um den Ansturm der großen Schiffe zu kontrollieren und dafür zu sorgen, dass einheimische Händler und Unternehmen von den Reisenden profitieren.

Die Lust, sich komfortabel und ohne ständiges Kofferpacken von Land zu Land über die Weltmeere schippern zu lassen, wächst kontinuierlich. Die Anzahl deutscher Passagiere auf Kreuzfahrtschiffen stieg laut Zahlen des Statistik-Portals statista in den Jahren 2016 und 2017 von 2.018.000 auf 2.189.000 Reiselustige. Deutschland belegt damit hinter den USA und China Platz drei auf der Rangliste der modernen Kreuzfahrer.

Dass diese Form des Reisens besonders bei den wohlhabenden Europäern beliebt ist, erweist sich bei einem weiteren Blick auf die statista-Auswertung 2017. Unter den 28 aufgeführten Nationen finden sich knapp hinter Deutschland die Italiener (769.000), Spanier (510.000) und Franzosen (504.000). Im Jahr 2019 haben sich laut Schätzungen der Branchenexperten etwa 30 Millionen Passagiere aus aller Welt auf eine Kreuzfahrt begeben. Manchmal teilen sich mehr als 3.000, manchmal aber auch mehr als 4.000 oder sogar knapp 5.500 Passagiere das Heim auf Zeit.

Oft vergessen wird beim Blättern im Werbekatalog mit vielen bunten Bildern, dass die schwimmenden Kleinstädte viel Energie verbrauchen und mit ihren schmutzigen Abgasen – Ruß, Feinstaub, Stickoxide und Schwefeloxide – die Gesundheit der Menschen und das Klima belasten.

Besonders kleine Häfen verändern sich unter Einfluss der Kreuzschifffahrt. Wenn einer der großen „Pötte" im Sultan Qaboos Hafen in Matrah neben den Yachten des Sultans anlegen, die hier ihren festen Ankerplatz haben, dann haben die Passagiere erst einmal die malerische Bucht mit der markanten, karstigen Felsküste Omans vor Augen. Von Ferne sieht der Hafen aus wie eine scheinbar unberührte Postkartenidylle aus 1001 Nacht.

Germans rank third on the international list of modern cruise-ship passengers. Whenever two or three ships lie at anchor at Port Sultan Qabus, the narrow alleys are stuffed full with travellers. That doesn't fit well with the Sultanate's pursuit of high-quality tourism. That's why there needs to be an action plan to control the onslaught of large ships and to ensure that local merchants and companies benefit from tourism.

The inclination to be transported comfortably from country to country across the oceans without the constant need to pack your suitcase is growing. According to figures provided by the renowned portal statista, the number of German cruise-ship passengers rose from 2,018,000 to 2,189,000 between 2016 and 2017. This means that Germany ranks third on the list of modern cruise-ship passengers, behind the USA and China.

The fact that this type of travel is particularly popular with well-to-do Europeans is confirmed when you take a closer look at the statista evaluation of 2017. Among the 28 nations listed, Germany appears just after the Italians (769,000), the Spanish (510,000) and the French (504,000). According to experts in the field, roughly 30 million passengers from all over the world will take a cruise in 2019. These massive cruise ships can become the temporary home of thousands of people, the largest can hold up to 5,500 passengers.

What they forget, or choose to ignore, is that these small floating cities consume huge amounts of energy and that their exhaust fumes – soot, fine particles, nitric oxide and sulphur oxide – are dangerous to human health and the environment.

Small ports are particularly affected by cruises. When one of the large ships lands at Port Sultan Qabus in Matrah next to the Sultan's yacht, which has its permanent berth here, the first thing the passengers see is the picturesque bay with the striking, craggy shoreline of Oman. From afar, the port looks like a seemingly pristine postcard idyll out of the 1001 Nights.

Tourists are chauffeured via shuttle directly in front of the souq. Here, they might meet the person from the cabin next-door or maybe travellers from other cruise

Deceptive Postcard Idyll

Manchmal ankern zwei oder drei Kreuzfahrtschiffe gleichzeitig im Hafen von Maskat.
Sometimes two or three cruise ships anchor simultaneously in the port of Muscat.

Per Shuttle werden die Touristen direkt vor den Souk chauffiert. Hier treffen sie vielleicht den Kabinennachbar, vielleicht aber auch fremde Reisende von einem oder zwei anderen Kreuzfahrtschiffen, die zeitgleich im Hafen liegen. Auf jeden Fall sind die oft mit kniefreien Shorts und schulterfreien Shirts entgegen arabischer Bekleidungsgewohnheit gewandeten Reisende deutlich in der Mehrheit im Vergleich zu Omanern und den Expats, also den ständig im Oman lebenden Menschen aus beispielsweise Indien oder Pakistan.

Im Souk, der als einer der ältesten im arabischen Raum gilt, wird bis 21 Uhr in den zahllosen Mini-Lädchen unter anderem duftender Weihrauch, eine reiche Auswahl an Silberwaren, blinkendes Goldgeschmeide und Kunsthandwerk angeboten. Die Händler offerieren ihre Waren, sind aber insgesamt deutlich zurückhaltender als es viele Reisende von Basaren aus anderen Regionen kennen. Das schätzen die Touristen aus aller Welt.

Viel Geld lassen die Touristen, die oft nur für eine Nacht bleiben, bei ihrem Ausflug in das bunte Treiben der kleinen Gässchen nicht. Schließlich wird im Schnitt alle zwei, drei Tage ein neuer Hafen angelaufen – und irgendwann hat man die Mitbringsel für die Lieben daheim zusammen.

ships that are at the port at the same time. Tourists, who often ignore Arabian clothing habits by wearing shorts above the knee and sleeveless shirts, clearly outnumber Omanis and expats from countries such as India or Pakistan.

In the souq, which is said to be the oldest in the Arab world, countless tiny shops offer fragrant incense and a large selection of silverware, sparkling gold jewellery, and arts and crafts until 9 p.m. The merchants selling their goods are much more relaxed than many travellers are accustomed to from bazaars in other regions. Tourists appreciate that.

However, visitors frequently stay for only one night and don't spend much money on their excursions into the hustle and bustle of the small alleyways. After all, they reach a new port on average every two or three days – and at some point, they've bought all the souvenirs and gifts they need for family and friends back home.

"Usually they just come to look around," Alim, one of the local shop owners, says prosaically with a gentle smile as he arranges colourful scarves and handmade kummas, the traditional headdress of Omani men. "For many, the souq is just one stop of many. They don't come here to buy something; they're just here to pass

Trügerische Postkartenidylle

„Sie kommen meist nur, um zu gucken", stellt Alim, einer der lokalen Shop-Betreiber, nüchtern fest – und sortiert mit sanftem Lächeln farbenprächtige Schals und handgefertigte Kummas, die traditionelle Kopfbedeckung der omanischen Männer, zu ordentlichen Stapeln. „Die Menge an Besuchern im Souk verschlechtert insgesamt die Qualität des Standorts", so sein Resümee. Manchmal drängen sich in den vielleicht gerade einmal zwei Meter breiten Gassen dicht an dicht die Besucher. „Der Souk ist für viele nur ein Stopp auf einer Ausflugstour. Sie kommen nicht her, um etwas zu kaufen, sondern um sich die Zeit zu vertreiben und vielleicht ein paar Erinnerungsfotos zu schießen", fügt Standnachbar Younos, ein gebürtiger Kaschmiri, hinzu.

Das Gewimmel an Touristen verschreckt Einheimische, so dass sie zunehmend den Souk meiden. Auch immer mehr Ladenbesitzer verlieren die Lust, geben auf oder vermieten ihr Ladengeschäft unter.

Näher mit dem Thema beschäftigt hat sich Manuela Gutberlet, Politologin und Public Relations Managerin an der German University of Technology im Oman (GUTech). In ihrer 2016 veröffentlichten Untersuchung „Socio-cultural impacts of large-scale cruise tourism in Souq Mutrah, Sultanate of Oman" belegt sie den Ansturm mit Zahlen. Erste Kreuzfahrtschiffe, so schreibt sie, legten 2004 im Hafen von Matrah an. 2005 kamen auf 24 Schiffen rund 7.600 Touristen an, sieben Jahre später waren es schon 135 Schiffe mit 257.000 Reisenden.

Das Interesse an dem friedlichen und weltoffenen Sultanat wächst. Die Autorin zitiert Statistiken des Ministeriums für Tourismus. 2013 wurde die Anzahl der ausländi-

Kreuzfahrttouristen geben im Souk meist wenig Geld aus

Cruise-ship tourists usually spend little money in the souq

the time or maybe to take some happy snaps," adds Younos, a native-born Kashmiri from the neighbouring booth.

The teeming crowds of tourists scare away the locals, who increasingly avoid the souq. More and more shop owners are losing interest and are either subletting their shops or simply closing them.

Dr Manuela Gutberlet, tourism geographer and Public Relations Officer at the German University of Technology in Oman (GUTech), has dealt with this development in more detail. In a study on sociocultural effects of mega cruise-ship tourism in souq Matrah ("Socio-cultural impacts of large-scale cruise tourism in souq Matrah, Sultanate of Oman"), published in 2016, she uses statistics and qualitative surveys to demonstrate the impact of this type of tourism. The first cruise ships, she writes, landed in the Port of Matrah in 2004. In 2005, 24 ships brought around 7,600 tourists, seven years later this had grown to 135 ships with a total of 257,000 visitors.

Interest in the peaceful and open-minded Sultanate is growing. The author cites statistics from the Ministry of Tourism in Oman. In 2013, the number of foreign visitors to Oman was 2.18 million. By 2020, up to 12 million visitors a year are expected. The number of cruise ships in 2012 was 80 times higher than in 2005. In 2011, 170,000 tourists came to Matrah, which roughly matches the number of local inhabitants. In 2013, this number rose to 202,159 passengers, according to data provided by the Ministry of Tourism.

Oman could profit economically from this trend – after all, the country is constantly looking at options for the future after its oil reserves have run out. The tourism sector plays a key role here. But according to official statements, the Ministry wants to focus less on mass tourism and more on quality tourism. In order to better manage the situation, there are plans to expand the area around Muttrah in the coming years and turn it into a cruise-ship port. Among the projected developments are several hotels, a mall, residential buildings and infrastructure catering to up to 33,000 tourists. This could create new jobs that are desperately needed.

Deceptive Postcard Idyll

schen Besucher im Oman mit 2,18 Millionen angegeben. Bis 2020 rechnet man mit bis zu 12 Millionen Besuchern jährlich. Zwischen 2005 und 2012 erhöhten sich die Anlandungen von Kreuzfahrtschiffen um das 80fache. 2011 kamen 170.000 Touristen nach Matrah, was ungefähr der Einwohnerzahl des Ortes entspricht. 2013 erhöhte sich die Zahl laut Angaben des Ministeriums für Tourismus auf 202.159 Passagiere.

Oman entwickelt neue Perspektiven für die Zeit nach dem Öl. Der Sektor Tourismus spielt dabei eine zentrale Rolle. Dabei setzt man laut Ministerium weniger auf Massen- als auf Qualitätstourismus. Die Pläne sehen vor, den Standort rund um Matrah in den kommenden Jahren touristisch auszubauen. Geplant sind Hotels, Einkaufszentren und eine Infrastruktur für bis zu 33.000 Touristen. Hierbei werden auch dringend benötigte neue Jobs entstehen.

Only a form of tourism that the region can benefit from economically and also socio-culturally pays off for the destination according to Dr Gutberlet's analysis. She believes that the Omanis have to carefully evaluate the rapid growth of cruise-ship tourism because her study proves that the local population is overwhelmed by the crowds that suddenly appear in huge numbers, staying only for a few hours at a time.

Her suggestions for how to systematically counter the onslaught of cruise-ship tourists: "In order to prevent the mass appearance of tourists and the pressure this puts on the local population, the number of cruise ships landing here should be heavily restricted and regularly supervised. Quotas could be introduced. Other options might be to accept only companies with small ships at the port, to establish a specific tourist souq outside the port that can serve as an alternative

Bummel durch die Geschäfte – bald in einem eigenen Souk für Touristen?
Stroll through the shops – soon in a special souk for tourists?

Nur ein Tourismus, von dem auch die Region profitiert, zahlt sich für das Gastgeberland aus, heißt es in der Analyse von Gutberlet. Die rasanten Wachstumsraten der Kreuzschifffahrt müssen in dem Zusammenhang sicher kritisch betrachtet werden.

Vorschläge zur systematischen Steuerung der Touristenströme von der Autorin: „Um touristisches Massenaufkommen und den Druck auf die lokale Gemeinschaft zu vermeiden, sollte die Anzahl der anlegenden Kreuzfahrtschiffe limitiert und überwacht werden. Weitere mögliche Maßnahmen wären zudem, lediglich Linien mit kleinen Schiffen im Hafen zu akzeptieren, einen eigenen Touristen-Souk außerhalb des Hafens anzulegen und als Ausweichort anzubieten oder eine spezielle Steuer für Kreuzfahrtschiff-Touristen zu erheben."

and to collect a special tax from cruise-ship tourists, the revenues of which benefit the tourist infrastructure and the locals."

www.academia.edu, Suche / Search: Socio-cultural impacts of large-scale cruise tourism in Souq Mutrah, Sultanate of Oman.

Die Netzmoräne gehört zu den zahlreichen Bewohnern der reichen Unterwasserwelt Omans.
The net moraine is one of the numerous inhabitants of the rich underwater world of Oman.

Im Paradies der Taucher

A Diver's Paradise

Walter Harschers Extra Divers
zeigen Omans besondere Unterwasserwelt

Walter Harscher's Extra Divers Centres
reveal Oman's extraordinary underwater world

في جنة الغواصين
الغواصين الممتازين التابعين لـ فالتر هارشر يعرضون
الحياة في أعماق البحار في عُمان

خليج عُمان غني بالأسماك وأسراب سمك النهاش الكبيرة
وبما فيها الحيتان ذات الظهر المحدب، هذه الحيوانات المائية
تسبح بمحاذاة الشاطئ العُماني حيث أن الدلافين تقفز من
أمواج البحر. ومن أوائل الناس الذين اكتشفوا جنة الغطس
هذه في عُمان هو الألماني فالتر هارش الذي أسس في عام
2004م تحت عنوان "الغطاسين الخاصين" المدرسة العالمية
الأولى لتعليم الغطس في عُمان. وتعتبر هذه المدرسة بوجود
4 مراكز للغطس من رواد مدارس الغطس. ليس فقط عالم
أعماق البحار الذي لم يمسه إنسان بعد هو الشيء الذي لا
يزال يثير إعجاب رجال الأعمال بل أيضا العمل الجيد مع
حكومة عُمان.

Walter Harscher gründete die „Extra Divers", die erste internationale Tauchschule im Oman.
Walter Harscher founded "Extra Divers", the first international diving school in Oman.

Der Golf von Oman ist reich an Fisch: Schnapper-schwärme, sogar Buckelwale ziehen an der Küste vorbei, und Delfine springen aus den Wellen. Einer der Ersten, die dieses Tauchparadies als solches erkannt haben, ist der Deutsche Walter Harscher. 2004 gründete er unter der Flagge der „Extra Divers" die erste internationale Tauchschule im Oman und gilt mit insgesamt vier Tauchbasen als Pionier.

Die See ist ruhig an diesem Morgen, als die Taucher voller Erwartungen ins tiefblaue Meer springen. Sanfte Wellen rollen an die schroffe Felsenküste – trotz aller farblichen Gegensätze wirkt wundersam harmonisch vereint, was so gar nicht zueinander zu passen scheint. Die Taucher lassen die Luft aus ihren Tarierjackets entweichen und sinken langsam gen Meeresgrund, wo eine stählerne Lady einige der schönsten Unterwassermomente des Sultanats ermöglicht. Ihr Name: Al Munassir. Ihr Baujahr: 1978. Ihre Maße: 84 Meter lang, knapp 15 Meter breit. In 30 Meter Tiefe ruht sie aufrecht auf dem Meeresboden. Ein stolzes Wrack, dessen Aufbauten als Schatten direkt nach dem Abtauchen zu erkennen sind. 2003 wurde der ehemalige Frachter der Royal Navy Of Oman an dieser Stelle versenkt, um Fischschwärmen, Nacktschnecken, Muränen und Rochen ein künstliches Riff zu bieten. Die blubbernden menschlichen Besucher aus aller Welt erhalten dadurch ein Unterwassermuseum in bestem Zustand, in das zahlreiche Meeresbewohner eingezogen sind. Der Golf von Oman ist reich an Fisch;

The Gulf of Oman is rich in fish: Schools of snappers, pods of hunchback whales, and dolphins leaping out of the water. One of the first people to recognise this diver's paradise was German Walter Harscher. In 2004, he pioneered the first international diving school in Oman and he now runs a total of four Extra Divers Centres in the country.

The sea is calm this morning when the divers jump into the dark blue sea; their expectations are high. Gentle waves break on the harsh rocky shore – in spite of the juxtaposition of colours, everything seems to be united in wondrous harmony. The divers release the air from their buoyancy control devices and slowly sink towards the bottom of the ocean to visit a steel lady and experience some of the most beautiful underwater scenes in the Sultanate. Her name is Al Munassir. She was built in 1978. She measures 84 meters long and roughly 15 meters wide. She rests on the bottom of the sea in upright position at a depth of 30 meters. A proud wreck whose outline can be seen as a shadow as soon as you start submerging. In 2003, the former cargo vessel of the Royal Navy of Oman was sunk here to provide an artificial reef for schools of fish, sea slugs, moray eels and rays. Bubbling human visitors from all over the world are presented with an under-water museum in pristine condition which numerous sea dwellers now call home. The Gulf of Oman is rich in fish: gigantic schools of snappers block out sight of wrecks and reefs, dolphins leap out of the sea

A Diver's Paradise

gigantische Schnapperschwärme versperren die Sicht auf Wrack und Riffe, Delfine springen in den Morgenstunden aus den Wellen, und ab und an ziehen Orcas oder Buckelwale vorbei. Die Riffe sind intakt; Meeresschildkröten sind bei jedem Tauchgang zu sehen, und an den exponierteren Stellen wie Fahal Island, rund eine Stunde mit dem Boot von Muscat entfernt, oder den etwas nördlicher liegenden Daymaniyat Inseln, können Rochen und Walhaie beobachtet werden.

Der Deutsche Walter Harscher gehört zu den Ersten, die dieses Tauchparadies als solches erkannt haben. 2004 gründete er unter der Flagge der „Extra Divers" die erste internationale Tauchschule im Oman und gilt dort als Pionier. Es ist nicht nur die unberührte Unterwasserwelt, die den Unternehmer beeindruckt, sondern auch die Zusammenarbeit mit der Regierung. „Das läuft alles sehr angenehm, die Menschen sind freundlich", sagt Harscher. Er schätzt den gelassenen, aber dennoch organisierten Lebensstil der Omanis. Fast 50 Mitarbeiter beschäftigt er in seinen Tauchbasen im Oman; die Kapitäne sind Einheimische, die die schönsten Riffe, Plätze und Wracks kennen. Die Gewässer des Sultanats sind bekannt für ihr Meeresleben: Was an der Oberfläche in Tiefblau und Steinbraun daherkommt, explodiert unter Wasser zu einem Feuerwerk der Tierwelt.

„Der Oman hat noch großes Potenzial", da ist sich Reiseverkehrskaufmann und Touristikfachwirt Walter Harscher sicher. „Das muss gemeinsam entwickelt werden – zum Beispiel mit Ökotourismus." Er weiß, wovon er spricht: Mit 25 Tauchcentern, sechs Taucherhotels und drei Safaribooten ist sein Unternehmen führender Tauchbasenbetreiber weltweit. Angefangen hat es mit einer Basis am Roten Meer in Ägypten. Doch dann entdeckte Harscher, Jahrgang 1963, den Oman für sich. Mindestens acht Mal jährlich fliegt er hin, um Tauchcenter, Mitarbeiter und potenzielle neue Partner zu besuchen.

Eine seiner Tauchbasen ist am Shangri-La-Hotel angesiedelt, zehn Minuten von Maskat entfernt. In der Marina starten die Boote zu den Plätzen von Bandar Khayran, einer kleinen Küstenstadt. Diese selbst bekommen die Taucher bei den Touren nicht zu Gesicht, wohl aber die Unterwasserwelt, die sich hinter der Kulisse labyrinthartig im Wasser liegender Bergmassive versteckt. Im Wirrwarr zwischen den Felsformationen bieten klei-

in the early morning, and occasionally orcas or hunchback whales pass by. The reefs are unspoilt; turtles can be seen on every dive. At more remote places, such as the Fahal Islands, about an hour from Muscat by boat or the Daymaniyat Islands, a little more to the north, you can observe rays and whale sharks.

Walter Harscher was one of the first people to recognise this diver's paradise. In 2004, he launched the first international diving school in Oman under the flag of Extra Divers and is considered a pioneer there. The entrepreneur isn't just impressed with the pristine underwater world but also how easy it is to work with the government. "It all runs very smoothly, the people are friendly," Harscher says. He appreciates the Omanis' lifestyle, which is both relaxed and organised. He has almost 50 employees at his dive centres in Oman; the captains are locals who know the most beautiful reefs, spots and wrecks. The waters of the Sultanate are well-known for their sealife. Underneath the surface, that looks dark blue and stone brown, is an explosion of wildlife. "There is still a lot of potential in Oman," says Walter confidently. "We have to develop it together – for example with ecological tourism." He knows what he's talking about: With a total of 25 dive centres, six diving hotels and three safari boats, his company is the leading global operator of dive centres. It all began with a centre at the Red Sea in Egypt; but then Walter, who was born in 1963, discovered Oman. He flies to Oman at least eight times a year to visit dive centres, and speak with his staff and potential new partners.

One of his dive centres is located at the Shangri-La Hotel, ten minutes from Muscat. At the marina, the boats cast off to Bandar Khayran, a small coast town. It's not the town that the divers see on these tours but the underwater world that hides between the labyrinth of rock formations jutting out of the water. The small bays that nestle between the rock formations serve as wonderful starting points for a dive. The rocks protect the area even when the sea is rough, the water is as smooth as glass. Following steep escarpments, we reach the blue anemones of "First Entrance"; in Seahorse Bay, scores of camouflaged scorpion fish watch the divers, and on the way back at "Jissah Point" rare butterfly rays can be spotted in the sand – providing you can even see through the turtles and schools of barracudas.

Im Paradies der Taucher

ne Buchten wunderbare Tauch-Startpunkte. Die Felsen schützen den Bereich selbst bei Seegang, das Wasser ist spiegelglatt. Entlang von Steilwänden geht es zu den blauen Anemonen von „First Entrance", in der „Seahorse Bay" beobachten in bester Tarnung unzählige Skorpionfische die Taucher, und auf dem Rückweg sind an „Jissah Point" seltene Schmetterlingsrochen im Sand zu finden – wenn man denn überhaupt zwischen Schildkröten und Barrakudaschwärmen hindurchblicken kann.

Mehr als ein Tauchboot ist selten an einem der Plätze zu sehen. Hier hat man das Meer zumindest über dem Wasserspiegel meist noch für sich allein. Kein Wunder, dass auch Prominente das Land und die Diskrektion der Luxushotels für sich entdeckt haben und mit der ganzen Familie auf einem privat gemieteten Boot hinaus schippern. Besonders wichtige Besucher werden von der Küstenwache begleitet. Während sie schnorcheln oder tauchen, blicken die Bewacher entspannt in die Sonne. Sie erinnern sich an Zeiten, als sie selbst an Bord der Al Munassir gingen – als die stählerne Lady noch oberhalb der Wellen unterwegs war.

Mehr Informationen gibt es unter
www.extradivers-worldwide.org

It's rare to see more than one diving boat at these locations. Usually you have the sea to yourself, at least above the surface. It's no surprise that celebrities have also discovered the country and the discretion of its luxury hotels, so they privately rent a boat to go to sea with their whole families. VIP guests are usually accompanied by the coast guard. While they snorkel or dive, the guards laze in the sun and relax. They remember the times when they themselves were on board the Al Munassir – when the steel lady still sailed above the water.

More information can be found at
www.extradivers-worldwide.org

Gemächlich zieht der Walhai in Begleitung eines Tauchers seine Runden.
The whale shark leisurely makes its rounds accompanied by a diver.

A Diver's Paradise

Wacher Wanderer zwischen den Welten

Inquisitive Wanderer between Two Worlds

Amur Al Rawahi schlägt die Brücke
zwischen Orient und Oxident – ein Portrait

Amur Al Rawahi is building a bridge
between the Orient and the Occident

المهاجرون الذين يحبون المعرفة في العالم
عمر الرواحي يقيم جسراً بين الشرق والغرب – لوحة
شخصية

إن أمنية السيد عمر الرواحي هي نقل ثقافة بلده عُمان إلى
الضيوف والزوار، حيث يستطيعون التعرف على الناس في
قريته، وأيضاً يرافقونهم سواءً على الدراجات أو سيراً على
الاقدام إلى المناطق الجبلية. إن هذا الشاب العُماني، رجل
الأعمال الذي لا يخاف من الخطر ويبحث عن المغامرات،
يحب السفر كثيراً. حيث زار في أوربا كلاً من المانيا وإيطاليا
للتعرف على الشعوب والمقارنة بين الاختلافات والتشابه
بينهم كثقافات مختلفة حتى يستطيع تعلم كيف يتفهم هذه
الشعوب.

Mit dem Mountainbike unterwegs in den Bergen Omans.
Mountain biking in the mountains of Oman.

Sein Traum ist es, Gästen die Kultur seines Landes zu vermitteln. Sie können die Menschen im Dorf von Amur Al Rawahi kennenlernen, aber auch mit ihm auf dem Mountainbike oder zu Fuß in den Bergen unterwegs sein. Der junge omanische Unternehmer, der das Risiko nicht scheut und das Abenteuer sucht, reist auch selbst – nach Deutschland und Italien, um Unterschiede und Ähnlichkeiten zwischen den Menschen besser verstehen zu können.

Wie sollte ich ihn anders beschreiben als Wanderer zwischen den Welten? Einer, der mit Tempo unterwegs ist - über die Berge Omans, durch die Wüste und dann durch das Grün sächsischer Wälder bei Erfurt. Auf der Suche nach neuen Erfahrungen, zuhause oder in Austauschprogrammen. Dabei trägt er wahlweise die klassische Dishdasha oder wetterfeste, atmungsaktive Stoffe. Immer aber ist der Kopf bedeckt, mit einem Tuch oder einem Turban, meist zum Schutz gegen die sengende Sonne. Sie begleitet Amur Al Rawahi durch sein wechselvolles Leben und scheint dem durchtrainierten Anfangdreißiger wenig auszumachen. Jetzt gerade brennt sie auf

His dream is to show visitors his country's culture. They can meet the people of Amur Al Rawahi's village, but they can also explore the mountains with him by mountain bike or on foot. The young Omani entrepreneur, who is not afraid to take risks and is drawn to adventure, also travels himself to Germany and Italy, in order to better understand the differences and similarities between peoples.

How else could I describe him but as a wanderer between two worlds? Someone who travels at speed across Oman's mountains, across the desert and also across the green forests of Saxony in Germany. He is always looking for new experiences, be it at home or in an exchange programme. Depending on what he is doing, he either wears the classic dishdasha or clothing that is weather-resistant and breathable. Either way, his head is always covered with a scarf or a turban, usually to protect himself against the scorching sun. The sun is a constant companion in Amur Al Rawahi's varied life and does not seem to be much of a bother for the fit man in his early thirties. Right now, the sun is blasting the roof of his

das Dach seines weißen SUV, im dem er mit uns durch die Zauberberge Omans in Richtung Sur braust. Bezaubernd deshalb, weil ihre weichen, teils wie ausgespült wirkenden Konturen und die durch gewaltige Erdverschiebungen ans Tageslicht gewuchteten Adern spüren lassen, dass sie einst unter dem Meeresgrund lagen. Wie hingewürfelt liegen zwischendrin kleine, private Villen – was machen die Menschen, die dort leben? „Sie haben vielleicht Tiere in der Nähe", meint Amur. Die Regierung siedelt die Menschen in Oman an, gibt ihnen Grundstücke – und sie ziehen dorthin, manchmal mitten ins Nirgendwo, arbeiten unter der Woche in Maskat und kommen am Wochenende heim.

Früher lebten Omaner wie Amur von selbst geernteten Datteln und bauten ihr Getreide an, heute kaufen sie Brot und Lebensmittel im Supermarkt ein. Früher... diese Zeit endete für den Mann mit dem hellen Lachen Anfang der 2000er Jahre, als er als 16-Jähriger aus den Bergen der Qaryyat nach Maskat kam – für ihn damals eine

white SUV as we race through the enchanted mountains of Oman towards Sur. "Enchanted" because their soft contours, some of which seem almost molten, and their veins, which have been brought to the surface by enormous earth shifts, remind us that they once lay beneath the seabed. Every now and then we see small private villas – what do the people do that live there? "Maybe they have livestock close by," shrugs Amur. The government settles the people in Oman, provides them with a piece of land and they move there, sometimes in the middle of nowhere. During the week, they work in Muscat, only returning home for the weekends.

In the old days, Omanis like Amur could subsist on the dates they harvested and the crops they grew. Today, they buy their bread and their groceries in supermarkets. The "old days" ended for the man with the cheerful smile in the early 2000s when he was 16 years old and left the mountains of Qurayyat for Muscat – which was just a large confusing city to him back then. In Al Mazara,

Oman kennenzulernen – das bedeutet auch, einen Trip durch die Wüste zu unternehmen.
Getting to know Oman also means taking a trip through the desert.

Wacher Wanderer zwischen den Welten

verwirrende Großstadt. In seinem Dorf Al Mazara war er behende mit den Ziegen über Stock und Stein geklettert, hatte mit seiner Familie gelebt – was für die Mutter und den Vater, einen einfachen Arbeiter, bedeutete: Fünf Söhne und vier Töchter in einer Gegend großzuziehen, in die man bis 2002 nur mit Eseln auf Trampelpfaden gelangte und in der es bis dahin auch keinen Strom gab. „Mein Vater hat uns nichts umsonst gegeben. Wenn wir etwas haben wollten, mussten wir ihm dafür auf der Farm helfen", sagt Amur.

Er ist dankbar für diese Schule, die ihn gelehrt hat, keine Geschenke vom Leben zu erwarten. Alles erarbeitet er sich mit dem eisernen Willen, den man hinter den warm leuchtenden braunen Augen spürt. Und diese Arbeit hat mit Gästen, Touristen zu tun: „Ich wollte den Kontakt zu ihnen, seit ein weißhäutiger Engländer nahe dem Dorf sein Zelt aufgeschlagen hat. Ich war ein Junge und bestaunte ihn wie einen Alien."

Entschlusskraft und Durchhaltevermögen sind es, die den schmalen Mann auffallen lassen – schon kurz nach seiner Ankunft in Maskat, als er im Hotel als Barkeeper jobbte und Alkohol ausschenkte, streng geheim gehalten vor den Eltern. Da lernte ihn der Geschäftsführer von Oman Flour Mills kennen und engagierte ihn vom Fleck weg als Human Resources Manager. Unterstützte ihn dabei, mit dem Computer umgehen und Auto fahren zu lernen. „Aber ich wollte mich verändern", so begründet Amur heute seinen Wechsel von der Mehlmühle ins omanische Verteidigungsministerium. Vier Stunden vormittags dort zu arbeiten reichte ihm nicht, er studierte nachmittags Informatik und begann dann als Taxifahrer seinem Ziel näher zu kommen: den Touristen sein Land zu zeigen, und zwar auf ungewöhnlichen Wegen. 2009 bekam er seine Lizenz als Touristenführer und widmet sich seit 2013 ganz diesem Bestreben, für das er zum Entsetzen seiner Familie den Job im Ministerium kündigte.

Die Sicherheit aufgegeben zu haben und selbstständig zu sein, das bereut Amur nicht. Er gab all sein Geld aus, um seine Firma „arab adventures" zu gründen. Als junger Unternehmer schaffte er es, bei deutschen und italienischen Agenturen Zweifel an seiner Erfahrung beiseite zu räumen – obwohl er getreu seinem Motto von Anfang an Touren plante, die abseits der üblichen Routen lagen. „Nach Nizwa zum Viehmarkt fahren alle, aber wer

the village where he grew up, he used to climb nimbly over the craggy countryside with his goats. He lived with his mother and father, a simple worker, and with his five brothers and four sisters in an area that, until 2002, could only be reached by donkey, and where there was no electricity. "My father never gave us anything for free", Amur says, "If we wanted something, we had to help him on the farm."

He is grateful for being taught not to expect life to give you any presents. Whatever he wants, he works for with the iron determination that can be found behind his warm brown eyes. Now he works with guests and tourists. "I wanted to have contact with them ever since a fair-skinned Englishman pitched his tent near our village. I was just a boy and marvelled at him as if he were an alien."

It's his determination and his perseverance that make this slender man stand out. Shortly after his arrival in Muscat, he got a job as a bartender in a hotel and served alcohol to guests, something which he kept strictly secret from his parents. It's here that he met the CEO of Oman Flour Mills, who hired him on the spot as their Human Resources Manager. He helped Amur to become computer-literate and learn to drive. "But I wanted to keep evolving," is how Amur explains his reason for leaving Flour Mills for a position at the Omani Ministry of Defence. Working there for four hours in the morning was not enough for him, so he studied computer science in the afternoon and then he started to work as a cab driver in order to get closer to achieving his goal: showing tourists his country and not just in the typical ways. In 2009, he received his license as a tourist guide, and since 2013 he has devoted all of his time to this endeavour, shocking his family when he resigned from his position at the Ministry.

Amur does not regret giving up his security and becoming self-employed. He spent all of his money on setting up his company Arab Adventures Tours. As a young entrepreneur, he managed to overcome all the doubt that German and Italian agencies had regarding his experience – even though he stayed true to his motto and from the very start came up with tours that were off the beaten track. "Everybody drives to the cattle market in Nizwa, but who offers mountain-biking or hiking through

Inquisitive Wanderer between Two Worlds

bietet schon Mountainbiking oder Hiking durch die Rub Al Khali-Wüste an?", fragt Amur provokant charmant, während sein weißer SUV sich immer höher hinauf in die Berge schraubt. Wir machen kurz Halt am azurblauen Wadi-Dayqah-Stausee, in dessen stillem Wasser sich schroffe, sandfarbene Gipfel spiegeln.

Im ehemaligen Flusstal unterhalb der Staumauer sehen wir schon die ersten Häuser von Al Mazara im Sonnenglast – unter ihnen Amurs frühere Schule. Wir werden sie später gemeinsam besuchen und ihn im Kreis seiner stolzen Lehrer erleben. Bildung ist ein hohes Gut im Oman, für das der Staat zahlt. Kinder werden auch aus den kleinsten Dörfern mit dem Bus zum Unterricht abgeholt. Das wird uns der jetzige Rektor mit Würde (und vielleicht mit einem verstohlenen Blick auf den erfolgreichen ehemaligen Schüler) sagen. Doch erst einmal bewirtet uns Amur in seinem Haus. Elegant kniet er in der langen Dishdasha auf dem Teppich nieder, um uns omani coffee einzuschenken und Datteln zu reichen. Seine Mutter lässt sich entschuldigen, sagt er. Dass der 32-jährige – für einen jungen Omaner ungewöhnlich – bisher weder Frau noch Kinder hat, begründet Amur mit seiner Unternehmungslust, die zu einem Familienvater nicht passt. Ein Hauch von Bedauern huscht kurz über seine Miene, doch dann reckt er sein Kinn. Wer weiß, was noch kommen wird? Sein Wissensdurst ist groß, Italienisch hat er im Sommer vor drei Jahren gelernt, jetzt ist Deutsch an der Reihe. Denn schließlich arbeitet Amur nebenbei noch als Kulturvermittler für das Institut für Auslandsbeziehungen (ifa). Irgendwann, so überlegt er laut, möchte er Besucher in einem schattigen Tal in der Nähe von Al Mazara in einem eigenen Gasthaus bewirten. Eilig hat es Amur damit nicht, seine Firma soll mit Bedacht wachsen und er sieht durchaus die Gefahr, sich zu übernehmen. Die Sonne über Oman und Europa wird erleben, welche Menschen seinen Weg kreuzen und ihn – ein Stück lang oder länger – begleiten werden.

Amur Al Rawahi ist Gründer und Inhaber von „arab adventures", sein Reiseunternehmen hat er vor allem gegründet, um seinen Traum von kulturellem Austausch zwischen Ost und West zu realisieren. Mehr Informationen gibt es unter www.arab-adventures.com.

the Rub' al Khali desert?" Amur asks in his charming style while his white SUV climbs higher and higher into the mountains. We make a quick stop at the Wadi Dayqah Dam, whose tranquil azure water reflects harsh sand-coloured peaks.

In the ancient river valley below the dam wall we see the first houses of Al Mazara appear in the glare of the sun – among them Amur's former school. Later on, we'll visit it and witness how proud his teachers are of him. Education is highly valued in Oman, the state pays for it. Children are picked up by bus from even the tiniest villages. Later, we will hear the current principal proudly tell us about Oman's education system (maybe with a quick glance at his successful former student). But for now, Amur entertains us in his house. In his long dishdasha, he kneels elegantly on the carpet to pour us some Omani coffee and pass us some dates. His mother apologises for not being there, he says. It's uncommon for a 32-year-old Omani to not have a wife or children, but Amur cites his adventurousness as the reason for that, a trait that does not suit a family man. A hint of regret flashes over his face, but then he raises his chin. Who knows what is yet to come? He is highly inquisitive and learned Italian three summers ago, now it's time for German. As a side job, Amur also works as a cultural mediator for ifa, the German Institute for Foreign Relations. Someday, he muses, he wants to own a guesthouse in a shady valley near Al Manzara where he can host visitors. However, Amur is not in a hurry, he wants his company to grow, and he is well aware of the danger of overdoing it. The sun over Oman and Europe will see people sharing his path for a little while more yet.

Amur Al Rawahi is the founder and owner of Arab Adventures Tours. He started his travel company to make his dream of cultural exchange between East and West come true. More information at www.arab-adventures.com.

Zu Besuch in Paris – in Europa erzählt Amur Al Rawahi von seiner Heimat.
On a visit to Paris – in Europe Amur Al Rawahi talks about his homeland.

56

Wacher Wanderer zwischen den Welten

Oxea – ein Stück Maskat am Rhein

Oxea – A Little Bit of Muscat on the Rhine

Know-how-Transfer und neue Jobs:
Oman investiert in Deutschland

Transfer of know-how
and new jobs for Oman

Oxea - قطعة من مسقط على نهر الراين

نقل المعرفة ووظائف جديدة: عُمان تستثمر في ألمانيا
ماذا يجب على العُمانيين أن يأخذوه معهم بعد العمل في
أوكسيا في راينلاند؟ معرفة التقنيات والعمليات التي يمكنهم
استخدامها لتحقيق التنمية الاقتصادية المستدامة في عُمان
وخلق فرص العمل. هذه الاعتبارات دفعت إدارة شركة النفط
العُمانية المملوكة للدولة إلى الاستحواذ على شركة أوكسيا
العالمية. بالإضافة إلى ذلك فإنه يتم تبادل معلومات ذات قيمة:
كيف يتم تطوير التقارب وروح العمل المشترك في حالة قيام
عمال من بلاد مختلفة ويملكون نظرة روحية مختلفة بالالتقاء
مع بعضهم البعض. يعتبر "التنوع" عند أوكسيا كقيمة مستقلة
بحد ذاته. هذا يتناسب مع كل الأشخاص في منطقتي الراين
والرور، والذي لا يعتبرون بأن الغرباء أو الآخرين شيء
جديد بالنسبة لهم: كان المهاجرون في الماضي يأتون من
مازوري، بروسيا الشرقية وبولندا وتركيا للعمل في منطقة
الرور — واليوم يأتون من كل أنحاء العالم وأيضاً خلال
بضعة ساعات في رحلة طيران من عُمان.

Was sollen Omaner in ihr Land mit zurück bringen, nachdem sie bei Oxea im Rheinland gearbeitet haben? Wissen über Technologien und Prozesse, die sie in einem neuen Werk anwenden können – und mit deren Hilfe Arbeitsplätze im Oman geschaffen werden können. Diese Überlegungen bewogen die Geschäftsführung des staatlichen Konzerns Oman Oil dazu, das Unternehmen Oxea zu erwerben. Für die bisher größte Auslandsinvestition des Sultanats haben sich zwei Geschäftsbereiche zusammengeschlossen, die Chemikalien aus Öl herstellen. Darüber hinaus fließt aber auch weiteres, menschlich geprägtes Know-how: darüber, wie sich Nähe und Teamgeist entwickeln, wenn Mitarbeiter aus verschiedenen Ländern und mit unterschiedlicher Geisteshaltung zusammentreffen.

Menschen, die sich auf der Straße treffen, gehen in Deutschland oft schweigend aneinander vorüber, ohne sich gegenseitig anzublicken. Das war eine Überraschung für Ali Al Lawati bei seinen ersten Begegnungen. Der Mittzwanziger, der an der Sultan-Qaboos-Universität studiert hat, gehörte bis Mitte 2018 zu den omanischen Trainees beim Chemieunternehmen Oxea in Monheim am Rhein. Eigentümer von Oxea ist die Oman Oil Company – ein staatliches Unternehmen des Oman. Von dort kennt es Ali Al Lawati, dass man sich meist zuvorkommend mit „Salam" begrüßt. Abwarten und beobachten lautete also die erste Lektion in dem fremden Land, in das Al Lawati vor allem gekommen war, um mehr über die Themen Controlling und Auditing zu erfahren. Zusammen mit seinem Kollegen Majid Al Mashari nimmt er an einem Austauschprogramm zwischen Oman und Deutschland teil. Im Umgang mit den Kollegen lernen die beiden Trainees auch typisch deutsche Tugenden wie Disziplin und Gründlichkeit.

Wie zurückhaltend Menschen in Deutschland sein können, das hat auch Majid Al Mashari in seinem privaten Umfeld im rheinischen Düsseldorf erlebt. Dort lebte er für rund zwei Jahre während seines Trainees bei Oxea. „Es braucht Zeit, um ihnen nahe zu kommen. Doch wenn sie dann zu Freunden werden, nehmen dich mit, erzählen dir private Dinge." Eine interessante Parallele, möchte man aus deutscher Sicht sagen – denn ähnlich erleben wir die Omanis in ihrem Land. Kommen wir mit ihnen ins Gespräch, dann werden sie schnell zum Fremdenführer für Gäste, laden großzügig in ihre Häuser ein.

What is it that Omanis should take back with them to their home country after working for Oxea in the Rhineland? Knowledge of technologies and processes that they can apply at a new plant – and that can help create new jobs in Oman. This is what motivated the management of state-owned Oman Oil to acquire Oxea. Two businesses that produce chemicals from oil were merged in the Sultanate's largest foreign investment to date. There are also people skills and personal know-how being shared: how close ties and team spirit are developed when co-workers from different countries and with different mind-sets come together.

In Germany, people who pass one another on the street frequently walk by without saying a word or looking at each other. This surprised Ali Al Lawati when he first experienced it. The Omani, who is in his mid-twenties and studied at the Sultan Qabus University, was one of the Omani trainees at the Oxea chemical company located in Monheim am Rhein until the middle of 2018. Oxea is owned by the Oman Oil Company – a state-owned company in Oman. Ali was used to the custom in Muscat of greeting each other with a courteous "Salam". The main reason Al Lawati came to Germany, a country he had never been to, was to learn more about controlling and auditing; his first lesson here was "wait and watch". With his colleague Majid Al Mashari, he took part in an exchange programme between Oman and Germany. Other things that the two trainees learned while working with their German colleagues including typical German virtues such as discipline and thoroughness.

Majid Al Mashari also experienced how reserved people in Germany can be in his private live in the city of Düsseldorf on the Rhine. He lived there for around two years when he was a trainee at Oxea. "It takes time to get close to them. But when they finally are your friends, they really care for you and tell you quite personal things." This is an interesting parallel from a German perspective because this is similar to what we experience with the Omanis in their home country. If you strike up a conversation with them, they are quick to act as travel guides for their guests and show their generosity by inviting you to their homes. They joke a lot, using subtle irony and tongue-in-cheek humour. But as soon as you want to write about something in your role as journalist or author, they suddenly become

Sie scherzen viel und gern mit feiner Ironie und augen-zwinkerndem Humor. Doch wenn darüber als Pressever-treter oder Autor berichtet werden soll, tritt Vorsicht zu-tage – plötzlich scheinen Bedenken aufzutauchen, man könne missverstanden werden oder zu tiefe Einblicke gewährt haben.

Rund 7.000 Kilometer Entfernung zwischen dem Rhein-land und dem Sultanat wurden überbrückt, als Oman Oil aus strategischen Gründen das Unternehmen Oxea erwarb. „Öl- und Gasvorkommen spielen in Oman im-mer noch eine große Rolle und wir wollten mehr in den Downstream investieren – das bedeutet: In die Stufen, welche die Rohstoffe nach der Förderung durchlaufen. Außerdem geht es darum, neue Jobs zu schaffen", er-klärte Dr. Salim Al Huthaili. Bis 2018 arbeitete er als Ge-schäftsführer (CEO) von Oxea, jetzt gehört er dem Board des Unternehmens an und ist als neuer CEO der Duqm Refinery and Petrochemical Industries Company (DRPIC) im Oman tätig. Aus nächster Nähe hat er Unterschiede und Ähnlichkeiten zwischen Deutschland und Oman kennengelernt. Größte Differenz: die Demografie. Einer älter werdenden deutschen Bevölkerung und entspre-chenden Belegschaften steht ein Land im Aufbruch ge-genüber, in dem die Hälfte der Einwohner nach Angaben Omans jünger als 18 Jahre alt ist.

Den Nachwuchs in Lohn und Brot zu bringen ist eine He-rausforderung in Zeiten, in denen die ölfördernden Län-der am Golf neue Einkommensquellen ins Auge fassen müssen. Vision 2040 ist die Zukunftsplanung betitelt, die wirtschaftliche Perspektiven in Oman entwickelt. Diese stehen im Fall von Oxea noch mit Öl und Gas in Verbin-dung. Daraus produziert das Unternehmen chemische

cautious – worried that they might be misunderstood or give away too much.

A distance of roughly 7,000 kilometres between the Rhineland and the Sultanate was bridged when Oman Oil bought Oxea for strategic reasons. "Oil and gas re-sources still play a large role in Oman, and we wanted to invest more into downstream areas, that is, the stages that raw materials go through after extraction. It's also about creating new jobs," explained Dr Salim Al Huthaili. Until 2018, he was Oxea's CEO, now he is part of the com-pany's board and the new CEO of the Duqm Refinery and Petrochemical Industries Company (DRPIC) in Oman. He had a chance to experience the differences and similari-ties between Germany and Oman first hand. The biggest difference: the demographics. Whereas the German pop-ulation and its workforce are getting older, Oman is an emergent country where, according to official data from Oman, half of the population is younger than 18.

> „Wir wollen unsere Rohstoffe nicht
> mehr nur exportieren,
> sondern sie direkt in
> unserem Land verarbeiten"

> "We no longer want to just export
> our raw materials, but process them
> directly in our country"

Oxea – ein Stück Maskat am Rhein

Ali Al Lawati (links) und Majid Al Mashari arbeiten im Team mit ihren deutschen Kolleginnen.
Ali Al Lawati (left) and Majid Al Mashari work in a team with their German colleagues.

Verbindungen, die für die Herstellung von Kosmetika, Schmiermitteln oder Oberflächenbeschichtungen verwendet werden. „Wir wollen unsere Rohstoffe nicht mehr nur in den asiatischen Markt oder andere Länder exportieren, sondern sie direkt in unserem Land verarbeiten", erzählte Dr. Salim Al Huthaili noch als damaliger CEO der Oxea. Der Weg zu mehr Industrialisierung im Oman ist allerdings ohne den Zugang zu neuen Technologien und dem internationalen Handelsnetzwerk nicht gangbar. Kein Wunder also, dass Oxea mit seiner globalen Präsenz interessant wurde und umgekehrt ebenfalls: „Ein Ziel war von Anfang an, den asiatischen Markt von Oman aus mit Produkten des Unternehmens zu versorgen", erläutert Al Huthaili.

Dafür entsteht im Ort Duqm auf halbem Weg zwischen Maskat und Salalah ein neuer Chemiepark. Für dieses Projekt ist Dr. Salim Al Huthaili nun CEO. Downstreaming ist in Duqm das beherrschende Stichwort. Das

Providing employment for the next generation is a challenge in a time when the oil-producing countries in the Gulf need to think about new sources of revenue. Vision 2040 is the title of the roadmap for future economic development in Oman. In Oxea's case, they are still connected to oil and gas. The company uses them to produce chemical compounds that are used for manufacturing cosmetics, lubricants and surface coatings. "We not only want to export our raw materials to Asia and other countries, we also want to process them directly in our own country," stated Al Huthaili when he was still the CEO of Oxea. However, further industrialisation in Oman is not possible without access to new technologies and the international trade network. It's not surprising then that Oxea became an attractive proposition with its global presence: "It was our goal from the get-go to supply the Asian market with the company's products directly from Oman," Al Huthaili explained.

Oxea – A Little Bit of Muscat on the Rhine

bedeutet in der Vorstellung der Geschäftsleitung, dass Molekülkombinationen aus Öl oder Gas nicht nur produziert, sondern auch gewinnbringend weiter verkauft werden sollen. Know-how aus Deutschland soll dazu beitragen, dass dieser Plan aufgeht. Um den Austausch zwischen dem Oman und Oxea zu fördern, wurden zwei Austauschprogramme ins Leben gerufen. Eins für junge Graduierte wie Majid Al Mashari und Ali Al Lawati und ein zweites zur Weiterbildung erfahrener Kollegen, die im Oman Aufgaben übernehmen.

Dr. Salim Al Huthaili sah Oxea in seiner Funktion als CEO nicht als rein deutsches Unternehmen, sondern als Weltfirma, in der Vielfalt seiner Meinung nach eine noch größere Rolle als bisher spielen sollte: „Es geht um das gute Verhältnis der verschiedenen Kulturen untereinander", erklärte er mit festem Blick und ergänzte: „Es ist erstaunlich, zu sehen, wie sich Omaner und Deutsche in ihrer Zusammenarbeit gegenseitig beeinflussen." Die Kollegen tauschen sich mit den Omaner nicht nur über ihre Kenntnisse aus, sondern erzählen auch von Reisen oder treffen sich zum Fußballspielen und machen gemeinsame Ausflüge. Al Huthaili erzählte, dass er „Diversity" nicht als Wert an sich im Unternehmen ansieht und gerade die Unterschiedlichkeit der Menschen schätzt. Das passt zu den Menschen an Rhein und Ruhr, für die das Fremde, Andere auch nichts wirklich Neues ist: Früher kamen die Zuwanderer aus Masuren, Ostpreußen, Polen und der Türkei, um im Ruhrgebiet zu arbeiten -

As part of achieving this goal, a new chemistry park is being built in Duqm – halfway between Muscat and Salalah. Dr Al Huthaili is the CEO for this project. Downstreaming is the keyword in Duqm. For management this means that molecular combinations of oil or gas are not only produced but also sold on profitably. Know-how from Germany is to contribute to the success of the plan. In order to encourage exchange between Oman and Oxea, two exchange programmes were set up. One for young graduates, such as Majid Al Mashari and Ali Al Lawati, and a second one for advanced training of experienced workers who will assume greater responsibilities in Oman.

In his role as CEO, Salim Al Huthaili doesn't see Oxea as a purely German company but rather as a global company where, in his opinion, diversity should play an even bigger role than it has so far. "It's about a good relationship between different cultures," he explained to me with a steady look and added: "It is impressive to see how Omanis and Germans influence each other when working together." Work colleagues don't just share know-how, they also tell each other about their travels, meet to play soccer or go on trips together. Al Huthaili explained that he doesn't consider "diversity" a value per se in the company and especially appreciated the differences between the people. That's nothing new for the people from the Rhine and Ruhr, because they are used to foreign people and things. In the past, immigrants from Masur-

Das heutige Oxea-Werk hat eine lange Geschichte in Oberhausen im Ruhrgebiet.
Today's Oxea plant has a long history in Oberhausen in the Ruhr area.

Oxea – ein Stück Maskat am Rhein

heute aus allen Teilen der Welt und innerhalb von ein paar Flugstunden auch aus dem Oman. Gemeinsame Erfahrungen können, so meint Al Huthaili, bei der vorsichtigen Annäherung aneinander ebenso Bindeglieder sein wie humorvolle Begegnungen: „Warum soll man keine Scherze über kulturelle Eigenheiten machen?" Eine Frage, mit der er im Rheinland einen weiteren Nerv trifft – dort, wo man das Herz gern auf der Zunge trägt und ein munteres Schwätzchen zum Tag dazu gehört.

ia, East Prussia, Poland and Turkey came to work in the Ruhr area; today they come from all over the world and are just a few hours by plane from Oman. Shared experiences, Al Huthaili believes, can be just as good at building relationships as humorous episodes: "Why shouldn't we laugh together about cultural differences?" A question that strikes a chord in the Rhineland – where they wear their hearts on their sleeves and a friendly chat is part of everyday life.

Von der Ruhr bis an den Golf

Oxea ist ein Unternehmen mit einer langen Geschichte: Die damalige Ruhrchemie AG in Oberhausen wurde bereits 1928 gegründet, Oxea 2007. Nach einer aufstrebenden Entwicklung kaufte Oman Oil das Unternehmen 2013. Das Unternehmen stellt Oxo-Intermediate und -Derivate her und hat derzeit Produktionsstandorte in Bishop, Bay City (beide in den USA gelegen), Amsterdam, Oberhausen, Marl und Nanjing in China. Oxea-Produkte sind beispielsweise Alkohole (u.a. Polyole), Aldehyde, Carbonsäuren, Spezialitäten-Ester und verwandte Stoffe wie Amine und werden als Zwischenprodukte bei der Herstellung von Beschichtungen, Pharmazeutika, Schmier-, Aroma-, Duft-, Farb- und Kunststoffen benötigt. Die besondere Herstellungstechnik geht auf die Forschungsarbeit von Otto Roelen zurück. Heute hat Oxea rund 1.400 Mitarbeiter weltweit und verzeichnet einen Umsatz von rund 1,2 Milliarden Euro.

www.oxea-chemicals.com

Duqm – ein ökonomisches Zukunftsprojekt

Die Special Economic Zone in Duqm (SEZAD) ist ein ökonomisches Zukunftsprojekt, von dem man sich im Sultanat viel verspricht: Seit fast zehn Jahren wird in die Entwicklung der Region investiert. Der omanische Staat baut den Hafen in dem einstigen Fischerort unter anderem als Drehscheibe für petrochemische Produkte aus. Darüber hinaus soll die Umgebung mit Hotels und Restaurants auch noch für Touristen interessant werden.

From the Ruhr to the Gulf

Oxea is a company with a long history: Its predecessor, Ruhrchemie AG in Oberhausen, was founded in 1928, Oxea in 2007. Following further expansion, Oman Oil acquired the company in 2013. Oxea produces oxo intermediates and derivatives. It currently has sites in Bishop and Bay City in the USA; Amsterdam in the Netherlands; Oberhausen and Marl in Germany; and Nanjing in China. Oxea products include alcohols (e.g. polyols), aldehydes, carbonic acids, speciality esters and related substances such as amines. These are used as intermediates in the manufacture of coatings, pharmaceuticals, lubricants, flavouring agents, fragrances, dyes and plastics. The unique manufacturing technology is based on the research of Otto Roelen. Today, Oxea has approximately 1,400 employees around the globe and annual revenue of around €1.2 billion.

www.oxea-chemicals.com

Duqm – an economic project for the future

The Special Economic Zone in Duqm (SEZAD) is an economic project for the future, for which the Sultanate has high expectations. Investing in the development of the region has been going on for almost ten years. The Omani government is expanding the former fishing village's port into a hub for petrochemical products. Hotels and restaurants in Duqm are also being expanded to make the area more attractive for tourists.

Oxea – A Little Bit of Muscat on the Rhine

Sie gingen als Unternehmer nach Maskat: Alexandra und Georg Eichenberg.
They went to Muscat as entrepreneurs: Alexandra and Georg Eichenberg.

Ein überzeugendes Team

A Winning Team

Alexandra und Georg Eichenberg
haben als Unternehmer viel im Oman gelernt

Entrepreneurs Alexandra and Georg Eichenberg
have learned a lot in Oman

الفريق المُقنع
تعلمت الكسندرا وجورج إيشنبرج، كونهما من أصحاب الأعمال أشياء كثيرة في عُمان

من الممكن أن يكون شعار الكسندرا وجورج إيشنبرج هو أن يتفاجأ الإنسان من ذاته ومن الآخرين وعلى وجه الأخص من الحياة، لم يكونا يحلمان بأنهما في يوم ما سيغادران بلديهما إلى عُمان كمغتربين ويصلان إلى هذا النجاح بعد عشرة أعوام من الاغتراب. لقد أسسا معهد للتدريب في عُمان ووجدا لهما أصدقاء كثر وتمتعا بقبول المجتمع لهما ونالا ثقتهم، إن أكاديمية OakHill للتطوير تعرض خدمات مثل تطوير القدرات البشرية والخروج بقيادات متدربة ذات كفاءة عالية بالتعاون مع الجامعة التقنية للعلوم التطبيقية في مدينة روزنهايم. إن أفكارهم للمستقبل هي: بناء كلية تزود الكوادر العمانية بتخصصات مهنية يحتاجها سوق العمل. كما توجد أيضا مشاريع أخرى مثل السياحة وما شابه ذلك من الأعمال وهي على طريق الإنشاء.

Die Brücke zu Menschen zu schlagen ist eine der Stärken von Alexandra Eichenberg.
Building a bridge between people is one of the strengths of Alexandra Eichenberg.

Sich von sich selbst, von anderen und besonders vom Leben immer wieder überraschen lassen – das könnte das Motto von Alexandra und Georg Eichenberg sein. Dass sie einmal in den Oman auswandern und dort erfolgreich sein würden, hätten die beiden sich nicht träumen lassen. Nach mehr als zehn Jahren sind sie mit ihrem Trainings-Institut bestens akzeptiert und haben Freunde gefunden, denen sie unbedingt vertrauen. Die Oakhill Development Academy bietet Dienstleistungen im Bereich Human Resources Development an und qualifiziert Fach- und Führungskräfte - jetzt in einer Partnerschaft mit der Technischen Hochschule Rosenheim. Ihre Ideen für die Zukunft: Sie wollen ein College für besondere Berufszweige aufbauen. Weitere Projekte – z.B. im Bereich Tourismus – sind auf dem Weg.

Da war dieser Moment in der äußerst schwer zu findenden, traumhaften neuen Wohnung in München. Dort eröffnete Georg Eichenberg seiner Frau Alexandra vor zwölf Jahren seinen Plan, in Deutschland alles aufzugeben und nach Oman zu ziehen. „Wir waren gerade eingezogen und ich fühlte mich endlich angekommen", erzählt Alexandra Eichenberg und kann sich noch gut an den damaligen Schock erinnern. Das gewinnende Lächeln auf ihren Lippen verliert sich allerdings nicht, und sie hat nach vielem Auf und Ab heute allen Grund zur Zuversicht: Das gemeinsame Trainings-Institut ist gerade Partner der Technischen Hochschule für Angewandte

Alexandra and Georg Eichenberg are constantly being surprised by themselves, by others and by life. They never dreamed that they would one day emigrate to Oman and run a successful business there. After more than ten years, their training institute is well established, and they have found friends who they trust without reservation. The Oakhill Development Academy offers training courses in human-resource development for specialists and managers. The Academy works in collaboration with the Rosenheim University of Applied Sciences. In the future, they want to launch a college for special professions. Other projects, including in the field of tourism, are already under way.

There was this one defining moment in their gorgeous new apartment in Munich that had taken them so long to find. That's when Georg Eichenberg told his wife Alexandra twelve years ago about his plan to leave behind their life in Germany and move to Oman. "We had only just moved in, and I finally felt settled down," says Alexandra, still remembering the shock she felt back then. However, the smile on her face never fades and she has good reason to be upbeat these days. The training institute they run together has just entered into a partnership with the Rosenheim University of Applied Science in Bavaria. In cooperation with the professors there, the couple help Omani specialists and managers to be more successful in their professional lives.

A Winning Team

Forschung im bayerischen Rosenheim geworden – zusammen mit den dortigen Professoren unterstützt das Paar junge omanische Fach- und Führungskräfte auf vielfältige Weise dabei, im Berufsleben erfolgreich zu sein.

„Hier im Oman müssen auch ‚soft skills' wie gegenseitiger Respekt trainiert werden – damit nicht jeder nur an sich und seine Familie oder seinen Stamm denkt, sondern sich auch innerhalb der Gemeinschaft verantwortlich fühlt. Das fängt schon damit an, zu Meetings pünktlich zu kommen. Der Imam verspätet sich ja auch nicht beim Gebet in der Moschee", sagt Georg Eichenberg. Seine Frau sieht es als eine ihrer Aufgaben an, Omanis gleich nach ihrem Studium darin zu schulen, erfolgreich im Team zu arbeiten oder ethische Grundsätze wie Ehrlichkeit und tägliche Arbeitsdisziplin ernst zu nehmen. Dabei signalisiert sie ihren Kursteilnehmern mit ihrem freundlichen, zugewandten Blick ihre ungeteilte Aufmerksamkeit und überzeugt auf ihre besondere Art und Weise auch zurückhaltende Kandidaten.

Dass die beiden es so gut geschafft haben, in Oman Fuß zu fassen und ein fester Bestandteil der Gesellschaft zu werden, verdanken sie nicht nur ihrer Entdeckerfreude. Dazu gehörten ebenso viel Leidenschaft und vor allem

"Here in Oman 'soft skills' such as mutual respect also need training. This helps people to not only think about themselves, their families or tribes but also to take on a sense of responsibility within the community. This starts with turning up to meetings on time. After all, the imam doesn't come late for prayer time in the mosque," Georg says. His wife regards it as one of her tasks to show Omani graduates how to work successfully in a team and to take principles such as honesty and discipline at work seriously. Her friendly and attentive manner signals to the course participants that she is focused solely on them. Her unique way of training wins over even the most reserved of participants.

Their love of discovering isn't the only reason that the two of them could gain a foothold in Oman and become an integral part of the community. It also took passion and courage to not let difficulties get in their way. It was hard work getting where they are now and, at the same time, finding a good work-life balance. "When we needed some time out, we would sometimes drive to the Jabal Akhdar mountains and avoid talking business," says Alexandra . Her husband adds with a wink: "Golf is even better, it's a sport where you don't need to talk much but you're still together." They can tee off at one of Oman's golf courses, that is, if there's any time left in their busy schedule.

Georg Eichenberg in einem Training, bei dem es unter anderem um Kommunikation und Kooperation geht.
Georg Eichenberg in a training session that focuses on communication and cooperation.

der Mut, sich von Schwierigkeiten nicht aufhalten zu lassen. Insgesamt ein hartes Stück Arbeit – auch daran, gemeinsam die Balance zu finden, beruflich wie privat. „Dafür fahren wir dann schon mal zusammen ins Jabal Akhdar-Gebirge, ohne über Geschäftliches zu reden", sagt Alexandra Eichenberg. Ihr Mann ergänzt augenzwinkernd: „Noch besser ist es, Golf zu spielen – das ist ja ein Sport, bei dem man wenige Worte braucht und doch zusammen aktiv ist." Wenn denn bei den vielen anderen Terminen überhaupt Zeit dafür bleibt, den Abschlag auf Omans Plätzen zu üben...

Doch zurück zum Beginn: Georg Eichenberg war in der Automobil-Zuliefererindustrie beschäftigt, während Alexandra Eichenberg mit ehrgeizigen Plänen ihr erstes Büro an Düsseldorfs feinster Adresse, der Königsallee, gemietet hatte. Dort arbeitete sie anfangs als Headhunterin und Trainerin, bevor sie mit ihrem Mann 2004 nach München zog. Dort baute die Coaching-Expertin ihr Geschäft ganz neu auf. Just als alles gut lief, verlor Georg Eichenberg auf einer Unternehmerreise sein Herz an den Oman.

Adé ihr gemütlichen Spaziergänge an der Isar, hallo du Abenteuer in Arabien – der gelernte Ingenieur und studierte Maschinenbauer wollte etwas ganz anderes machen als seine Vorväter. Der quirlige Mann, der so schnell in Kontakt mit anderen kommt, suchte neue Herausforderungen. Seine Frau sieht eine ähnliche Entwicklung bei anderen Männern in ihren Coachings: „Ab Anfang 40 überlegen viele, wie es in ihrem Leben sinnvoll weitergehen kann." Ein Hasardeur ist Georg Eichenberg nicht, aber er mag auch nicht zu viel über Risiken nachdenken: „Dann macht man es nämlich nicht", ist er sicher. Und sein Entschluss stand fest, zumal er schon damals bei seiner ersten Reise in den Mittleren Osten sah: Oman „brummte", die Wirtschaft des Landes durchstand auch Krisen relativ stabil.

Es galt nun, erst einmal Fuß zu fassen. Anfangs pendelte Alexandra Eichenberg zwischen Deutschland und Oman, betreute weiterhin ihre festen Kunden. 2009 zog sie schließlich ganz mit ihrem Mann nach Maskat. Dort mussten die beiden dann fast ein Jahr lang auf eine Lizenz warten, um mit ihren Trainings Coachings loslegen zu können – und hatten aber die Auflage, während der gesamten Zeit bereits ein Büro zu unterhalten. „Ich habe

But back to where it all began: Georg Eichenberg was employed in the automotive supply industry, while Alexandra Eichenberg had ambitious plans of her own and rented her first office at Düsseldorf's most elite address, the Königsallee. At first, she worked there as a headhunter and trainer before moving to Munich with her husband in 2004. There, the coaching expert re-established her business. Just when everything was going well, Georg fell in love with Oman during a business trip.

Farewell to strolling along the banks of the Isar river, hello to adventures in Arabia. After studying mechanical engineering, George wanted to do something totally

Leidenschaft für die Arbeit mit Menschen, Entdeckerfreude und Mut zu neuen Lösungen

Passion for working with people, joy of discovery and the courage to find new solutions

different than his forefathers. The energetic man, who quickly makes new contacts, was looking for a new challenge. His wife sees the same thing with other men during her coaching: "Starting in their forties, many men start thinking about how their lives can continue in a meaningful way." Georg Eichenberg isn't a gambling man but he prefers not to think too much about risks: "That only keeps you from doing things," he says with confidence. And once his decision was made, there was no turning back, particularly because he had already realised on his first trip to the Middle East that Oman was buzzing, and the country's economy was relatively stable even during crises.

The first thing he had to do was get his foot in the door. Initially, Alexandra commuted between Germany and Oman, continuing to mentor her regular clients. In 2009, she finally moved to Muscat with her husband full-time. They had to wait almost a year for their licenses to start their training sessions; however, they had to maintain an office the entire time. "I read the biographies of entrepreneurs such as Steve Jobs in order to keep myself

Biografien von Unternehmern wie Steve Jobs gelesen, um mich in der quälenden Wartezeit innerlich aufzubauen und Rückschläge, zum Beispiel während der Ölpreiskrise, besser zu verkraften", erzählt Alexandra Eichenberg. Auch ganz Menschliches musste gemeistert werden, denn der Körper verändert sich in der Hitze Arabiens. „Wir haben zwei Jahre gebraucht, um das richtige Deodorant ohne Aluminiumzusätze zu finden", schmunzelt Georg Eichenberg.

Aufzugeben kam den beiden nicht in den Sinn – sie hatten beschlossen, den Kopf oben zu behalten, gemeinsam die Startphase zu überstehen. Und siehe da: Erst zaghaft, dann zunehmend intensiver bahnten sich Freundschaften mit den Omanis an. „Wir schätzen ihre freundliche Offenheit. Inzwischen lege ich manchen bei der Begrüßung die Hand auf den Handrücken– ein vertrautes Zeichen besonderer Zuwendung", erzählt Alexandra Eichenberg. Ihr Mann fügt an: „Durch Mundpropaganda machte derweil im Land die Runde, dass es da ein Trainings-Institut gibt, in dem gute Arbeit geleistet wird und dessen Kursteilnehmer begeistert sind." Er offenbart noch weitere Zutaten des persönlichen Erfolgsrezepts: Immer wieder bei potenziellen omanischen Geschäftspartnern anklopfen, auch wenn es nach europäischen Maßstäben fast unhöflich erscheinen mag. Und ständig damit rechnen, dass überraschend Gäste vor der eigenen Tür stehen, die willkommen geheißen werden wollen – Privates und Geschäftliches geht dabei zuweilen Hand in Hand.

Ein weiterer Zufall kam Eichenbergs zu Hilfe: Die Ölpreiskrise sorgte dafür, dass die Budgets für Bildungs-

driven during the agonising waiting period and to cope with setbacks, for example during the oil crisis," Alexandra tell us. They also had to cope with physical changes as their bodies got used to the Arabian heat : "It took us two years to find the right deodorant without aluminium," says Georg with a chuckle.

Neither ever considered giving up – they had decided to keep their chins up in order to get through the difficult first stage. Then slowly but surely they started to make friends with the Omanis, at first tentatively then full-steam ahead. "We appreciate how friendly and open-minded they are. Nowadays, I put my hand on the back of the hands of some of my friends when we say hello – a personal gesture of special affection," says Alexandra. Her husband adds: "Word got around Oman that there was a training institute doing a good job and that participants were really happy." He also reveals further ingredients for his personal recipe for success: Keep knocking on the

Studierende machen Abschlüsse in Human Resources oder Office Management

Students graduate in Human Resources or Office Management

Mund-zu-Mund-Propaganda und begeisterte Kursteilnehmer machen das Trainingsinstitut immer bekannter.
Enthusiastic students have spread the word about the training institute.

reisen ins Ausland zusammenschnurrten. Seitdem schicken Unternehmen ihre Mitarbeiter wieder in Seminare innerhalb des Landes. Zum Beispiel zu den Eichenbergs, die das Arbeitsministerium immer wieder von der Qualität ihrer Curricula überzeugen können und – im Gegensatz zu vielen anderen Fortbildungsinstituten – stets aufs Neue eine Lizenz erhalten. Das hat auch damit zu tun, dass sie Wert auf die Effektivität ihrer Trainings legen. Wie nachhaltig das vermittelte Wissen angewandt wird, das soll künftig noch stärker mit den Führungskräften in den Unternehmen überprüft werden.

Vor allem aber liegt es den beiden am Herzen, dass die Teilnehmer sich in den Seminaren wohlfühlen. „Wir gestalten die Stunden so, dass die Menschen das Lernen und Trainieren regelrecht spüren können – zum Beispiel in einem Rollenspiel oder indem sie ein Bild malen und dadurch ausdrücken, was Führungsqualität für sie bedeutet. Das macht viel aus", erzählt Alexandra Eichen-

doors of potential Omani business partners, even if it may seem rude by European standards. And always be ready for surprise guests dropping by unannounced and expecting you to welcome them in; private and professional life in Oman sometimes go hand in hand.

Another fortunate coincidence worked in the Eichenberg's favour: Due to the oil crisis, budgets for training abroad were heavily cut back. Since then, companies have been sending their staff to seminars within the country again. The Eichenbergs have always been able to convince the Ministry of Labour of the quality of their training programmes and curricula, and are always awarded a new license, which is not the case for many other educational institutes. This has also to do with the fact that they set great store by the effectiveness of their training. The extent to which the knowledge they impart is applied over the long term is something the Eichenbergs want to look at even more closely with companies in the future.

A Winning Team

berg. Um Themen wie „Vertrauen fassen" fühlbar zu machen, reicht oft schon die schlichte Erfahrung, sich von einem Kollegen einmal mit verbundenen Augen, also quasi blind, führen zu lassen. Beim Teambuilding müssen die Übungen allerdings den Gepflogenheiten des Landes angepasst werden. So sind Männer und Frauen bei bestimmten Aktionen beispielsweise über lange Schnüre miteinander in Kontakt, ohne einander dabei zu berühren.

Zusammen mit Abdulhakeem Al Jardani, ihrem neuen omanischen Partner, schlugen die Eichenbergs 2017 ein weiteres Kapitel ihrer Erfolgsgeschichte auf: die Partnerschaft mit der Uni Rosenheim. Sie macht es möglich, dass in Zusammenarbeit mit Professoren, die einfliegen, noch mehr praxisnahes Wissen bereitgestellt wird - zum Beispiel im Bereich Finanzen. Zudem wollen die drei Partner, die ihr Unternehmen jetzt Oakhill („Eichenberg") Development Academy genannt haben, ein College gründen und Studierenden Abschlüsse als Bachelor in „Human Resources" oder „Office Management" ermöglichen. So rückt Oman in Sachen Weiterbildung unweigerlich näher an Deutschland heran. Dorthin zurückzukehren – das kommt Alexandra und Georg Eichenberg allerdings nicht in den Sinn, im Gegenteil: Sie haben das Gefühl, endgültig angekommen zu sein und sich weitere Wünsche erfüllen zu können. Dazu gehört die Eröffnung eines kleinen, feinen Boutique-Hotels - weil sie in ihren Jahren in Oman gelernt haben, spontan gute Gastgeber, auch für überraschende Besucher, zu sein ...

However, one of the most important things to the Eichenbergs is that their participants feel comfortable in the seminars. "We design the training sessions in such a way that people can really feel that they learning; for example, through role-playing or by drawing a picture so they can express what quality leadership means to them. That certainly makes a difference," says Alexandra. In order to make topics such as trust tangible, it's often enough to simply let a colleague lead you with your eyes blindfolded. In terms of team-building, the exercises need to be adjusted to the customs of the country. For instance, there are certain activities where men and women are in contact via long strings but do not physically touch each other.

In cooperation with Abdulhakeem Al Jardani, their new Omani partner, they started a new chapter in their success story: their collaboration with Rosenheim University. This means that they now have access to even more expert knowledge, for example by flying in a professor of economics. In addition, the three partners, who call their company Oakhill Development Academy, intend to launch a college where students can get a Bachelor's degree in human resources or office management. This means that Oman will move even closer to Germany in terms of tertiary education. Returning to Germany is something that Alexandra and Georg don't even think about. On the contrary, they feel that they have finally arrived and now can fulfil more of their dreams. One of these is to open up a small boutique hotel because they have learned during all their years in Oman that it's important to be good hosts, even when surprise visitors turn up unexpectedly

Oakhill Development Academy

Gute Personalentwicklung ist das Anliegen der Oakhill Development Academy mit ihrem Team von zehn Mitarbeitern – getreu den Grundsätzen der systemischen Beratung nach Bernd Schmid (Gründer des Instituts für Systemische Beratung ISB in Wiesloch), bei dem Alexandra Eichenberg ausgebildet wurde. „Der holistische Ansatz, den wir verfolgen, besagt: Der Mensch steht im Mittelpunkt, ist aber in drei Bereiche eingebettet – in die Organisation in seinem Unternehmen, zum Beispiel in seiner Abteilung. Als zweites spielt er eine bestimmte Rolle durch sein Wissen und seine Skills innerhalb der Berufswelt." Hinzu kommt die private Welt, die auch während der Arbeit nicht ausgeblendet werden kann. „In unseren Trainings beziehen wir alle drei Bereiche mit ein – bei unseren Teambuildings geht es viel um Kooperation, Kommunikation", sagt Alexandra Eichenberg.

Integrität und Loyalität gegenüber dem Unternehmen, bei dem man beschäftigt ist – also ethische Werte bei der Arbeit - werden ebenfalls in Seminaren (weiter)entwickelt. Als weiterer wichtiger Aspekt kommt Change-Management hinzu, das Gestalten von Veränderungsprozessen in Unternehmen. Die Oakhill Development Academy bietet auch Kurse und Workshops über die Grenzen Omans hinweg in den Emiraten, Qatar, Kuwait und Saudi-Arabien an. Zu ihren Kunden zählt Farooq Shaikhan Al Toobi (Strategic Business Partner, Oman Airports): „Wenn es um Personalentwicklung geht, ist die Oakhill Development Academy erste Wahl für uns, weil sie für Kompetenz, Verlässlichkeit und Nachhaltigkeit steht. Oakhill arbeitet mit unkonventionellen Methoden, um unsere Mitarbeiter und Organisation gleichermaßen in den Bereichen Leadership, Change und Kommunikation weiter zu entwickeln. Dabei sind Alexandra und Georg Eichenberg immer offen, lösungsorientiert und gleichzeitig unkompliziert."

Mehr Informationen gibt es unter www.oakhill.de

Oakhill Development Academy

The objective of the Oakhill Development Academy, with its team of ten, is good personnel development. "Oakhill" is the English word for "Eichenberg". The Academy follows the principles of systemic consulting developed by Bernd Schmid, founder of the Institute for Systemic Consulting (ISB) in Wiesloch, where Alexandra Eichenberg was trained.

"The holistic approach that we follow states: The person is at the centre, but is embedded in three different areas. First, in the organisation of their company, for example their department. Second, they play a certain role because of their knowledge and skills within the professional world." Finally, there is the private world, which cannot be ignored, even during working hours. "We include all three areas in our training – our team-building activities revolve a lot around cooperation and communication," Alexandra says.

Integrity and loyalty towards one's company – ethical values in the work environment – are also worked on in seminars. Another important aspect is change management in companies. The Oakhill Development Academy also offers courses and workshops outside Oman, including the UAE, Qatar, Kuwait and Saudi Arabia. One of Academy's clients is Farooq Shaikhan Al Toobi, Strategic Business Partner at Oman Airports: "As far as staff development is concerned, the Oakhill Development Agency is our first choice, because it represents competence, reliability and sustainability. Oakhill uses unconventional methods to help both our staff members and our organisation to develop further in areas such as leadership, change and communication. Alexandra and Georg Eichenberg are open-minded, solution-oriented and at the same time uncomplicated."

More information is available at www.oakhill.de

Nach dem Öl: Wirtschaft neu denken

Life after Oil: Rethinking the Economy

ITHRAA promotet Investitionschancen
in fünf Schwerpunkten

ITHRAA promotes investment opportunities
in five main areas

فترة ما بعد النفط: التفكير الاقتصادي الجديد
تشير "إثراء" إلى خمسة مجالات رئيسية للاستثمار

بما أن مخزون النفط أو احتياطي النفط سيكون له نهاية يوماً ما، فإنه يجب على عُمان أن تكون متأهبة للمستقبل. لذلك تريد سلطنة عُمان إقامة بنية اقتصادية جديدة لها. أسُست "إثراء" في عام 1996م لتتولى مسؤولية الاستثمار في مجال إنتاج النفط. فهي مسؤولة عن عرض عُمان على مستثمرين اقتصاديين عالميين وتساعد المستثمرين الأقوياء على إنشاء شركاتهم في عُمان في الخمسة مجالات الرئيسية للاستثمار.

Weil die Ressource Öl endlich ist, muss sich Oman für die Zukunft wappnen. Daher will sich das Sultanat wirtschaftlich neu aufstellen. IHTRAA wurde 1996 gegründet und ist die Investitions- und Exportförderungs-Agentur des Landes. Sie stellt es einem internationalen Wirtschaftspublikum vor und unterstützt potenzielle Investoren bei der Ansiedlung vor Ort.

Know-how-Transfer, Begleitung bei bürokratischen Prozessen, Organisation von wirtschaftlichen Veranstaltungen oder die Organisationen von Auslandsdelegationen sind einige der Aktivitäten von ITHRAA (the Public Authority for Investment Promotion and Export Development). Auf diese Weise soll Oman als Wirtschaftsstandort international einem breiten Wirtschaftspublikum präsentiert werden, um finanzstarke Investoren zu überzeugen.

Der aktuelle wirtschaftliche Entwicklungsplan definiert fünf Branchen mit besonderem Wachstumspotenzial. Dazu zählen die verarbeitende Industrie, Tourismus, Logistik, Landwirtschaft sowie der Sektor Fischerei und Bergbau.

ITHRAA nennt acht wirtschaftliche Schlüsselstandorte im Sultanat. An der Küste von Norden Richtung Süden liegen Sohar, Maskat, Sur, Duqm, Salalah; dazu kommen Al Muzunah im Gouvernment Dhofar. Im nördlichen Landesinnern befinden sich Al Buraimi und Nizwa.

Flug- und Seehäfen, Industriezonen und Free Zones sollen diese Standorte für Unternehmen attraktiv machen. Speziell die Free Zones locken mit besonderen wirtschaftlichen Rahmenbedingungen und steuerlichen Anreizen.

Eine junge, vielfach international ausgebildete Bevölkerung, die politische Stabilität im Land und eine wachsende Infrastruktur sind einige der Faktoren, die für das Land auf der arabischen Halbinsel sprechen und ausländische Investoren überzeugen sollen.

Wer im Oman mit einem Standort vertreten sein möchte, kann sich bei den Experten von ITHRAA beraten lassen. Welche lokalen Investoren kommen als potenzielle Partner infrage? Welche Maßnahmen sind die geeigneten, um schnellstmöglich Erfolge zu erzielen? Welche beson-

As oil is a limited resource, Oman has to ready itself for the future. That's why the Sultanate is looking for a new economic direction. IHTRAA, the country's agency for promoting investment and exports, was founded in 1996. The agency promotes the country to the international economic community and supports potential investors who are thinking about setting up business there.

Transfer of know-how, support with bureaucratic processes, organisation of economic events or of foreign delegations are among the activities of ITHRAA (Oman's Inward Investment and Export Development Agency). The aim is to promote Oman internationally as an attractive country for investors to invest their money.

The current economic development plan defines five sectors with particularly good growth potential: manufacturing, tourism, logistics, agriculture, and the sector of fishing and mining. ITHRAA lists eight key economic locations in the Sultanate. These are: Sohar; Muscat; Sur, Duqm; Salalah running north to south on the coastline; Al Muzunah in the Dhofar Governorate; and Al Buraimi and Nizwa in the country's northern interior. Airports and harbours, industrial zones and "free zones" make these locations attractive for businesses. The free zones are particularly appealing with their special economic conditions and tax incentives.

A young population, frequently with international training, the country's political stability and a growing infrastructure are among the advantages of this country on the Arabian Peninsula which draw foreign investors.

Anyone who wants to set up a subsidiary in Oman, can get advice from an ITHRAA expert. Which local investors are suitable as potential partners? What's the best way to achieve quick success? Which special conditions apply locally, and which legal regulations need to be observed?

In the future, Oman wants to secure its place as a logistical hub from which goods are transported to destinations all over the world. "Most people outside Oman and the Gulf States aren't aware of the commercial possibilities here," explained Abdulrahman Salim Al Hatmi, CEO of logistics provider ASYAD, in an interview with the English-language newspaper Muscat Daily in November

Oman gestaltet seine Zukunft mit einer jungen, international ausgebildeten Bevölkerung

Oman is shaping its future with a young, internationally educated population

deren Bedingungen gelten vor Ort und welche gesetzlichen Vorschriften sind zu beachten?

Oman möchte sich künftig als logistische Drehscheibe positionieren, von der aus Güter in alle Welt transportiert werden. „Die meisten Menschen außerhalb des Oman und der Golfstaaten kennen die geschäftlichen Möglichkeiten nicht, die sich hier bieten", erklärte Abdulrahman Salim Al Hatmi, CEO von Logistik-Anbieter ASYAD, in einem Interview mit der englischsprachigen Tageszeitung Muscat Daily im November 2018. Internationale Wirtschaftskongresse sollen zukünftig vermehrt auf das Potenzial im Sultanat und seine wachsende Infrastruktur aufmerksam machen. Themen wie Internethandel, künstliche Intelligenz, Drohnen, neue Datenbanktechnologien stehen dabei auf der Agenda.

Deutsche Unternehmen haben seit den 1960er Jahren beim Aufbau einer leistungsfähigen Infrastruktur im Oman einen wichtigen Beitrag geleistet. Laut Informationen des Auswärtigen Amtes vom Juni 2018 lagen die deutschen Ausfuhren nach Oman 2017 bei 916,5 Millionen Euro (2016: 834,1 Millionen Euro). Wichtigste Exportprodukte waren dabei Kraftfahrzeuge und Kraftfahrzeugteile, Arzneimittel, Kunststoffe, Industriechemikalien und Maschinen. Die Importe betrugen 2017 etwa 38,8 Millionen Euro (2016: 39,4 Millionen Euro). Experten gehen davon aus, dass der tatsächliche Exportwert höher liegt, da die deutschen Exporte teilweise über die Vereinigten Arabischen Emirate nach Oman gelangen.

Deutsche Firmen waren und sind bei wichtigen Projekten beteiligt. So liefert zum Beispiel Siemens Turbinen für Gaskraftwerke und die Flughäfen, die München GmbH berät beim Ausbau der Flughäfen in Maskat und Salalah, die Europoles GmbH trug mit Schleuderbetonmasten zur Sicherheit bei der Weiterleitung von Strom bei.

Mehr Informationen gibt es unter: www.ithraa.om

2018. There will soon be international economic congresses to raise awareness of the Sultanate's potential and its growing infrastructure. Topics such as internet commerce, artificial intelligence, drones and new database technologies are on the agenda.

Since the 1960s, German enterprises have been an important part of establishing an efficient infrastructure in Oman. According to information provided by the Foreign Office in June 2018, German exports to Oman amounted to €916.5 million in 2017 (2016: €834.1 million). The most important exports were motor vehicles and their components, pharmaceuticals, synthetic materials, industrial chemicals and machinery. Imports in 2017 came in at approximately €38.8 million (2016: €39.4 million). Experts believe the actual export value to be higher because German exports also enter Oman via the United Arab Emirates. German companies have been involved in several important projects. For example, Siemens provided turbines for gas-fired power plants and the airports; München GmbH provided consulting services for the expansion of the airports in Muscat and Salalah; Europoles GmbH contributes to the safety of power poles by providing spun-concrete masts.

More information available at: www.ithraa.om

Im Oman müssen neue Arbeitsplätze – zum Beispiel bei der Herstellung von Batterien – entstehen, da die natürliche Ressource Öl endlich ist. New jobs must be created in Oman – for example in the production of batteries – because the natural resource oil is finite.

Life after Oil: Rethinking the Economy

Endrik Mehlo in der Mühle von Sohar – Mahlsteine gibt es nicht mehr, die Rohre transportieren das Mehl.
Endrik Mehlo in the mill of Sohar – there are no more millstones, the pipes transport the flour.

In der Mühle am rauschenden Golf

In the Mill on the Edge of the Gulf

Endrik Mehlo ist der Müller von Oman
und Uwe Müllers backt das Brot

Endrik Mehlo is the miller of Oman
and Uwe Müllers bakes its bread

في الطاحونة عند الخليج الهادر
إندريك ميلو هو طحان عُمان يخبز الخبز هناك

إن الطاحونة التي تحدث أصوات عند الجدول الهادر هي جزء من الماضي: الآن يُجلب الطحين النقي كل يوم في الأنابيب المعدنية النقية قبل أن يعبأ بشكل جيد ويرسل إلى المخابز والأسواق. إن مهنة الطحان أصبحت نادرة في جميع أنحاء العالم. حيث أنه يجري البحث عن الأخصائيين الذين تدربوا في ألمانيا. إندريك ميلو من مدينة بريمن هو الطحان في عُمان: إنه مسؤول منذ عشرة سنوات عن توفير صناعة الخبز في الخليج — على سبيل المثال من الخباز الألماني أوفي موللرس. إن ميلو هو المسؤول حالياً عن أحدث طاحونة في عُمان، من بين أربعة طواحين موجودة هناك: طاحونة صحار.

Das Schild weist auf die deutsche Bäckerei in Maskat hin – sie liegt versteckt in einem Industrieviertel.
The sign refers to the German bakery in Muscat – hidden in an industrial quarter.

Die klappernde Mühle am rauschenden Bach gehört der Vergangenheit an: Reines Mehl rauscht heute mehrmals durch stählerne Rohre, bevor es fein abgepackt in Bäckereien und Supermärkte geliefert wird. Der Müller ist weltweit ein seltener Beruf geworden – gesucht sind Spezialisten, die in Deutschland ausgebildet werden. Endrik Mehlo aus Bremen ist der Müller von Oman: Seit fast zehn Jahren sorgt er dafür, dass am Golf Brot gebacken werden kann – zum Beispiel vom deutschen Bäcker Uwe Müllers. Jetzt leitet Mehlo eine der vier Mühlen des Landes, Sohar Flour Mills. Sie gehört seinem bisherigen Arbeitgeber Oman Flour Mills zu 60 Prozent und Mr. Essa Al Ghurair aus Dubai zu 40 Prozent. Sie hat für dieses Projekt umgerechnet 30 Millionen Euro berappt.

Der Hüne von mehr als zwei Metern macht sich keine Illusionen über seinen Job: „Müller zu sein, das hat kein Prestige. Mehl ist ein Massenprodukt", erzählt Endrik Mehlo in seinem Büro im Industriehafen von Sohar. Auf dem Schrank stehen Loriots Figuren Müller-Lüdenscheidt und Dr. Klöbner als Buchstützen, vor dem Fenster ankern die Bulk carrier – spezielle Schiffe, die den Weizen aus Australien, Russland oder Kanada bringen. Bevor daraus die Basis fürs Brot wird, überprüft Mehlo die Körner: Er riecht daran, weil ihm die geschulte Nase verrät, ob sie verunreinigt sind; kaut ein paar davon, um

The clattering sounds of a mill next to a rushing stream are a thing of the past. Nowadays, flour rushes through steel tubes several times until it is ground fine enough to be packaged and delivered to bakeries and supermarkets. All over the world, the profession of miller is dying out, but millers who have been trained in Germany are in high demand. Endrick Mehlo from Bremen is the miller of Oman. For almost ten years, he has made sure that bread can be baked on the Gulf – for example, by German baker Uwe Müllers. Mehlo is now head of one of four mills in the country, Sohar Flour Mills. 60 percent of it is owned by his former employer Oman Flour Mills and 40 percent by Mr. Essa from Dubai, which has invested the equivalent of €30 million in the project.

He may be a giant, coming in at over 2 metres, but his expectations regarding his job are not as high. "Being a miller isn't prestigious. Flour is a mass-produced product," he tells us from his office in Sohar's industrial port. On his cabinet, he has figurines of Müller-Lüdenscheidt and Dr. Klöbner as book ends, characters created by German humourist Loriot. Special cargo ships anchor directly in front of his window which have carried wheat from Australia, Russia or Canada. Mehlo checks the grains closely before they are turned into flour for bread. His well-trained nose tells him if they are tainted; he chews a

den Anteil von Protein zu erschmecken. Ein anerkennender Blick in die Tüte – und das Urteil lautet: „Guter australischer Weizen mit großen Körnern, da steckt viel Mehl drin."

Sein Wissen hat der frisch gebackene Betriebsleiter von Sohar Flour Mills aus der dreijährigen Ausbildung, die er später mit dem Meistertitel in Stuttgart abgeschlossen hat. Die Berufswahl war nicht durch den Namen bedingt (obwohl Mehlos Mutter obendrein früher Weizenkorn hieß), sondern eine Idee seines Vaters: Er hatte ein Ausbildungsangebot in der Zeitung gefunden. Die väterliche Bestimmung hat der bodenständige Mann schnell angenommen. Ihn zieht es in den Iran, wo er seine jetzige Frau Maryam kennenlernte. Die beiden heiraten und arbeiten gemeinsam bei einer Niederlassung der Schweizer Firma Bühler, dem Weltmarktführer für Müllereimaschinen, die auch Reinigungsgeräte für Körner herstellt. Dann entschließen sie sich, in den Oman zu ziehen – hier, nicht weit von Maryams iranischer Familie – lebt die Müllerfamilie, zu der inzwischen auch

few to taste the amount of protein. He looks into the bag approvingly – his verdict: "Good Australian wheat with large grains, this will yield a lot of flour."

The newly appointed company director of Sohar Flour Mills gained his knowledge from a three-year apprenticeship that he finished with his master craftsman certificate in Stuttgart. It wasn't just his name that led to his choice of profession (Mehlo translates to flour and his mother's maiden is Weizenkorn, which means wheat grain). Instead, it was his father's idea, who one day found an advertisement for an apprenticeship in a newspaper. Being down-to-earth, Mehlo quickly accepted his father's decision. He was drawn to Iran, where he met his now wife Maryam. The two of them married and worked together at a subsidiary of the Swiss company Bühler, the global market leader in milling machines, one of their product lines being cleaning machines for grains. Then they decided to move to Oman and live close to Maryam Iranian's family in the up-and-coming quarter of Al Mouj ("the Wave") in Muscat. Mehlo's own family now includes

Die Regale sind leer, Roggenbrot muss als Besonderheit bei Uwe Müllers bestellt werden.
The shelves are empty, rye bread must be ordered as a speciality from Uwe Müllers.

die Kinder Mehrzad, Marziar und Nilufar zählen, im aufstrebenden Viertel „Al Mouj / Die Welle" in Maskat: „Oman ist steuerfrei und sicher. Und die Kinder gehen in die internationale Schule, wachsen viersprachig auf, können mit dem Fahrrad rausfahren", so fasst Endrik Mehlo die Vorteile seiner Wahlheimat zusammen. Er selbst pendelt zwischen der neu eröffneten Mühle in Sohar und dem 200 Kilometer entfernten Maskat, wo er zuvor gearbeitet hat, um am Wochenende mit den Kindern Rugby zu spielen.

Während der Woche hat er einen hochexplosiven Job: „Mehlstaub ist in bestimmten Konzentrationen entzündlich. Wenn man nicht aufpasst, fliegt die ganze Mühle in die Luft", stellt Mehlo nüchtern fest und zieht den Schutzhelm auf, um die acht Etagen bis aufs Dach seiner Arbeitsstätte hinaufzuklettern. Dort sind Einheimische an der Seite von Arbeitern aus Indien, Pakistan und Bangladesh täglich damit beschäftigt, 600 Tonnen Getreide zu verarbeiten. 40 Prozent der Belegschaft müssen nach dem Willen des Staates aus dem Oman stammen.

the children Mehrzad, Marziar and Nilufar. "Oman is tax-free and safe. The children ride their bikes to the international school where they speak four languages," lists Endrik as some of the advantages of his chosen home. He himself commutes 200 kilometres between the newly opened mill in Sohar and Muscat, where he previously worked, in order to play rugby with his children on the weekends.

During the week he has a highly "explosive" job. "In certain concentrations, flour dust is flammable. If you aren't careful, the whole mill will blow up," Mehlo states prosaically and puts on his helmet to climb the eight flights of stairs leading to the roof of his workplace. Locals work alongside workers from India, Pakistan and Bangladesh; they process 600 tonnes of grain every day. As mandated by the state, 40 percent of the workforce comes from Oman.

To prevent insect eggs being laid in the flour and making it "come alive", the grains are put into a special egg-kill-

Rahma Müllers hat von ihrem Mann gelernt, wie Brotlaibe aussehen müssen.
Rahma Müllers learned from her husband what bread loaves must look like.

Damit sich keine Insekteneier ins Mehl verirren und dieses quasi „lebendig" zu werden droht, werden die Körner in einer speziellen Eiertöter-Maschine gegen Metallwände geschlagen. Siebe sortieren die verfärbten, unbrauchbaren Exemplare heraus. Walzen, die gegeneinander laufen, brechen dann die Körner auf. Sie rieseln und rauschen, zunehmend feiner werdend, durch zehn Vermahlungsstufen. Das geschieht innerhalb weit verzweigter Metallrohrsysteme, die das Innere der Mühle durchziehen. Zufrieden spitzt Endrik Mehlo bei seinem Rundgang die Ohren: „Wenn alles rund läuft, schnurrt die Mühle wie eine Katze." Das fertige Mehl bekommt am Schluss noch Enzyme, Eisen (eine Vorgabe der Weltgesundheitsorganisation WHO in diesem Teil der Welt) und Vitamin C zugesetzt. „So altern wir in gewisser Weise das Mehl, und es bekommt bessere Backeigenschaften. Das überprüfen wir bei Back-Tests", erwähnt der Müller.

Inzwischen ist er auf dem Dach seines Mahlturms am Golf von Oman angekommen und schaut zu den Nachbarn: Eisenerz, Stahl und Aluminium wird da produziert, vorwiegend von indischen Firmen. Der 20 Quadratkilometer große Hafen von Sohar ist ein 50prozentiges Joint Venture des europäischen Bruders in Rotterdam. Gleich nebenan raucht wie ein dunkles Ungetüm eine Stahlfirma vor sich hin, sie wirkt wie ein Relikt aus den Anfangszeiten der Industrialisierung. Als heller Kontrast dagegen die Mühle, ein echtes Zukunftsprojekt. „Natürlich erwartet man von mir, dass ich als Deutscher hier Struktur und Ordnung hineinbringe", sagt Endrik Mehlo. Dafür muss er halt auf den würzigen heimischen Senf zu seinem Würstchen verzichten – und darauf, zu sehen, wie sich die Blätter im Herbst verfärben. Denn Jahreszeiten gibt es im Oman nicht, nur heiß im Sommer und angenehm warm im Winter. Mehl hingegen braucht hier jeder, auch der deutsche Bäcker, der manchen Einheimischen schon mit bayerischen Brezeln versorgt hat. Der heißt übrigens Uwe Müllers und eröffnete seine „Oman Bakery" Ende der 1970er Jahre. Heute ist er selbst in den 70ern und backt nur noch auf Bestellung, Roggenbrot mit importiertem Mehl aus Deutschland zum Beispiel oder Proteinbrot für gesundheitsbewusste Omaner – 25 Kilo für 55 Rial, das sind rund 130 Euro. Dabei hilft ihm seine einheimische Frau Rahma. „Sie ist inzwischen die bessere Bäckerin", sagt Müllers schmunzelnd.

ing machine, where they are beaten against metal walls. Sieves sort out the discoloured, unusable grains. Opposed rollers then crack the grains open. They fall and whistle through ten levels of grinding, becoming ever finer. This takes place within a wide network of metal pipe systems that run through the interior of the mill. Contentedly, Mehlo pricks up his ears during his walkthrough. "When everything runs smoothly, the mill purrs like a cat." At the end of the process, enzymes, iron (a WHO / World Health Organization requirement in this part of the world) and vitamin C are added to the finished flour. "That way we effectively age the flour to improve its baking properties. We carry out baking tests to make sure of the quality," the miller goes on to say.

Meanwhile, he has arrived on the roof of his grinding tower on the Gulf of Oman and looks over to his neighbours where iron ore, steel and aluminium are being processed, mainly by Indian companies. The large harbour of Sohar measures 20 square kilometres and is a 50/50 joint venture of its European partner in Rotterdam. Right next door, a steel company is smoking away like a dark monster, a relic from the early days of industrialisation. The mill stands in striking contrast, a true project for the future. "Of course, as a German, I am expected to introduce structure and order," Endrik says. To do this, he has to forego his bratwurst and savoury mustard from back home, and he no longer sees the leaves change colour in autumn. That's because there are no seasons in Oman, only hot in summer and pleasantly warm in winter. Flour, however, is something that everyone needs, including the German baker who has provided many a local with Bavarian pretzels. His name happens to be Uwe Müllers (again the German word for a miller), and he opened his Oman Bakery towards the end of the 1970s. Today, he is in his 70s and only bakes on request; for instance, rye bread with imported flour from Germany or protein bread for health-conscious Omanis – 25 kilograms for 55 Rial, which is roughly €130. His local-born wife Rahma helps him . "By now, she's the better baker," he chuckles.

In den Dörfern kaufen die Omaner ihr Weißbrot oft in einer Art arabischem Tante Emma-Laden.
In the villages, Omani people often buy their white bread in little shops.

In der Mühle am rauschenden Golf

In the Mill on the Edge of the Gulf

Abu Ubayda Abdallah Al Qassim – Hauptfigur in der Dokumentation „Die Söhne Sindbads".
Abu Ubayda Abdallah Al Qassim – main character in the documentary „Sons of Sinbad".

Die Söhne Sindbads

The Sons of Sinbad

Die Geschichte des Oman –
verfilmt von einem omanisch-deutschen Team

The history of Oman –
made into a film by an Omani-German team

"أبناء السندباد"
هي قصة عُمان ‒ تم تصويرها من قبل مجموعة ألمانية عُمانية مشتركة

"أبناء السندباد" هو عنوان لفيلم وثائقي من ثلاث حلقات يتحدث عن تاريخ عُمان. هذه القصة أخرجت وصورت من قبل طاقم ألماني عُماني. كان هناك أشخاص من عُمان مشاركين في هذا الإنتاج وعلى كل المستويات. وقد تم عرض سكان عُمان في هذا الفيلم على أنهم بحارة وتجار. يقول مخرج فيلم أبناء السندباد فريدريش كلوتش: "إن وصفة النجاح لفيلم ابن السندباد هي خلق وضع مربح للجانبين، لأنفسهم ولشركائهم التجاريين". يركز الفيلم على أحداث مثل التجارة الصينية أو وصول البرتغاليين إلى عُمان، هذه هي الفترات التي يرتبط فيها التاريخ الأماني بالتطورات العالمية.

Die Gefangennahme der letzten Portugiesen in Maskat 1650 – eine der Szenen der dreiteiligen Dokumentation „Die Söhne Sindbads".
The capture of the last Portuguese in Muscat 1650 – one of the scenes of the three-part documentary "Sons of Sinbad".

Mit der Al Salmi-Stiftung in Bidiyah und der GUTech in Maskat wirkte das Sultanat Oman zum ersten Mal an einer international verbreiteten Filmreihe über seine eigene Geschichte mit. Regisseur Friedrich Klütsch drehte die dreiteilige Dokumentation mit einem omanisch-deutschen Team. Im Interview spricht er über die Hintergründe.

Wer weiß schon, dass Oman einmal die Westküsten des Indischen Ozeans beherrschte – und direkte Handelsbeziehungen bis nach China unterhielt. Nun haben Sie die Geschichte des Landes in drei Teilen verfilmt. Was ist den Omanis an ihrer Geschichte besonders wichtig?

Friedrich Klütsch: Sie möchten nicht als Eroberer und Beherrscher wahrgenommen werden. Kontrolle übten die Omanis nur an räumlich begrenzten Handelsplätzen aus. In unseren Filmen stellen wir – die meisten Historiker tun dies auch – die Omaner als Seefahrer und Händler dar. Ihr Erfolgsrezept bestand darin, für sich und ihre Geschäftspartner eine Win-Win-Situation herzustellen.

Also Kooperation statt Kontrolle, Austausch statt Unterwerfung?

So ist es. Und das hat aus meiner Sicht ganz pragmatische Gründe. Oman ist klein. Seine Bewohner sind wehr-

The Sultanate of Oman was involved in a joint film production between the Al Salmi Foundation in Bidiyah and the GUTech in Muscat. This was the first time the Sultanate collaborated on a film series about its own history to be shown internationally. Director Friedrich Klütsch worked on the three-part documentary with an Omani-German team. We spoke to him about the production.

Who knew that Oman once ruled over the west coast of the Indian Ocean and had direct trade relationships reaching as far as China? Now you've made a three-part film of the history of the country. What do the Omanis see as especially important about their own history?

Friedrich Klütsch: They don't want to be perceived as conquerors and rulers. The Omanis only controlled trading centres in a limited geographic area. Like most historians, we portray the Omanis in our films as seafarers and merchants. Their formula for success was creating win-win situations for themselves and their business partners.

So cooperation instead of control, exchange instead of submission?

Precisely. If you ask me, there are pragmatic reasons for that. Oman is small. Its citizens are defen-

haft, aber militärisch waren sie nie stark genug, andere zu dominieren.

Warum hat sich dieses kleine Land dann überhaupt auf die Weltbühne begeben?

Die Hinwendung zur Außenwelt hatte existenzielle Gründe. Die Landschaften des Oman sind eindrucksvoll, aber auch sehr karg. Wer dort nicht nur überleben, sondern sich auch entwickeln möchte, muss Handel betreiben. Die geografische Lage am Eingang des Golfes und vor allem die saisonalen Monsunwinde, die bis an die Küste des Oman heranreichen, taten ein Übriges.

Gilt das nicht auch für die anderen Länder der Region?

Nicht in dem Maße. Auf dem Landweg ist der Oman durch die Rub Al-Kali, der größten Sandwüste der Erde, vom Rest Arabiens abgetrennt. Die Omaner mussten Seefahrer werden. Das macht sie aus unserer Sicht auch zu den wahren Söhnen Sindbads.

Teilen Ihre omanischen Auftraggeber diese eher materielle Sicht auf Geschichte?

Die Fakten bleiben ja dieselben, die sind gar nicht das Problem. Aber die Frage, warum die Dinge so kamen, wie sie kamen - als freies Spiel der Kräfte oder durch den Willen Gottes, das sehen säkulare Filmemacher aus Deutschland ganz anders als gläubige Omaner. Insofern ist unser Filmprojekt auch ein spannendes Experiment gewesen, das auf ein Entgegenkommen beider Seiten angewiesen war.

Ist dieses Experiment aus Ihrer Sicht gelungen?

Aus ganzem Herzen: Ja! Es soll aber nicht verschwiegen werden, dass am Ende auch um einzelne Filmbilder und Formulierungen gerungen wurde.

Wo lagen die Probleme?

Für Filmemacher aus Deutschland sind Kontroversen und Konflikte wichtige Bestandteile der Erzählung, die

Darstellerinnen der Hofdamen auf Sansibar.
Actresses of the court ladies on Zanzibar.

sive, but they were never strong enough to dominate others.

Then why did this small country step onto the world stage at all?

They turned towards the outside world for existential reasons. The landscapes of Oman are impressive, but also not very fruitful. Those who want to survive and even develop there, need to carry out trade. The geographic position at the mouth of the Gulf and most of the monsoon winds that reached the coast of Oman added to that.

Isn't that also true for other countries of the region?

Not to the same degree. The Rub al-Chali, the Earth's largest sand desert, separates Oman from the rest of Arabia. The Omanis had to become seafarers. From our perspective, that's also what makes them the true sons of Sinbad.

Do your Omani clients share this rather material view of history?

The facts stay the same, that's not the problem. But the question of why things came about as they did – through the free play of forces or through the will of God – is something that secular filmmakers from Germany see quite differently from devout Omanis. In that respect, our film project was an exciting experiment that depended on give and take from both sides.

Do you think the "experiment" was successful?

Absolutely, no doubt about it! But I don't want to hide the fact that there was also some wrangling over individual film images and scripts.

„Alle Rollen werden von Laiendarstellern gespielt"

"All roles are played by amateur actors"

Spannung und Erkenntnis liefern. Omaner hingegen leben eine Kultur der Zurückhaltung und des Ausgleichs. Wenn wir also in Folge 3 darüber berichten wollten, dass sich Deutsche und Omaner Ende des 19. Jahrhunderts in Ostafrika blutige Kämpfe lieferten, mussten wir Wege der Darstellung finden, die beiden Haltungen gerecht wurden. Prinzipiell gilt, dass je näher die geschilderten Ereignisse an der Gegenwart liegen, umso sensibler damit umgegangen werden muss.

Für welche Ereignisse der omanischen Geschichte haben Sie sich entschieden - und warum?

Aus der reichen und bislang kaum bekannten Geschichte Omans haben wir Episoden gewählt, bei denen omanische Geschichte mit globalen Entwicklungen in Verbindung steht. In der ersten Folge geht es zum Beispiel um den direkten Seehandel mit China im frühen Mittelalter. Die zweite beginnt mit der Ankunft der Portugiesen im 16. Jahrhundert, und die dritte Folge beschäftigt sich mit dem omanischen Sultanat von Sansibar, das bis 1964 bestand.

Aus der Sicht des Filmemachers: Welche ist Ihre persönliche Lieblingsstory aus einigen Jahrhunderten omanischer Geschichte?

Als Filmemacher und Hobby-Segler begeistern mich die omanischen Seefahrergeschichten. Etwa die von Abu

What were some of the problems?

German filmmakers think of controversy and conflict as significant elements of narration, generating suspense and insight. Omanis, however, live in a culture of restraint and balance. So, in Episode Three, when we wanted to show the brutal fighting between Germans and Omanis in East Africa at the end of the 19th century, we had to find ways to portray that while staying true to both attitudes. In general, the closer the events we showed were to the present, the more we had to approach them in a very sensitive manner.

Which events of Omani history did you choose – and why?

From the rich and relatively unknown history of Oman, we chose episodes where Omani history was connected to global developments. For instance, the first episode is about direct maritime trade with China during the early Middle Ages. The second episode starts with the arrival of the Portuguese in the 16th century, and the third episode deals with the Omani Sultanate of Zanzibar, which existed until 1964.

From the perspective of a filmmaker: Which is your personal favourite story from the centuries of Omani history?

Dreh mit Laiendarstellern in den Bergen im Oman (links) und in einem eigens aufgebauten Souk (rechts).
Shooting with amateur actors in the mountains in Oman (left) and in a specially constructed souq (right).

Die Söhne Sindbads

Ubayda Al Qassim, der es im 8. Jahrhundert von einem Bergdorf in Zentraloman bis nach Kanton in China schaffte. Die wussten eben schon mit dem Monsun umzugehen, als man in Europa noch nicht einmal vom Seeweg nach Indien träumte.

Wo können wir die Filme sehen?

Nachdem unsere Reihe erfolgreich auf Festivals gelaufen ist, konnten wir Lizenzverkäufe mit dem chinesischen und omanischen Fernsehen abschließen. Gespräche mit deutschen TV-Anbietern stehen noch aus. Bereits jetzt sind deutsch- und englischsprachige Versionen der Filme zu sehen: vimeo.com/ondemand/diesoehnesindbads (German) or vimeo.com/ondemand/sonsofsinbad (English).

Sind weitere Filme mit omanischer Beteiligung geplant?

Wir sind bereits mitten in der Produktion einer Dokureihe, die die jahrhundertelange Verbindung zwischen Oman und Ostafrika zum Thema hat. Das Ergebnis wird am 50. Nationalfeiertag Omans im November 2020 präsentiert. Darüber hinaus entwickeln wir einen Spielfilm zu den dramatischen Ereignissen, die 1964 das Ende des Sultanats Sansibar zur Folge hatten.

As a film maker and hobby sailor, Omani seafarer stories excite me. For instance, the story of Abu Ubayda Al Qassim, who made the successful journey from a mountain village in central Oman to Canton in China in the 8th century. The Omanis already knew how to deal with the monsoon at a time when nobody in Europe even dreamed of getting to India by sea.

Where can we see the films?

We've already screened the films at several festivals and been positively received, so we now have license agreements with Chinese and Omani television stations. We're still in talks with German TV stations. But the German and English language versions of the films can already be seen on VIMEO for a fee: vimeo.com/ondemand/diesoehnesindbads (German) or vimeo.com/ondemand/sonsofsinbad (English).

Are there plans for further films with Omani involvement?

We are already in the middle of producing a documentary series about the decades-long bond between Oman and East Africa. This will be ready for the 50th anniversary of Oman National Day in November 2020. In addition, we're developing a movie dealing with the dramatic events that resulted in the end of the Zanzibar sultanate in 1964.

Kameramann Tobias Corts (links) bei Dreharbeiten und Hiyam Al Jabri (rechts), Sprecherin der englischen und arabischen Fassungen.
Cinematographer Tobias Corts (left) shooting and Hiyam Al Jabri (right), spokeswoman for English and Arabic versions.

Friedrich Klütsch lebt und arbeitet in München. Für das öffentlich-rechtliche Fernsehen wirkte er als Autor und Regisseur u.a. an den Reihen »2000 Jahre Christentum«, »Morgenland«, »Heiliger Krieg« und »Die Deutschen« mit. Er ist Geschäftsführer der deMAX Filmproduktion GmbH (www.demaxtv.de).

Friedrich Klütsch resides and works in Munich. He has been involved in several public television productions as writer and director, e.g. the series "2000 years of Christianity", "Orient", "Holy War" and "The Germans". He is the CEO of deMAX Filmproduktion GmbH (www.demaxtv.de).

Der typische Turban

Dass man Turbane, die typische Kopfbedeckung der Omanis, falsch oder richtig wickeln kann, musste das Team um Friedrich Klütsch bei den Abnahmen durch ihre omanischen Produktionspartner erfahren. Aber nicht nur die Knoten, auch Farben und Stoffe sind dabei wichtige Merkmale, die den Turban eines Sultans von allen anderen unterscheidet. Und so mussten bereits fertig geschnittene Sequenzen noch einmal aufwändig im Computer nachbearbeitet werden.

Ans Gebet denken

Bei der Drehplanung ist es wichtig, die Gebetszeiten für Muslime zu berücksichtigen. Sonst wird man von einer Situation überrascht, bei der alle omanischen Darsteller und Teammitglieder plötzlich verschwunden sind. Insbesondere das ‚Asr' genannte Gebet am Nachmittag ist dazu geeignet, Aufnahmen zu verhindern, die während des Sonnenuntergangs entstehen sollen.

The typical turban

The fact that turbans, the typical headdress of the Omanis, can be tied the wrong way or right way was something Friedrich Klütsch's team learned when they showed it to their Omani partners for approval. However, it is not only the way of tying, but also colours and fabrics that are important for distinguishing between turbans for sultans and those that everybody else wears. As a result, scenes that had already been filmed had to be changed in time-consuming postproduction.

Thinking about prayer time

When setting a shooting schedule, it is imperative to take Muslim prayer times into consideration. If you don't, you could find that all of the Omani actors and staff members suddenly disappear. The afternoon prayer called "Asr" puts a regular stop to filming scenes at sunset.

Die omanische Sandkünstlerin Shayma Al Mughairy verleiht der Erzählstimme in der Dokumentation Gestalt.
The Omani sand artist Shayma Al Mughairy gives form to the narrative voice in the documentary.

سلطنة عمان
وزارة الأعلام والسياحة
تلفزيون وإذاعة عمان

**OMAN
RADIO & TELEVISION**

Fernsehen im Oman

Oman TV

Geburtstagswunsch des Sultans in 1974:
Ein eigener Fernsehsender

The Sultan's birthday wish:
his own television station

أمنية السلطان في عيد ميلاده: الحصول على قناة تلفزيونية عمانية
بدء سريع في البث وقوة في العمل وسرور عند اتخاذ القرار ومجموعة عمل عالمية جيدة

بطلب من السلطان أسس المهندس الألماني منفرد كلوبش خلال خمسة أشهر في عام 1974م أول قناة بث تلفزيوني في عُمان. وكانت إحدى وظائفه الأولى هي بناء وتدريب وتشكيل فريق تلفزيوني كفؤ يتمتع بالمهارة التقنية والقدرة على شراء البرامج. وتحت ضغط عامل الوقت كان يجب أن يكون هناك نوعية عالية وخصائص وأيضاً شجاعة في اتخاذ القرارات وسعادة في اتخاذ تلك القرارات بطرق غير تقليدية. ويتذكر المدير السابق المهندس كلوبش ذلك المشروع المثير بسعادة.

Die Redakteure Walter Helfer (li) und Hans-Jürgen Börner (re.) halfen beim Sprung in die technische Neuzeit.
Editors Walter Helfer (left) and Hans-Jürgen Börner (right) helped with the jump into the technical modern age.

Im Auftrag von Sultan Qaboos ibn Said baute der deutsche Diplomingenieur Manfred Klupsch als Director General 1974 innerhalb von fünf Monaten im Oman den ersten Fernsehsender auf. Die Zusammenstellung eines leistungsfähigen Teams, umfangreiche Neubauten, Technik, Programmeinkauf – die großen Herausforderungen unter enormem Zeitdruck erforderten besondere Qualitäten. Besonnenheit, Tatkraft, und Mut zu ungewöhnlichen Wegen waren einige von ihnen.

Dass ihm die olympischen Spiele 1972 und die Fußball-Weltmeisterschaft 1974 den roten Teppich bis ins Sultanat Oman auslegen würden, hätte Manfred Klupsch nicht gedacht. Als Projektleiter für Fernsehtechnik war er an über 36 Austragungsstätten für die Abnahme aller Radio-, TV-Anlagen und Studios verantwortlich und dadurch verbunden mit den Verantwortlichen aller deutschen Radio- und Fernsehsender. Gäste aus aller Welt konnten dank seiner Arbeit den aufregenden Wettkämpfen und Spielen folgen. Als bei der Firma Sicmens Anfang 1974 die Anfrage aus dem Oman eintraf, der Sultan wünsche sich zum Geburtstag im November einen Farbfernsehsender, rechnete man nicht wirklich mit einem Auftrag. Ein Exposé war dennoch zügig geschrieben, eine erste Kalkulation erstellt. Die Delegation aus dem

Vigor, decisiveness and a good international team all came together to make a successful launch possible in a very short amount of time. By order of Sultan Qaboos ibn Said, German graduate engineer Manfred Klupsch established the first Omani television station as Director General in 1974 within five months. Putting together an efficient team, handling the considerable amount of new constructions as well as the technical side and the purchase of programming – all these challenges under enormous time pressure required some special qualities. Calmness, vigor and the courage to go about things in an unusual manner were among them.

Never had Manfred Klupsch expected the Olympic Games in 1972 and the Soccer World Cup in 1974 to spread a red carpet before him that would reach all the way to the Sultanate of Oman. As project manager for television technology he was responsible for all radio and television equipment and studios at more than 36 venues, and thus he was connected to those in charge of all German radio and television stations. Guests from all over the world could follow those exciting competitions and matches. When in early 1974 a request from Oman reached the firm Siemens that the Sultan wished for a color television station for his birthday in November of that year,

Sultanat sorgte für eine Überraschung. „Ja, wir erteilen den Auftrag", hieß es. Jetzt musste es schnell gehen und Manfred Klupsch kam als Kenner der Radio- und Fernsehszene ins Gespräch.

„Im Juli 1974 fuhr ich in den Oman, um Details des Projekts mit dem zuständigen Staatssekretär zu verhandeln. Wir wollten uns in der Hauptstadt Maskat ein Bild von den Gegebenheiten verschaffen", erzählt Manfred Klupsch. „1974 war der Oman noch ein traditioneller Wüstenstaat. Mit dem Fernsehsender sprang das Sultanat quasi aus dem Mittelalter in die Neuzeit. Es gab noch kein Bildungs- und kein Gesundheitssystem, keine flächendeckende Stromversorgung, kein Straßennetz. Die Ära des Schwarz-Weiß-Fernsehens wurde mal eben übersprungen, gleich sollte die weite Welt mit bunten Bildern ins Land kommen." Der Standort des ersten omanischen Fernsehsenders im heutigen Stadtteil Qurm war ein weites Nichts von Wüste und Geröll. Wenige Monate blieben bis zum 34. Geburtstag des Sultans am 18. November.

Mit dem zuständigen Minister besuchte Klupsch 1974 den Bauplatz. Nicht weit von den bereits im Bau befindlichen Fernsehstudios wurde nach kurzer Besprechung der Standort für die Mitarbeiter festgelegt. „Eine gute

they did not really expect to secure the order. Still an exposé was quickly drafted, a first calculation made. Then the delegation of the Sultanate surprised everyone. "Yes, we are placing the order," they said. Now, everything had to happen quickly, and Manfred Klupsch soon came up as an expert in radio and television.

"In July 1974 I traveled to Oman in order to negotiate details of the project with the state secretary in charge. We wanted to get a clear picture of the conditions in Muscat, the capital," Manfred Klupsch reports. "In 1974 Oman was still a traditional desert country. The television station basically transported the Sultanate from the Dark Ages to the Modern Era. Back then there was no educational or healthcare system, no comprehensive power supply, no road network. The era of black-and-white television was skipped over, instead the world was expected to come into the country in color." The location of the first Omani television station in what today is the district Qurum was a whole lot of nothing, consisting of desert and debris. And it was only eight months until the 34th birthday of the Sultan on 18 November.

In 1974 Klupsch took the minister in charge for a visit of the construction site. After a brief discussion they decided to set up the location for the staff fairly close

Gwendy Klupsch bei einer Reportage am neuen Hafen in Matrah in den 1970er Jahren.
Gwendy Klupsch reporting from the new port in Matrah in the 1970s.

Organisation ist das A und O für herausfordernde Projekte wie Oman TV", erklärt Klupsch. „Wir brauchten noch Häuser und Möbel für die Mitarbeiter, die technischen Bauten für den Sender, außerdem modernste Technik und natürlich Filme und Programme. Dazu für den Anfang 40 erfahrene und qualifizierte Mitstreiter wie Ingenieure, Techniker, Kamera- und Produktionsleute sowie Redakteure."

Auf in den Oman hieß es Mitte des Jahres für Manfred Klupsch und seine Frau Gwendy. "Wir waren jung, begeisterungsfähig, konnten anpacken und hatten Lust auf das Abenteuerleben", erinnert sich der Organisator.

Die Kontakte aus der Zeit der Olympiade und der Fußball-WM waren noch frisch. Eine ungewöhnliche Aufgabe, eine attraktive Entlohnung – das waren Anreize für viele, zum Team von Manfred Klupsch zu stoßen. Der Norddeutsche Rundfunk und der Sender Freies Berlin stellten zudem Experten für das Projekt ab.

In einem Land ohne Infrastruktur muss man bereit sein, neue Wege zu gehen. Klupsch: „Wir benötigten 29 Bungalows für die 40 Mitarbeiterinnen und Mitarbeiter. Aber Neubauten brauchen Zeit, die wir nicht hatten. Am Anfang war das Projektteam in Hotels im Bezirk Ruwi untergebracht. In den ersten heißen Sommerwochen entdeckten wir dann, dass quasi um die Ecke des geplanten Fernsehsenders Reihenhäuser für Regierungsmitarbeiter in Bau waren."

Mit dem zuständigen Ministerium wurde vereinbart, dass die Fernsehmacher vorübergehend in die Häuser ziehen konnten. Aber alles war noch eine Baustelle mit viel Schutt und Dreck. „Wir haben kurzerhand selbst zur Schaufel gegriffen und geackert. Dann ging es jeden Tag zum Ministerium. Wir brauchten schnellstens Wasser- und Stromanschlüsse. Immer wieder mussten die Dinge angeschoben werden."

Irgendwann waren die Bungalows bezugsfertig. „Aber wir brauchten Möbel – Tische, Stühle, Couchen, Betten, Schränke. Im ganzen Oman gab es nur Betten und im Souk von Matrah nur Gardinen und Stoffe", erzählt der Manager. Kurzerhand buchten Gwendy und Manfred Klupsch einen Flug nach Dubai. Damals standen dort noch keine Shoppingcenter mit schicken Einrich-

to the studios that were already being built. "Good organization is the be-all and end-all of challenging projects such as Oman TV," Kupsch explains. "We were still in need of houses and furniture for the staff, the technological structures for the station as well as the most current technology and of course movies and other types of programming. In addition, just to get started, an experienced and highly qualified staff of 40, including engineers, technicians, camera operators, producers and editors."

So off to Oman they went in the middle of that year, Manfred Klupsch and his wife Gwendy. "We were young, enthusiastic, ready to work and wanted to live a life of adventure," the organizer recalls.

The contacts he made during the Olympic Games and the Soccer World Cup were still new. An unusual task and attractive pay – that was an incentive for many to join Manfred Klupsch's team. In addition Norddeutscher Rundfunk and Sender Freies Berlin provided experts for the project.

In a country without infrastructure you have to be ready to make your own path. Klupsch: We needed 29 bungalows for our staff of 40, but building something from scratch takes time, and we did not have any. At first the team of the project was accommodated at some hotels in the district Ruwi. Then, in the heat of the first few weeks of summer we found out that almost around the corner of where the television station was to be, town houses were being built for government workers.

They came to an agreement with the ministry in charge that the television staff could move into these houses for the time being. But it was still a construction site full of dirt and debris. "We simply took up the shovels ourselves and worked hard. Then we showed up at the ministry every day. We needed water and electricity as soon as possible. We had to keep pushing in order to get things done."

At some point the bungalows were ready for occupation. "But we still needed furniture – tables, chairs, couches, beds, wardrobes. In all of Oman only beds were available and curtains and fabric at the Matrah souq," the manager relates. So Gwendy and Manfred Klupsch spontaneously booked a flight to Dubai. Back then today's malls with

tungsläden wie heute; nur Lager, in denen man Möbel ordern konnte. „Unsere Einkaufsliste war lang, die Lieferung musste schnellstens erfolgen. Wir warteten gespannt", so Klupsch.

Mitte Dezember 1974 kündigten sich die Möbel mit einer Staubwolke an. Aus dem Dunst unter flirrendem Sonnenlicht rollte eine Karawane grauer Militärlaster heran. Auf jahrhundertealten Beduinenpisten war sie mehr als 550 Kilometer quer durch die Wüste nach Maskat gefahren. „Als wir die Lieferung sahen, waren wir erst einmal geschockt." Noch heute schüttelt der Ingenieur den Kopf. „Die Möbel standen unverpackt auf den Lastern, festgezurrt mit dicken Schiffstauen. Auf allem lag zentimeterdicker Wüstenstaub. Ehemals braune Cord-Couches waren weiß; der Stoff durch den Druck der Taue bis auf die Holzgestelle durchgescheuert. Wir haben dann mit Mut zur Lücke das Beste aus dem Ganzen gemacht."

Wenn Programmeinkäufer durch die Welt reisen, brauchen sie in der Regel ein bis drei Jahre, bis Filme und Dokumentationen gefunden, Lizenz-Verträge geschlossen, Kopien gezogen und Synchronisationen oder Untertitelungen gefertigt sind. „Uns standen fünf Monate zur Verfügung", erklärt Klupsch. „Gott sei Dank hatten wir den Hessischen Rundfunk als Paten des neuen omanischen Senders mit an Bord, der bei der Vorzensierung der ersten Filme geholfen hat."

Filme und Dokumentationen im Oman unterliegen besonderen Kriterien. So werden beispielsweise keine extremen Brutalitäten gezeigt und entsprechend der moralischen Werte ist der Kontakt zwischen Mann und Frau

their fancy furniture stores did not exist yet; there were only warehouses where you could order furniture. "Our shopping list was long, and we needed the items as soon as possible. We waited anxiously," says Klupsch.

In mid-December 1974 a dust cloud announced the furniture. In the shimmering sunlight a caravan of gray military trucks came rolling through the haze. They had traveled more then 550 kilometers to Muscat across the desert on Bedouin tracks that were several centuries old. "Our first reaction to this form of delivery was shock." Even today the engineer is shaking his head. "The furniture had just been put on the trucks unpacked, simply tied down with thick marine rope. Everything was covered with centimeters of desert dust. Corduroy couches that had once been brown had turned white; the fabric had been worn through from the pressure of the rope, laying bare the wooden frames. So we braved the gaps and made the best of the situation."

„Wir hatten nur fünf Monate Zeit, um Programme einzukaufen"

"We only had five months time to buy programs"

Anfangs war das Projektteam in Hotels im Bezirk Ruwi untergebracht. Jeder Tag verlangte Lösungen für neue Aufgaben.
Initially, the project team was housed in hotels in the district of Ruwi. Every day demanded solutions for new tasks.

sehr zurückhaltend. Hier musste eine Vorzensur passende Programme auswählen. „Wir kauften von MCA-TV Programm ein – US-Serien wie ‚Kojak‘, ‚Columbo‘ oder ‚Die Straßen von San Francisco‘, Trickfilme wie ‚Tom und Jerry‘ oder Disney-Filme", so Klupsch. „In Beirut, später in Ägypten und anderen Ländern bekamen wir vorzensiertes Material, das für die Ausstrahlung in arabischen Ländern bereits untertitelt war."

Doch das war nicht bei allen Programmen der Fall und eine Synchronisation kam nicht in Frage, da die arabische Sprache mehr Wörter braucht als andere. Wenn zum Beispiel ein englischsprachiger Schauspieler einen Satz fertig gesprochen hat, ist das letzte Wort im Arabischen oft noch nicht gefallen. Die News wurden mit 24-stündiger Verspätung mit der Gulf Air aus London eingeflogen, in den Studios von Oman TV bearbeitet und und arabisch kommentiert.

Usually when buyers travel the world searching for programming, it takes them one to three years to find movies and documentaries, to sign a license agreement, to make copies and to produce dubbing or subtitles. "We had five months," Klupsch explains. "Thank God, the Hessischer Rundfunk was on board as the new Omani television station's godparent, coming to our aid in censoring the first movies."

In Oman movies and documentaries are subject to special criteria. For example, extreme brutality must not be shown, and according to local moral values contact between men and women is quite reserved. To this end a censoring committee had to select suitable programming. "We bought programming from MCA-TV – US TV series such as 'Kojak', 'Columbo' or 'The Streets of San Francisco', cartoons like 'Tom and Jerry' or Disney movies," Klupsch relates. "In Beirut, and later on in Egypt and

Oman TV

Irgendwie kamen dennoch immer die täglich drei Stunden Sendeprogramm zusammen. Was an Material morgens aus Berlin, Paris oder London per Flieger kam, wurde gleich eingeplant. „Filme wurden ausgewählt, Kommentare geschrieben, Nachrichten geschnitten. Wir hatten phantastische, motivierte Mitarbeiter, die einen tollen Job gemacht haben", so Klupsch.

Parallel zum Sender in der Hauptstadt wurde in Salalah im Süden des Sultanats ein zweiter aufgebaut. Schließlich wollten die Omaner dort auch fernsehen. „Alle Filme und das gesamte Material wurden nach Ausstrahlung bei uns nach Salalah geschickt und dort noch einmal gesendet", so Klupsch.

other countries, we found material that had already been censored and subtitled for transmission in Arabic countries."

However, this was not the case for all programs, and dubbing was out of the question as Arabic needs more words than other languages. So when an English-speaking actor finishes his sentence, the final word in Arabic usually has not been said. The news arrived from London with a 24-hour delay via Gulf Air and was edited in the local studios where Arabic commentary was added.

Somehow the three hours of airtime were still always filled. Whatever the airplanes from Berlin, Paris or Lon-

Manfred und Gwendy Klupsch mit Dr. Zainab Al Qasmiah (Mitte), omanische Botschafterin in Deutschland 2009-2012.
Manfred and Gwendy Klupsch with Dr Zainab Al Qasmiah (middle), Omani ambassador to Germany from 2009 to 2012.

Fernsehen im Oman

Oft ist Manfred Klupsch am Flughafen auf die Suche nach Filmen gegangen. Er erzählt: „Damals gab es auf dem Flughafen noch keine Lager für die angelieferten Kisten und Container. Alles wurde ausgeladen und einfach auf dem Flugfeld abgestellt. Da ich wusste, wie die Behälter unserer Zuliefererfirmen aussahen, konnte ich sie schnell erkennen. Ich schaute in alle Ecken und habe später mit einem Kreidestück in dem kleinen Flughafengebäude einen Kreis gezeichnet. Dort wurde dann die für uns bestimmte Lieferung abgestellt."

Als der 18. November 1974, der 34. Geburtstag des Sultans, nahte, stand nicht nur die Einweihung des neuen Fernsehsenders an. Ein Fußballstadion und der neue Hafen wurden eröffnet, eine Militärparade war organisiert. Alles Ereignisse, über die der neue Fernsehsender unter Regie von Gwendy Klupsch während der mehrtägigen Festlichkeiten berichten sollte. „Wir brauchten einen Ü-Wagen. Und der stand noch zwei Wochen vorher in Darmstadt", erinnert sich Klupsch.

Der Draht der Omaner zum amerikanischen Stützpunkt war gut. Ob man aushelfen und mal eben den Großraumflieger Galaxy nach Hessen schicken könne? Die Amerikaner zeigten sich hilfsbereit und so waren alle europäischen und arabischen Mitarbeiter am großen Tag bestens für die erste Übertragung vorbereitet. Drei Teams fingen die ersten Bilder ein. „Wir waren stolz, dass alles letztlich so geklappt hat wie geplant", berichtet der Geburtshelfer von Oman TV. Zum Dank gab es vom Sultan eine Einladung in seinen Sommerpalast bei Seeb.

„Die Amerikaner holten den Ü-Wagen von Darmstadt nach Maskat"

"The Americans brought the outside broadcast van from Darmstadt to Muscat"

don carried in the morning immediately became part of the programming. "Films were chosen, commentary was written, the news were edited. We had a fantastic, highly motivated staff that worked extraordinarily well," Klupsch says.

In addition to the station in the capital a second station was established at the same time in Salalah in the South of the Sultanate. After all, the Omanis there wanted to watch television, too. "All movies and all other materials were sent to Salalah after we broadcast them to air them there as well," Klupsch relates.

Manfred Klupsch frequently went to the airport in search of movies. He reports: "Back there were no designated storage spaces at the airport for the crates and containers that were delivered. Everything was unloaded and then just dropped onto the airfield. As I knew what the containers of our suppliers looked like, I could make them out quickly. I looked in every nook and cranny, and later I took a piece of chalk to draw a circle in the small airport building. This is where they put our deliveries from then on."

When 18 November 1974, the Sultan's 34th birthday was approaching faster and faster, the launch of the new television station was not the only event on the agenda. A soccer stadium and a new haven had their grand openings, and a military parade had been organized. These were all events that the new television station under the auspices of Gwendy Klupsch were to report about in the course of the festivities lasting several days. "We were in need of a broadcasting van," Klupsch recalls, "which two weeks earlier was still in Darmstadt."

The Omanis were on good terms with the American outpost. Would it be possible to lend a hand and kindly send the large aircraft Galaxy to Hesse? The Americans proved eager to help, and thus all Europeans and Arabs involved were prepared for the first transmission on the big day. Three teams captured the first images. "We were proud because in the end everything worked out the way we had planned it," Oman TV's midwife reports. As a reward the Sultan invited them to his summer palace near Seeb. Watch parties for everyone

Ab November 1974 war public viewing im Oman angesagt, schließlich waren Fernseher in Privathaushalten noch die Seltenheit. In Ruwi, Matrah und anderen Bezirken der Hauptstadt wurden Balustraden aufgestellt und luden zum gemeinsamen Fernsehen ein. „Hier traf man sich vor dem Abendgebet und folgte den Streichen von Tom und Jerry oder den Abenteuern von Kojak. Viele Kinder lasen ihren Eltern die Untertitel vor", erinnert sich Klupsch.

Fünf Monate brauchten Manfred Klupsch und sein Team, um Oman TV aufzubauen, fünf Jahre blieben sie. „An keinem Tag ist das Programm ausgefallen", sagt er rückblickend. 1980 übernahmen dann die rund 100 omanischen Mitarbeiter die Organisation des Sendebetriebs und führten ihn seitdem in Eigenregie weiter. 2014 wurde Manfred Klupsch auf dem Filmfestival in Maskat für seine Verdienste mit einem Preis geehrt. In einer Ausstellung in der Filmakademie erinnerten rund 40 Fotos an die Zeit, als die bunten Fernsehbilder Omans das Laufen lernten.

Beginning in November 1974, watch parties became fixtures in Oman, after all televisions were rare in private households. In Ruwi, Matrah and other districts, public banners were erected to invite the public to join watch parties. "This was where one met before the evening prayer and kept up with Tom and Jerry's shenanigans or Kojak's adventures. Frequently children read the subtitles for their parents," Klupsch remembers.

It took Manfred Klupsch and his team five months to set up Oman TV, they stayed for five years. "Not once did we cancel a broadcast," he reflects. Then in 1980, the Omani staff of roughly 100 took over organizing the station and have done so autonomously ever since. In 2014 Manfred Klupsch was honored for his services with an award at the film festival in Muscat. About 40 photos in an exhibition at the film academy kept the memory alive of the time when Oman's color television found its feet.

Zahlen, Daten, Fakten

- Mitarbeiter 1974:
  40 Deutsche, 100 omanische Auszubildende
- **Start des Sendebetriebs:** 18.11.1974
- Ausstrahlung von täglich drei Sendestunden bis 1979.
- Übergabe des Sendebetriebs im Herbst 1979 an das Sultanat Oman
- Filmpreis für Manfred Klupsch am 24. 3. 2014
- Im Dezember 2015 wurde der digitale Studiokomplex für Radio und Television eingeweiht
- Die Programme von Oman TV werden im gesamten Sultanat empfangen und können weltweit per Satellit oder Internet verfolgt werden.

Facts and figures

- Staff in 1974:
  40 Germans, 100 Omani trainees
- **Start of transmission:** 18/11/1974
- Three hours of programming daily until 1979
- Handing over the reins to the Sultanate Oman in autumn 1979
- Film award for Manfred Klupsch on 24/3/2014
- In December 2015 the digital studio complex for radio and television was inaugurated.
- Oman TV's programming is received all over the Sultanate and can be watched globally via satellite or the internet.

Moschee in Maskat in den 1970er Jahren: Vor dem Abendgebet traf man sich zum "Public Viewing".
Mosque in Muscat in the 1970s: Before the evening prayer people met for watch parties.

Fernsehen im Oman

Oman TV

FEATURE

Sina Weibo is a Chinese micro-blogging portal famous for it's online services akin to a combination of twitter and facebook.

WAY OF THE DRAGON

The US-traded Weibo stock posted a 19% gain last week, while the number of shares borrowed for short selling rose to a record four million.

WEIBO has more than doubled this year as steady user growth and an improved sales outlook have lured investors to the Chinese social media. Short sellers are becoming increasingly convinced the stock has peaked.

Bearish bets on Weibo, the Asian nation's answer to Twitter, are at the highest ever, even after the company reported earnings that beat analysts estimates and forecast a bigger-than-expected increase in third-quarter revenue. The US-traded stock posted a 19 per cent gain last week, while the number of shares borrowed for short selling rose to a record four million. Bullish investors are betting that

television and video partnerships the company has been forging will further boost the number of people using Weibo, which has been growing at a steady rate of about 30 per cent for the past two years. Short sellers are wagering that a 119 per cent rally this year, twice as much as the second-biggest gainer among Chinese stocks in the US, has become excessive.

"There is a lot of optimism regarding Weibo," Henry Guo, an analyst at New York-based M Science who has been covering Chinese American depositary receipts for a decade, said by phone last week. "Investors bet

that it has a potential to expand and monetise its business. The question short-sellers are asking is, 'Can the stock rally last forever?' "

Since it was spun off from Sina in April 2014, Weibo's stock has rallied 151 per cent. Sina's ADRs gained 33 per cent during the same period.

Weibo, backed by Alibaba Group Holding, has been adding video content live-streaming features to its micro-blogging service, which helped boost the number of monthly active users to 282 million in the second quarter, Chief Executive Officer Gaofei Wang said in the second-quarter earnings statement

last week. The company projected third-quarter revenue of as much as $178 million, exceeding analysts' estimates of $165 million.

The shares sell for 49 times projected earnings, above the average multiple of 42 among nine global peers, including Twitter and Facebook, according to data compiled by Bloomberg. David Riedel, a president of New York-based Riedel Research Group, who cut Weibo to sell from buy in May, said by e-mail last week that he's negative on the stock mostly because it's "cheaper to buy the Weibo exposure via Sina."

Other analysts from banks including

Citigroup Inc. and Jefferies Group have recently raised their recommendations to buy. Weibo's second-quarter per-share earnings rose to 16 cents, compared with an estimate of 11 cents.

This is good news for Krane-Shares' Brendan Ahern, who has been increasing his position in the stock this year.

"There is a potential in Weibo," Ahern, chief investment officer at KraneShares, said in an interview in New York. "The company's fundamentals are solid and there is room for growth."

— *ELENA POPINA & SUNNY OH /Bloomberg News*

Informationen aus dem Reich der Mitte – grafisch kreativ aufbereitet.
Information from the Middle Kingdom – graphically presented in a creative way.

Preisgekrönt und am Puls der Zeit

Award-winning and with a Finger on the Pulse of Time

Die Erfolgsgeschichte der „Times of Oman":
digital und von höchster Layout-Qualität

The success story of the Times of Oman:
digital und possessing the highest layout quality

جريدة تايمز أوف عُمان هي الجريدة الحائزة على العديد من الجوائز وتعالج مشاكل العصر وتتميز بأعلى جودة في التحرير

إن القصة الناجحة لأول جريدة يومية باللغة الإنكليزية في عُمان تبدو وكأنها قصة من قصص ألف ليلة وليلة: كان في البداية هناك رئيس قسم في وزارة الخارجية العُمانية الذي انزعج كثيراً عندما أتت رسالة من أميركا وعليها العنوان "مسقط، عُمان، المملكة العربية السعودية". كان اسم هذا الشخص عيسى بن محمد الزدجالي الذي دفعته غيرته الوطنية لإنشاء جريدة تايمز أوف عُمان - وهي حالياً جريدة يومية، ذات جودة عالية في التحرير، ومعترف بها عالميا. وقد فازت هذه الجريدة الرقمية بعدة جوائز عالمية. وهناك مستشار صحافة ألماني يذكر الأسباب لذلك.

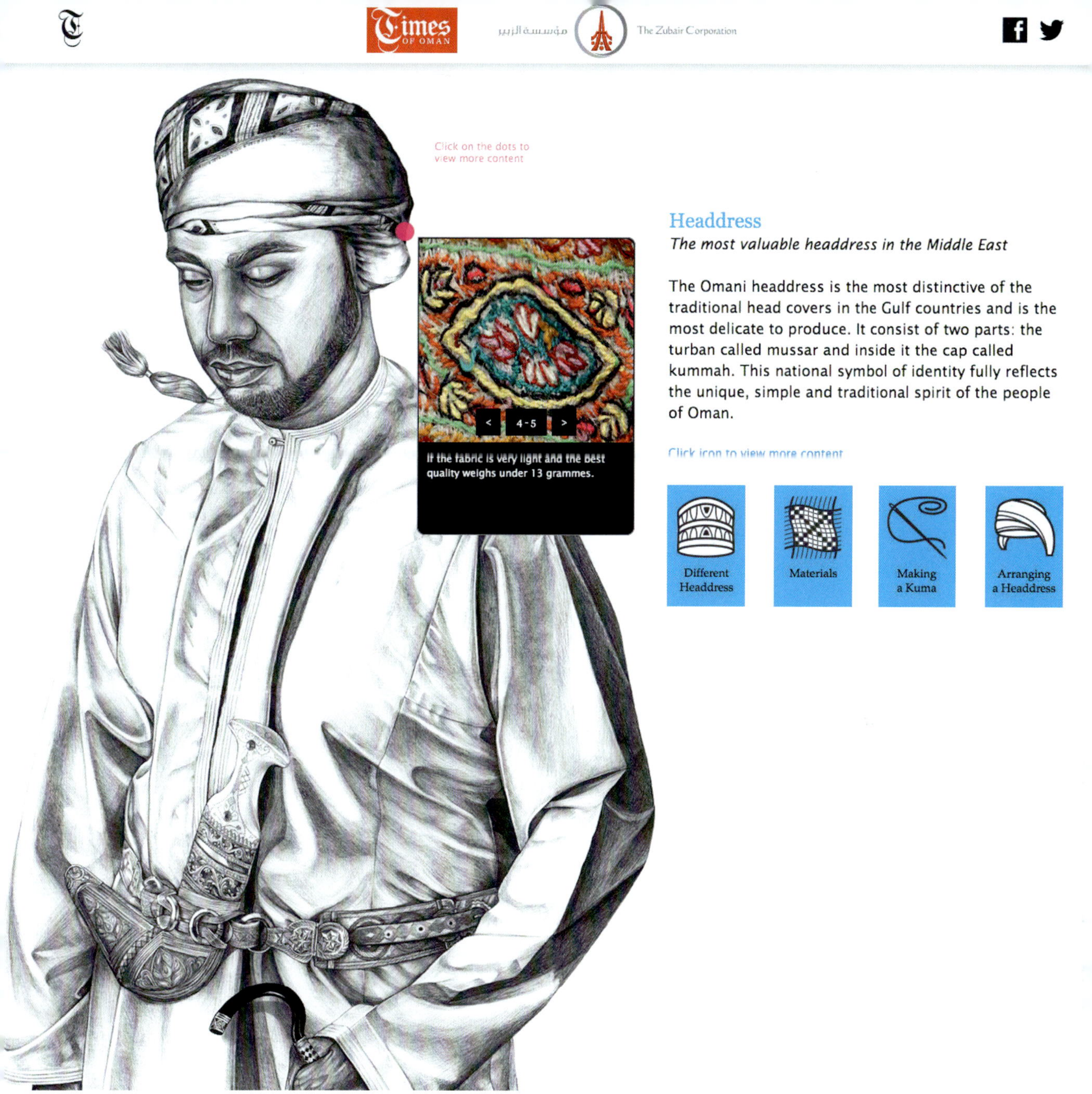

Click on the dots to
view more content

Headddress
The most valuable headdress in the Middle East

The Omani headdress is the most distinctive of the traditional head covers in the Gulf countries and is the most delicate to produce. It consist of two parts: the turban called mussar and inside it the cap called kummah. This national symbol of identity fully reflects the unique, simple and traditional spirit of the people of Oman.

Click icon to view more content

< 4 - 5 >

If the fabric is very light and the best quality weighs under 13 grammes.

Different Headdress

Materials

Making a Kuma

Arranging a Headdress

Die Geschichte der ersten englischsprachigen Zeitung im Oman klingt wie eine Erzählung aus 1001 Nacht: Es war einmal ein Abteilungsdirektor im omanischen Außenministerium, der sich über eine Anfrage aus den USA aufregte, weil sie adressiert war an „Muscat, Oman, Saudi Arabia". Er engagierte sich für die Gründung der Times of Oman – heute ist sie eine international beachtete Zeitung von höchster Layout-Qualität, die dafür und auch für digitalen Journalismus schon viele Preise erhielt. Ein deutscher Medienberater schildert die Hintergründe.

The story of the first English-language newspaper in Oman sounds like a tale out of the Arabian Nights: Once upon a time there was a senior director at the Omani foreign ministry, who was aggrieved for a request by the far-away country United States of America bore this address: "Muscat, Oman, Saudi Arabia." All his efforts did he put in to launch the Times of Oman – today a newspaper of international renown and highest layout quality that was given a plethora of awards both for its layout and its digital journalism. A German media consultant depicts the motives.

Award-winning and with a Finger on the Pulse of Time

Die phantastische Geschichte der Times of Oman beginnt mit Essa bin Mohammed Al Zedjali, der im Jahr 1974 seinen Aufgaben im Außenministerium nachgeht. Dazu gehört die Genehmigung von Überflugrechten für das Land. Als eine Firma namens „Flying Tiger Corporation" aus Los Angeles den Oman fälschlicherweise Saudi-Arabien zuordnet, reagiert er zunächst drei Tage nicht auf das Telex. Er überlegt, ob man der US-Firma die Schuld geben muss oder ob der Oman dafür mitverantwortlich ist. Der 34-Jährige vermutet, dass man mit einem TV-Sender oder einer Zeitung das Land in der Welt bekannter machen könnte. Dann kommt ihm eine Idee: „Warum kann der Oman keine englische Zeitung haben, die Gastarbeitern und Einwanderern hilft, unser Land kennen zu lernen und zu verstehen? Und sie wäre eine Botschafterin im Ausland."

Offensichtlich ist auch ein Appell des jungen Sultan Qaboos kurz nach seiner Machtübernahme eine große Motivation für Al Zedjali gewesen, das Risiko einer Zeitungsgründung einzugehen: Er wollte zum Aufbau des Landes einen Beitrag leisten. Es war also vor allem eine patriotisch motivierte Idee, als der junge Verleger in spe die Genehmigung beim Informationsministerium beantragte. Der Minister ließ sich persönlich von Al Zedjali sein Vorhaben erklären. „Er ermutigte mich und sagte: Wir werden Sie moralisch, finanziell und technisch unterstützen", berichtet Al Zedjali.

Nach zehn Monaten sind die aufwändigen Vorbereitungen am 23. Februar 1975 abgeschlossen: Die Times of Oman erscheint als erste Zeitung des Landes in englischer Sprache. Zunächst wird sie wöchentlich im sogenannten Halbformat gedruckt, wie es dem Handelsblatt in Deutschland entspricht. Die ersten Jahre sind offensichtlich so verlustreich, dass Berater dem jungen Verleger die Einstellung der Zeitung empfehlen. Sein Sohn Mohammed Issa Al Zedjali erinnert sich: „Doch mein Vater hatte immenses Vertrauen in das Produkt und er hat die Zeitung mit den Gewinnen eines anderen Unternehmens finanziert, das ihm gehörte." Anfangs habe er sogar die Kosten nicht gescheut, Exemplare nach London zu schicken.

Nach 15 Jahren wird die Times of Oman 1990 zur Tageszeitung im klassischen Format. Im selben Jahr bringt Verleger Al Zedjali, der gleichzeitig Chefredakteur ist,

The fantastical story of the Times of Oman takes its beginning with Essa bin Mohammed Al Zedjali, who in 1974 practices his profession in the foreign ministry. One of his tasks is granting flyover rights for the country. When a company called "Flying Tigers Corporation" from Los Angeles erroneously puts Oman into Saudi Arabia, he does not reply to the telex for three days. He reflects whether it is the US company's fault or whether Oman is partly to blame. The 34 year old man assumes that one could use a television station or a newspaper to spread awareness of the country. Then he has an idea: "Why not have an English-language newspaper in Oman to help foreign workers and immigrants to get to know the country better and understand its customs. At the same time, it could serve as an ambassador abroad."

Obviously an appeal the young Sultan Qaboos made shortly after he assumed power, also motivated Al Zedjali greatly to take the gamble and launch a newspaper: He wanted to contribute to the development of the country. Thus the idea was particularly motivated by patriotism when the young publisher-to-be applied for a permit from the ministry of information. The minister himself had Al Zedjali explain his proposal. "He encouraged me and said: We will support you morally, financially and technically," Al Zedjali reports.

After ten months the elaborate preparation phase concludes on 23 February 1975. The Times of Oman is the first newspaper in the country to appear in English. At first it is printed weekly in the so-called half-frame format, like the Handelsblatt in Germany. In the first few years apparently the losses are so grave that consultants recommend for the young publisher to cancel the newspaper. As his son Mohammed Issa Al Zedjali recalls: "My father still had complete trust in the project, and he financed the newspaper with gains from another company he owned." At first he did not even spare the expense to ship copies to London.

In 1990, 15 years later, the Times of Oman is converted to a daily paper in classical format. In the same year, Al Zedjali, both publisher and editor in chief, brings a new daily paper to the Omani market: Al Shabiba in Arabic. As early as 1997, the Times of Oman is represented on the Internet by a static website and is considered a pioneer in the region. Since 2005 both newspapers have had

Preisgekrönt und am Puls der Zeit

eine zweite Tageszeitung auf den omanischen Markt: Al Shabiba, die in arabischer Sprache erscheint. Bereits im Jahr 1997 ist die Times of Oman mit einer statischen Seite im Internet präsent und gilt als Pionier in der Region. Seit 2005 verfügen beide Zeitungen über moderne Internet-Auftritte, seit 2008 sogar bereits für Handys.

Der große Umbruch hin zu einer international beachteten Zeitung von höchster Layout-Qualität beginnt Ende 2007, als der renommierteste Zeitungsdesigner der Welt, der US-Amerikaner Mario Garcia, für die Entwicklung eines neuen Layouts verpflichtet wird. Mittlerweile arbeiten auch die beiden Söhne des Verlegers, Mohammed Issa und Ahmed Essa Al Zedjali, im Management der Muscat Media Group. Garcia arbeitet mehr als zwei Jahre an einem Design für die Times of Oman und Al Shabiba, die beide am 4. April 2010 erstmals damit ihre Leser überraschen. Die Times of Oman sieht aus wie eine andere Zeitung, weil alles neu ist: der Zeitungskopf, die Zeitungsspalten mit neuer Typografie und die Signalfarben der einzelnen Zeitungsbücher. Die Zeitung erscheint sonntags bis donnerstags in einem Umfang von 44 bis 52 Seiten in vier Sektionen, den sogenannten Zeitungsbüchern: das erste mit nationalen und internationalen Nachrichten, das zweite mit Wirtschafts- und Finanznachrichten, das dritte mit Sport, Kultur und Lifestyle und das vierte mit Anzeigen aller Art. Am Freitag erscheint ergänzend Hi, ein Heft mit Magazin-Charakter.

Die Bedingungen für eine erfolgreiche Entwicklung des Blattes sind erfüllt, zumal seit Februar 2010 der junge, aber bereits erfahrene Design-Direktor Adonis Durado von den Philippinen im Verlag arbeitet. Durado baut eine professionelle Design-Abteilung auf, die sich schon bald mit den besten Zeitungen der Welt messen lassen kann. Zunächst sind es nur die Leser, die äußerst ansprechende Zeitungsseiten mit Illustrationen und Informationsgrafiken finden. Aber schon Anfang 2011 beginnt eine einmalige Erfolgsserie bei internationalen Wettbewerben.

„Wer zur Hölle ist die Times of Oman?", kommentiert der renommierte US-Journalist Charles Apple am 10. Februar 2011, als er die Liste der Preisträger 2010 der Society for News Design sieht: Die Times of Oman steht mit 36 Preisen auf Platz zwei hinter der Los Angeles Times und vor der Washington Post. Das ist der Beginn einer beispiellosen Erfolgsserie für eine Zeitung im mittleren Os-

modern internet presences, as of 2008 they can even be accessed by cellphones.

The grand development towards becoming a newspaper of international renown and highest layout quality begins in late 2007 when the most prestigious newspaper designer in the world, Mario Garcia from the US, is signed for designing the new layout. By then the publisher's two sons, Mohammed Issa and Ahmed Essa Al Zedjali, also have jobs in the management of the Muscat Media Group. It takes Garcia more than two weeks to finish the designs for the Times of Oman and Al Shabiba, which both surprise their readers with their new layouts on 4 April 2010. The Times of Oman looks like a different newspaper because everything is new: the flag, the columns with new typography and the signal colors of the different newspaper books. The newspaper is published from Sunday to Thursday ranging in length between 44 and 52 pages in four sections, the so-called newspaper

International beachtete Zeitung von höchster Layout-Qualität

Internationally acclaimed newspaper of the highest layout quality

books: the first with national and international news, the second with business and financial news, the third with sports, culture and lifestyle, and the fourth with all sorts of ads. In addition, Hi, a magazine, appears on Fridays.

The preconditions for the successful development of the paper are fulfilled, not least because in February 2010 Adonis Durado from the Philippines, a young design director who nevertheless is quite experienced already, starts working at the publishing house. Durado builds up a professional design division that can soon compete with the best newspapers in the world. At first it is only the readership that takes note of the highly appealing newspaper pages with illustrations and informative graphics. But in early 2011, an unparalleled series of success at international competitions begins.

"What the hell is the Times of Oman?" is the comment of renowned US journalist Charles Apple on 10 February

ten: Mehr als 450 Preise für herausragendes Layout und Informationsgrafik kommen in den folgenden Jahren bei mehreren internationalen Wettbewerben zusammen.

Als Mitglied des internationalen Zeitungsverbandes WAN-IFRA lässt sich der Verlag inspirieren und bei der Reorganisation der Redaktion unterstützen. Als der Brite Scott Armstrong Anfang 2014 das Amt des Redaktionsdirektors antritt, nimmt die digitale Entwicklung der Times of Oman rasante Fahrt auf. Armstrong, der aus Dubai kommt, bildet aus der überwiegend aus Indern bestehenden Redaktion ein medienkonvergentes Team für Print und Digital. „Wir haben uns bemüht, Qualitätsjournalismus zu entwickeln", beschreibt Armstrong seine erfolgreiche Offensive. „In vier Jahren wurden wir zum erfolgreichsten digitalen Medium im Oman und machten 90 Prozent des englischen Nachrichtenverkehrs aus."

Als Armstrong die Times of Oman vier Jahre später verlässt, ist seine Erfolgsbilanz atemberaubend: „Wir sind in allen Bereichen der Medientitel Nummer eins im Land", sagt er. Und die Zahlen geben ihm Recht. In seiner Zeit steigen die Online-Seitenaufrufe von 7 Millionen auf 60 Millionen, aus 15.000 Facebook-Fans werden mehr als 600.000 – das sind erheblich mehr als zum Beispiel die Frankfurter Allgemeine Zeitung hat. Allein die Zahl der Zuschauer des Internet-TV steigt von 50.000 auf über

2011 when he sees the 2010 list of honorees of the Society of News Design: With its 36 awards The Times of Oman comes second behind the Los Angeles Times and ahead of the Washington Post. This is the beginning of an exemplary success story for a newspaper from the Mid East. In the course of the following years, more than 450 awards are gathered for exceptional layout and information graphics at international competitions.

As a member of the international newspaper association WAN-IFRA the publishing house takes inspiration and seeks help at the reorganization of the editorial department. When Scott Armstrong from Great Britain assumes the role of editor in chief in early 2014, the digital development of the Times of Oman surges. Armstrong, who previously was in Dubai, turns the editorial department, comprising mostly Indians, into a media-convergent team for Print and Digital. "We strove to make high-quality journalism," Armstrong describes his successful battle plan. "Within four years we became the most successful digital medium in Oman and made up 90 percent of English-language news communication."

Four years later, when Armstrong leaves the Times of Oman, his track record is breathtaking. "In every category we are medium number one in the country," he says. And the numbers prove him right. During his tenure the

Das Layout und die Informationsgrafiken der Times of Oman werden immer wieder ausgezeichnet.
The layout and the information graphics of the Times of Oman are awarded again and again.

Preisgekrönt und am Puls der Zeit

26 Millionen. Während überall auf der Welt Zeitungen versuchen, ein digitales Geschäftsmodell zu entwickeln, steigt der digitale Anteil am Umsatz auf 20 Prozent.

Sogar für digitalen Journalismus im Internet gibt es mehrere Auszeichnungen: Die Krönung ist 2016 ein World Digital Media Award in Gold vom Weltverband WAN-IFRA, den die Times of Oman als erstes Medium aus der Golf-Region bekommen hat.

online page impressions rise from 7 million to 60 million, 15,000 Facebook fans turn into more than 600,000 – which is significantly more than those of, say, the Frankfurter Allgemeine Zeitung. And just the number of the Internet TV viewers rises from 50,000 to more than 26 million. While around the world newspapers try to develop digital business models, here the digital revenue share reaches 20 percent.

They even win several awards for digital online journalism. The crowning achievement is a World Digital Media Award in Gold, awarded by the international association WAN-IFRA, which the Times of Oman receives as the first medium from the Gulf Region.

Unser Autor Joachim Blum ist internationaler Medienberater und lehrt als Honorarprofessor im Fach Medienwissenschaft an der Universität Trier. Er erzählt, was ihn an der Times of Oman fasziniert: „Oman war der dritte Golfstaat, in den es mich 2013 und 2014 als Berater von WAN-IFRA geführt hat. Auftraggeber war die Muscat Media Group, die ihre Redaktionen für die Zeitungen Times of Oman und Al Shabiba qualifizieren und für das digitale Zeitalter reorganisieren wollte. Nie bin ich als Berater so freundlich begrüßt und wieder verabschiedet worden; nie hat sich ein Verlag so wertschätzend und aufmerksam mir gegenüber verhalten. Besonders in den beiden anderen arabischen Staaten habe ich eher das Gegenteil erlebt. Was war so anders im Oman und in dem Verlagshaus? Auffallend war zunächst der gute Umgang der Omaner mit den Gastarbeitern aus Indien, aber auch mit anderen Gästen im Land. Einheimische und Inder arbeiten in Verlag und Redaktion kollegial miteinander, Inder bekleiden ganz selbstverständlich Führungspositionen wie in ihrem Heimatland. Was zählt, sind Qualifikation und Leistung, die angemessen bezahlt werden. Auffallend war auch die moderne und ambitionierte Haltung der beiden geschäftsführenden Verleger Mohammed Issa Ahmed Essa Al Zedjali, den Söhnen des Gründers."

Our author Joachim Blum is an international media consultant and teaches media studies at the University Trier as an honorary professor. He relates what he finds so fascinating about the Times of Oman: "Oman was the third Gulf State that I visited as a consultant for WAN-IFRA in 2013 and 2014. I was hired by the Muscat Media Group, who wanted to improve the qualifications of the editorial departments of their newspapers Times of Oman and Al Shabiba and reorganize them for the digital era. Never before had I been welcomed so cordially, and the farewell was the same; never had I been appreciated so much by a publishing house, never given that much attention. Especially in the other two Arab states I experienced quite the opposite. What was so different in Oman and this publishing house? What struck me right away was the friendly interaction of the Omanis with guest workers from India but also with other guests in the country. Natives and Indians work together in the publishing house and the editorial departments as genuine colleagues, Indians naturally occupy leadership positions, just as in their home country. All that counts is qualification and performance, both of which is reflected in the salary. Another aspect of note was the modern and ambitious attitude of the two CEOs of the publishing house, Mohammed Issa and Ahmend Essa Al Zedjali, the sons of the founder."

Der Magie von Worten verfallen

Under the Spell of Words

Lubna Abdullah Al Balushi
schreibt Gedichte in deutscher Sprache

Lubna Abdullah Al Balushi
writes poetry in German

الوقوع في حب سحر الكلمات
تكتب لبنى عبدالله البلوشي أشعاراً باللغة الألمانية

وقعت لبنى عبدالله البلوشي في حب سحر الكلمات.
تكتب الشابة العُمانية أشعاراً باللغة الألمانية. لقد تعلمت اللغة
الألمانية في معهد غوته في مسقط وذلك أثناء إقامتها في
فرايبورغ في جنوب غرب المانيا. القصائد الشعرية بالنسبة
للبنى هي عبارة عن مرآة الروح و مرآة المجتمع وحضارة
الإنسان.

Die junge Omanerin Lubna Abdullah Al Balushi lernte im Sultanat und während ihres Studiums in Freiburg Deutsch. Gedichte sind für sie Spiegel der Seele, der Gesellschaft und der Kultur eines Menschen.

Sie gehört zu den Menschen, die sich jenseits der eigenen Muttersprache an poetische Verse wagen: Lubna Abdullah Al Balushi lernte die Grundzüge der deutschen Sprache 2007 am Goethe-Institut in Maskat und vertiefte ihre Kenntnisse während eines einmonatigen Aufenthaltes in Freiburg.

Die Sprache von Johann Wolfgang von Goethe, Autor des berühmten West-Östlichen Diwan, und Friedrich Schiller, aus dessen Feder Werke wie „Wilhelm Tell" und „Die Räuber" flossen, faszinierte sie so sehr, dass sie bald erste eigene Verse schrieb. 2012 erschien ihr Band „Schönheit des Herzens" (Beauty oft he Heart) mit 54 Gedichten.

Das Ausloten von Gefühlen und das Finden der passenden Worte ist für die junge Frau zu einer eigenen Leidenschaft geworden. Die mehrsprachige Poetin schreibt Gedichte in Arabisch, Deutsch, Englisch und ihrer Muttersprache, dem indoiranischen Balochi. Literatur hat sie nie studiert, sie verlässt sich bei ihren Dichtungen ganz auf ihre Intuition und ihr Sprachgefühl. Lesen ist ihr großes Hobby, Bücher und speziell Poesie sind ihre täglichen Begleiter.

Auf die Frage, warum Literatur für ihr Leben so wichtig ist, meint Lubna Albaloshi: „Literatur beflügelt unsere Seele. Sie reflektiert die Persönlichkeit der Menschen, ist Spiegel von gesellschaftlichen und kulturellen Lebensumständen."

Eine besondere Bedeutung hat für sie ein Zitat des großen deutschen Dichters Johann Wolfgang von Goethe: „Wer keine fremden Sprachen kennt, weiß nichts von seiner eigenen."

Was heißt das für sie? „Wenn ich Worte suche, setze ich mich intensiv mit dem auseinander, was ich ausdrücken möchte. Das verändert mein Denken auch bezüglich Themen meiner eigenen Kultur und damit mich selbst." In ihren Sprachschöpfungen geht es vor allem um Gefühle – Liebesglück und Liebesleid, Hoffnungen und Träume.

The young Omani learned German in the sultanate and during her studies in Freiburg. To her, poems are the mirror of the soul, the society and the culture of a person.

She is one of those people who dare write poetry beyond their own mother tongue: Lubna Abdullah Al Balushi learned the basics of the German language at the Goethe Institute in Muscat in 2007 and deepened her knowledge during a one-month stay in Freiburg.

The language of Johann Wolfgang von Goethe, author of the famous West-Eastern Diwan, and Friedrich Schiller, who wrote such works as William Tell and The Robbers, fascinated her so much that she soon made her first attempts at writing verse. In 2012, she published her volume Schönheit des Herzens (Beauty of the Heart) containing 54 poems.

Exploring emotions and finding the right words has become a passion for the young woman. She writes poems in Arabic, German, English and her mother tongue, Balochi, an Indo-Iranian language. She has never studied literature, for her poetry she relies only on her intuition and her feeling for the language. Reading is her great hobby, books, and especially poetry, accompany her every day.

Asked, why literature is so important for her life, Lubna Al Balushi states, "literature inspires our souls. It reflects the personalities of people, it is a mirror of societal and cultural circumstances."

She bestows particular importance on a quote by grand German poet Johann Wolfgang von Goethe, "Those who do not know foreign languages, know nothing about their own."

What does that mean for her? "When I look for words, I intensely deal with what I want to express. That changes the way I think, also regarding topics of my own cultures and thus myself." Her creations are mostly about emotions – love's bliss and woe, hopes and dreams.

Lubna Abdullah Al Balushi: Seele

Sie sehen deine braunen Augen,
sie blicken auf deine stillen Herzen,
sie sehen deine ehrliche Seele,
aber sie verstehen dich nicht!

Wie können sie dich verstehen?
Wenn sie niemals in ihr Inneres sehen?
Leer sind ihre Augen,
leer sind ihre Herzen.
Ihre Zunge bleibt ein Verlust für ihre Seele!

Lubna Abdullah Al Balushi, Schönheit des Herzens,
MEDU Verlag, ISBN: 9783941955608, 60 Seiten,
Hardcover, 14,95 Euro

Lubna Abdullah Al Balushi: „Literatur beflügelt unsere Seele".
Lubna Abdullah Al Balushi: "Literature inspires our souls".

Under the Spell of Words

Verena Kyselka sammelt im Oman Eindrücke für ihre Videoinstallationen.
Verena Kyselka collects impressions for her video installations in Oman.

Auf den Spuren der Lieder Omans

Tracing the Songs of Oman

Die Berliner Künstlerin Verena Kyselka
verarbeitet ihre Erfahrungen in einer Videoinstallation

Verena Kyselka, an artist from Berlin,
processed her experiences in a video installation

على طريق الإغاني العُمانية
الفنانة البرلينية فيرينا كيسيلكا وإخراجات الفيديو الخاص بها

إن معهد غوته يشجع في كل أرجاء العالم الفنانين ونشر الثقافة في الدول الأخرى. إن الفنانة فيرينا كيسيلكا من برلين سافرت إلى مسقط في عُمان في عام 2016م. لقد قامت بتصوير خبراتها بشكل فيديو وعرضتها في عاصمة السلطنة في نهاية إقامتها في عُمان وبعدها قامت بعرض الفيديو عدة مرات في المانيا.

كان في زمان الماضي .. ساحر عشق جنيه
بين الوريد يتمخطر .. لابس ثوبه الاخضر
فستانه كحلي واحمر .. والقبعه بنيه

وتعارفوا بالصحراء .. وظلوا وفاتوا ح
وعلى الدخون والفخره .. وتجنست
كان في زمان الماضي .. ساحر

عاشق ولا له فاقه .. جالس ع
والناس شالوا الناقه .. ومرو
كان في زمان الماضي .. س

قالت تعال يا روحي .. شو
ملك محب ونصوحي .. و
كان في زمان الماضي .

Traditionelle Lieder – hier bildlich dargestellt – besingen die Schönheit des Landes.
Traditional songs tell of the country's beauty.

Das Goethe-Institut fördert weltweit die Arbeit von Künstlern und Kulturschaffenden in einem anderen Land. Verena Kyselka reiste als Artist-in-Residence 2016 nach Maskat. Ihre Ausstellung wurde inzwischen mehrfach in Deutschland und zum Ende der Residenzzeit im Oman gezeigt.

Die traditionellen Lieder Omans besingen die Schönheit des Landes mit seinen rauen Bergen und malerischen Wadis, es geht um Familie und Freunde sowie natürlich die Liebe und die Sehnsucht. Auf Spurensuche omanischer Gesänge hat sich die Berliner Künstlerin Verena Kyselka auf Einladung des Goethe-Institut Golf-Region gemacht. Im März 2016 arbeitete sie als Artist-in-Residence der Stal Gallery in der Hauptstadt Maskat an einem Kunstprojekt, in dem sie anhand des Liedguts die omanische Identität erforschte. Dabei haben ihr omanische Frauen geholfen, die sie auf verschiedene Kulturen in der omanischen Gesellschaft aufmerksam gemacht haben.

„Die Künstler habe ich über die Stal Gallery kennen gelernt", sagt Verena Kyselka. „Leiter der Galerie ist der omanische Künstler Hassan Meer. Er unterstützt vor allem junge Menschen, die unter anderem mit neuen Medien arbeiten." Seine Kontakte halfen der Berlinerin, geeignete Lieder zu finden und potenzielle Sängerinnen kennen zu lernen.

All over the world the Goethe Institute supports artists and creators abroad. In 2016 Verena Kyselka went to Muscat, Oman as artist in residence. Her exhibition has been shown repeatedly in Germany, and in Oman at the conclusion of her residence.

The traditional songs of Oman sing of the country's beauty with its rough mountains and picturesque wadis, they are about family and friendship as well as love and longing, of course. It was an invitation of the Goethe Institute Gulf Region that made the artist Verena Kyselka from Berlin trace Omani songs. In March 2016 she worked on an art project at the Stal Gallery in the capital Muscat as artist in residence, in which she researched Omani identity by means of their songs. She was helped by Omani women, who drew her attention to different cultures within Omani society.

"I met the artists through the Stal Gallery," Verena Kyselka says. "The director of the gallery is the Omani artist Hassan Meer. He predominantly supports young people who work with new media among other things." His connections helped the artist from Berlin find suitable songs and get to know potential singers.

"It was far from easy to find women who wanted to have their singing recorded. So without much ado I hired a

„Es war alles andere als einfach, Frauen zu treffen, die ihren Gesang aufzeichnen lassen wollten. Ich bin dann auf eigene Faust mit einem Fahrer nach Nizwa aufgebrochen, das eine gute Stunde von Maskat entfernt am Südrand des Hadschar-Gebirges liegt", erinnert sie sich. Aber auch dort konnte sie nicht einfach fremde Frauen ansprechen, zumal sie ja auch kein Arabisch verstand. Der Fahrer schlug einen Trip in ein Camp am Rande der Wahiba Wüste vor. Dort könnte sie Erfolg haben, so seine Überzeugung.

Aber auch dort ließ sich so schnell niemand überzeugen. Verena Kyselka ließ nicht locker. Schließlich hieß es: „In einer Stunde wird Oum da sein. Sie singt gerne." Dann gab es omanischen Kaffee, die Kinder trauen sich neugierig an die Fremde heran – und die Zeit verging wie im Flug. Dann kam Oum und es entstanden zauberhafte Bilder und Eindrücke von der ruhigen Schönheit der Wüste und dem Zauber des omanischen Gesangs. „Der Tag war etwas ganz Besonderes und bleibt mir auf ewig unvergesslich", so die Künstlerin im Rückblick.

Ergebnisse des vierwöchigen Projektes sind Zeichnungen, Collagen und ein Videofilm mit Liedern und charakteristischen Motiven des Landes. Gezeigt werden darin unter anderem eine Weihrauch-Räucherzeremonie, stimmungsvolle Naturmotive rund um Wasser und Sand und traditionelle Ornamente, Motive und Objekte.

driver to get me to Ibra, which is about an hour's drive from Muscat towards the heart of the country," she recalls. But it was not any easier to chat up strangers there; for one thing, she did not speak Arabic. The driver suggested a trip to a Bedouin camp at the edge of the Wahiba Sands. She might be successful there, he was certain.

However, quick success did not come there, either. Verena did not give up. At last someone said, "In an hour Oum will be here. She likes to sing." Omani coffee and dates were served, the children's curiosity brought them closer to the stranger – and time flew by. Then the Bedouin woman Oum Hamdan appeared, which resulted in enchanting pictures of the calm beauty of the desert and the expressiveness of Omani singing. "That day was something very special, and I will never forget it," the artist reflects.

The results of the four weeks of the project included drawings, collages and a video film with songs and images characteristic of the country. Among them are an incense ceremony, atmospheric nature motives highlighting water and sand as well as traditional ornaments, motives and objects.

"Within only very few decades Oman turned into a modern country," the woman from Berlin explains. "I wanted

Eine Impression aus der Video-Installation.
An impression from the video installation.

„Oman ist innerhalb weniger Jahrzehnte zu einem modernen Land geworden", erklärt die Künstlerin. „Ich wollte herausfinden, welche alten Lieder heute noch gesungen werden. Gesänge sind in jedem Land sehr wichtig und erzählen, was den Menschen am Herzen liegt. Die Texte wurden für mich übersetzt. Ich bin dann den Gefühlen in den Liedern gefolgt und habe entsprechende Motive gefilmt." Ihr Resümee: „Insgesamt war das eine beeindruckende Zeit."

Zu sehen war die Ausstellung danach im August 2016 in Berlin im Künstlerquartier Bethanien. Ende November 2016 präsentierte sie die Stal Gallery in Maskat, später wanderte sie nach Bonn und nach Augsburg. „Die Resonanz auf die Präsentationen war durchweg sehr positiv", berichtet Verena Kyselka. „Viele deutsche Besucher kannten das Land bisher nicht. Auch arabisch sprechende Menschen zeigten sich begeistert, da die Bilder und Lieder sie an ihre eigene Heimat erinnerten."

Die intensive Beschäftigung mit der Kultur Omans hat bleibende Spuren hinterlassen. Die Berliner Künstlerin: „Ich bin sehr dankbar für diese Chance, die Kultur dieses faszinierenden Landes mit seinen herzlichen und weltoffenen Menschen durch meine Arbeit im Oman kennen gelernt zu haben. Einige der Kontakte sind geblieben, die wir unkompliziert über die sozialen Medien pflegen können." Manchen der neuen Freunde reicht der Kontakt über Instagram und Facebook aber nicht. Zuletzt flatterte eine Einladung für eine Hochzeit ins Haus. Auch wenn die Anreise zum Fest ein paar Stunden mit dem Flieger dauert, entgehen lassen möchte sich Verena Kyselka diese Gelegenheit nicht.

to find out which old songs are still being sung today. Singing is of high significance in every country, as it relates what is close to people's hearts. The lyrics were translated for me. Then I followed the emotions of the songs and filmed suitable motives." She sums it up: "All in all, it was an impressive time."

Afterwards the exposition was shown at the Kunstquartier Bethanien in Berlin in August 2016. In late November 2016, it was presented by the Stal Gallery in Muscat, only to move on to Bonn and Augsburg later. "The response to the presentations was very positive throughout," Verena Kyselka reports. "Many German visitors did not know the country. But also speakers of Arabic were enthusiastic as the images and songs reminded them of their own home countries."

Dealing so intensely with Oman's culture has made a permanent impact. The artist from Berlin: "I am grateful for this chance of getting to know the culture of this fascinating country with its warm-hearted and open-minded people through my work in Oman. I have stayed in touch with several of the people I met there, which is easy to do with the help of social media." For some of her new friends, however, Instagram and Facebook are not enough. Most recently she was invited to a wedding. Even though she will spend several hours on an airplane to get to the ceremony, Verena Kyselka sure does not want that opportunity to pass her by.

Einen „Raum für neue Perspektiven" bietet das Goethe-Institut mit seinen Residenzprogrammen. Hierfür lädt es jedes Jahr Künstlerinnen, Künstler und Kulturschaffende ein. Nähere Infos unter: www.goethe.de, Menüpunkt Kultur

The Goethe Institute offers a "room for new perspectives" with its artist in residence scheme. To achieve this, they invite artists and creators every year. More info at: www.goethe.de, Keyword culture

Der imposante Kronleuchter in der Sultan Qaboos-Moschee in Maskat – sie steht auch Andersgläubigen offen.
Chandelier in the Sultan Qaboos Mosque in Muscat – it is also open to people of other faiths.

Toleranz, Verständnis und Koexistenz

Tolerance, Understanding, Coexistence

Eine deutsch-omanische Ausstellung
zeigt das friedliche religiöse Miteinander

A German-Omani exhibition
showing different religions coexisting peacefully

التسامح والتفاهم والتعايش: رسالة عُمان عن الإسلام يظهر معرض عُماني ألماني مشترك إمكانية التعايش الديني المشترك

تسعى عُمان جاهدة لإعطاء مثال حي عن التعايش السلمي بين الناس ـ سواء في الخارج أو في دولتهم ـ حيث أن الحرية الدينية هي من حق الإنسان. يلعب الحوار بين الأديان دوراً هاماً في البلاد. حيث يقدم المعرض المتنقل هذا الشكل الخاص للإسلام الذي يعيش في المجتمع العُماني الحديث. وقد تم تطوير المعرض مع وزارة الأوقاف والشؤون الدينية وفريق تنظيمي ألماني عُماني. يمكنك مشاهدة الصور والنصوص والمخطوطات القديمة والخطوط والصور الظلية ـ منذ عام 2010 في 35 دولة حول العالم. في المؤسسات التعليمية والثقافية والدينية، وكذلك اليونسكو والأمم المتحدة.

Arabische und internationale Besucher besichtigen die Ausstellung, im Vordergrund: Mohammed Al Mamari, wissenschaftlicher Berater des Religionsministeriums und Leiter des Projekts.
Arab and international visitors visit the exhibition, in the foreground: Mohammed Al Mamari, scientific advisor to the Ministry of Religion and leader of the project.

Oman bemüht sich um ein friedliches Miteinander der Menschen unterschiedlichen Glaubens – sowohl im Ausland als auch im eigenen Staat, wo Religionsfreiheit als Recht besteht. Der Dialog zwischen den Religionen und das gegenseitige Verständnis spielen im Land eine wichtige Rolle. Eine Wanderausstellung zeigt diese besondere Form des Islam, die in der modernen omanischen Gesellschaft gelebt wird. Die Schau wurde mit den Verantwortlichen des Religionsministeriums (Ministry of Endowments and Religious Affairs) und einem deutsch-omanischen Organisationsteam entwickelt. Zu sehen sind Bilder, Texte, alte Manuskripte, kalligraphische Zeichnungen und Sandbilder – seit 2010 in 35 Ländern weltweit in Bildungs-, Kultur- und Religionseinrichtungen.

Das Sultanat Oman garantiert die Freiheit der Religionsausübung. Deshalb gibt es dort Anhänger verschiedener Religionen. Das Religionsministerium trägt die Verantwortung für das Miteinander der religiösen Gemeinschaften im Oman. Diese erhalten die notwendigen Rahmenbedingungen, um ihren Glauben praktizieren zu können. Christliche Kirchen verschiedener Herkunft findet man in Maskat und Salalah neben Tempeln von

Oman strives for peace among peoples – both abroad and at home, where freedom of religion is a right. Dialog between religions and mutual understanding play an important role in the country. A traveling exhibition shows the specific variety of Islam that is part of everyday life in modern Omani society. The concept was developed by those responsible parties in the Ministry of Endowments and Religious Affairs and a German-Omani organizing team. Pictures, texts, old manuscripts, calligraphy and silhouettes are on display. The exhibition has been hosted in 35 countries since 2010, in educational, cultural and religious institutions as well as with UNESCO and the UN.

Today a large number of followers of various religions are found in Oman, where the state guarantees freedom of religion. The Ministry of Endowments and Religious Affairs is responsible for the various religious communities in Oman, which it provides with the facilities necessary to practice their faith. Christian churches of various denominations are found in Muscat and Salalah, with temples for Hindus, Sikhs and Buddhists, as well. The law prohibits public proselytizing by all religious groups. Oman is actively working to promote a true understand-

Tolerance, Understanding, Coexistence: Oman's message of Islam

Die Wanderausstellung zu religiöser Toleranz tourt seit 2010 weltweit durch Bildungs-, Kultur- und Religionseinrichtungen.
The exhibition on religious tolerance has been touring the world since 2010 in educational, cultural and religious institutions.

Hindus, Sikhs und Buddhisten. Das Gesetz verbietet allerdings allen religiösen Gruppen das öffentliche Missionieren.

Oman arbeitet aktiv daran, stereotypen und falschen Ansichten über den Islam zu begegnen, die zu Fanatismus und religiöser Intoleranz führen können. Die omanische Regierung führt internationale religionsübergreifende Dialoge, um religiöse Toleranz, gegenseitiges Verständnis und das friedliche Miteinander zu fördern. Es gibt regelmäßige Treffen und Konferenzen, Ausstellungen, Vorträge, Veröffentlichungen – außerdem werden religionsübergreifende Institutionen gefördert.

Der Religionsminister, Scheich Abdullah Al Salmi, beschreibt seinen Ansatz wie folgt:

„Auf der Welt gibt es drei religiöse Bevölkerungsgruppen. Das sind zum einen Christen, Juden und Muslime, die an einen Gott und an ein heiliges Buch glauben. Die zweite Gruppe machen die Atheisten aus, die jegliches Vertrauen in die Religion verloren haben. Die dritte Gruppe sind die Anhänger verschiedener Religionen und spiritueller Ideen. Wir unterstützen den konstruktiven und authentischen Dialog mit Wissenschaftlern und Vertretern all dieser Gruppen. Ziel des Austauschs ist es, auf der Grundlage unseres Denkens eine gemeinsame Moral und ein gemeinsames Verständnis von Gerechtigkeit zu reflektieren. Denn nur dann, wenn wir uns der Ähnlichkeit unserer Überzeugungen und Gedanken bewusst sind und sie uns als Fundament unseres Handelns dienen, werden wir und unsere Kinder einer friedlichen Zukunft entgegenblicken. Dazu gehört auch der gegenseitige Respekt kultureller Unterschiede."

ing of Islam to counter the spread of stereotypical and erroneous views of Islam, which lead to bigotry. The government of Oman has been conducting an interfaith dialogue to foster religious tolerance, mutual understanding, and peaceful coexistence on a global scale. The activities include regular international meetings and conferences, exhibitions, lectures, publications and support to interfaith institutions.

Abdullah bin Mohammad Al Salmi, Minister of Endowments and Religious Affairs, summarizes his approach as follows:

"We have three population groups on earth: the first, consisting of Christians, Jews and Muslims, who believe in one God and a holy book; the second, atheists, who have lost all confidence in religion; and the third group representing a variety of religious and spiritual ideas. We endeavor to maintain a constructive and genuine dialogue with scholars and representatives of all these groups. The aim of exchange is to reflect on the foundations of our thinking, a common morality and a common sense of justice. For only when we are aware of these similarities and when they form a basis for our actions, while accepting cultural differences, will we and our children enjoy a peaceful future."

In 2009 the Minister of Awqaf and Religious Affairs (MARA) decided to counter the generally negative media image of Islam with the largely unknown image of Islam as practiced in modern Omani society. This decision was implemented in the form of a touring exhibition. The project was launched in 2010 at the Adult Education Center (VHS) Ludwigshafen, Germany. Fortunately, the huge positive response quickly led to the decision to

Toleranz, Verständnis und Koexistenz

2009 entschloss sich der Religionsminister, dem weit verbreiteten negativen Image des Islam zu begegnen und das zumeist unbekannte Verständnis des Glaubens in der modernen omanischen Gesellschaft bekannter zu machen. Diese Entscheidung legte den Grundstein für eine Wanderausstellung.

Das Projekt startete 2010 in Zusammenarbeit mit der Volkshochschule Ludwigshafen. Viele Besucher reagierten sehr positiv – daraufhin wurde das Ausstellungsmaterial in sechs Sprachen übersetzt. Die Ausstellung und der begleitende Dokumentarfilm von Grimme-Preisträger Wolfgang Ettlich tourt seitdem durch ganz Europa. Heute steht die Schau in mehr als 25 Sprachen zur Verfügung.

Bis Ende 2018 wurde die Ausstellung an 120 Orten in mehr als 35 Ländern gezeigt. Gastgeber waren beispielsweise Korea, Japan und Pakistan, zahlreiche europäische Länder, Brasilien, die USA, Australien, Neuseeland und Südafrika. Zu den Kooperationspartnern zählen Universitäten, Bildungseinrichtungen für Erwachsene, religiöse und kulturelle Zentren, staatliche Installationen, die Vereinten Nationen, die Unesco und Unesco-Partnerorganisationen.

Auf Tagungen, Konferenzen und anderen ausgewählten Veranstaltungen, die sich mit religionsübergreifendem Dialog befassten, war die Schau zu sehen. Dabei stand immer auch die omanische Botschaft von religiöser Toleranz, gegenseitigem Verständnis und friedlicher Koexistenz im Fokus.

Der Erfolg des Projektes ist insbesondere der fruchtbaren und harmonischen Kooperation des internationalen Teams zu verdanken. Dazu gehören Hilal Al Harthy, Omair Al Mamari, Mohammed Al Rahbi, Mohammed Al Malki und Salmi Al Jahdhami auf omanischer Seite. Auf Seiten von Arabia Felix unterstützen Michael Dickinson, Alex Moll, Sebastian Schöberl und Violeta Galego die Organisation – alle sind Mitglieder der Deutsch Omanischen Gesellschaft. Das Team wird von Mohammed Al Mamari, wissenschaftlicher Berater des Religionsministeriums, und Georg Popp, Managing Direktor von Arabia Felix Synform GmbH, geführt. Beide entwickelten zusammen die Ausstellungidee und die -inhalte. Das Konzept verbindet westliche und omanische Perspektiven, so dass ein internationales Publikum mit unterschiedlichen kulturellen Hintergründen angesprochen wird. Ein

translate the material into six more languages and offer the exhibition and the accompanying documentary film, by Grimme prize winner Wolfgang Ettlich, throughout Europe. Since then the exhibition has been made available in more than 25 languages.

By the end of 2018, the exhibition was hosted in over 120 locations in more than 35 countries, ranging from Korea, Japan and Pakistan to Europe, Brazil and the USA, Australia, New Zealand and South Africa. Cooperation partners have been universities, adult education centers, religious and cultural centers, governmental institutions, United Nations, UNESCO and UNESCO affiliates.

The exhibition has been used as a focal point in meetings, conferences, and special events, all relating to interfaith dialogue and all promoting Oman's message of religious tolerance, mutual understanding and peaceful coexistence.

One of the keypoints for the success of the project is the fruitful and harmonic cooperation of the international team, led by Mohammed Al Mamari (Scientific Advisor to MARA) and Georg Popp (Managing Director ARABIA FELIX Synform GmbH, Germany), who together developed the idea and the content of the exhibition.

The core of the team consists of Hilal Al Harthy, Omair Al Mamari, Mohammed Al Rahbi, Mohammed Al Malki and Sami Al Jahdhami on the Omani side. Under the umbrella of ARABIA FELIX, Michael Dickinson, Alex Moll, Sebastian Schöberl and Violeta Galego all contribute. All ARABIA FELIX team members are members of the German Omani Association.

The concept unites Western and Omani perspectives, thus making the exhibition interesting for an international audience with the most varied cultural background. An overview of the project is to be found on the multilingual website www.islam-in-oman.com, where the exhibits and exhibition venues are presented, as well as insight into the interreligious global network, at various levels of society, which has been created as a result.

The exhibition "Tolerance, Understanding, Coexistence: Oman's Message of Islam" consists of printed matter, 3D objects and digital media. The heart of the exhibi-

Überblick über das Projekt findet sich auf der mehrsprachigen Webseite www.islam-in-oman.com. Parallel dazu gibt es Informationen über die Ausstellung, Termine sowie über das globale Netzwerk, das sich aus dem Konzept heraus entwickelt hat.

Die Schau „Toleranz, Verständnis, Koexistenz – Omans Botschaft des Islam" besteht aus Drucksachen, 3D-Objekten und digitalen Medien. Im Mittelpunkt stehen 24 farbige Informationstafeln in der Größe von 70 x 100 Zentimetern. Zudem sind Faksimiledrucke alter Manuskripte und Kunstobjekte – z.B. ein Kamel-Schulterblatt mit Koransprüchen – zu sehen. Künstlerisches Spiel mit Schatten, kalligraphische Objekte und Filme fügen die Ebene der Kunst hinzu. Multimedia-Terminals laden Besucher ein, die Panels in anderen Sprachen zu lesen und verschiedene Themen zu vertiefen. Die Farben der Ausstellungstafeln sind auf das Spektrum von Pigmenten abgestimmt, die Georg Popp aus omanischer Erde und heimischen Mineralien gewonnen hat. Die gesamte Farbpalette der Ausstellung ist deshalb typisch für den Oman und bezieht sich auf die dort in der Natur vorkommenden Farben. Die optische Präsentation ist auch deshalb einzigartig, weil das Farbspektrum digitalisiert und ausschließlich für diese Ausstellung produziert wurde.

Das Symbol der Ausstellung, eine Glasskulptur, wurde im November 2015 bei der 38. Hauptkonferenz der Unesco präsentiert. Die Skulptur steht sinnbildlich für die Vielfalt der Weltreligionen und Kulturen und veranschaulicht zugleich die Rolle des Sultanats als Vermittler einer Politik von Verständnis, Akzeptanz und des friedlichen Miteinanders zwischen den Völkern. Die Skulptur ist nun Teil der ständigen Kunstausstellung im Unesco-Hauptquartier in Paris.

Der Erfolg dieses omanisch-deutschen Projekts demonstriert, dass eine konstruktive Zusammenarbeit zwischen Ost und West möglich ist, auch wenn dies der heute gängigen Meinung widerspricht. Die objektive Präsentation des Inhalts, die frei ist von jeglichem kommerziellen Interesse, soll dabei helfen, Bedenken und Zweifel gegenüber dem Islam in Europa und weltweit zu zerstreuen.

Informationen zur Ausstellung „Toleranz, Verständnis, Koexistenz: Oman's Botschaft des Islam" unter www.islam-in-oman.com

tion consists of 24 full-color information panels, size 70 x 100 cm. Facsimile prints of ancient manuscripts and artefacts, like camel shoulder blades emblazoned with Quranic writings, enrich the setting. Shadow art, calligraphy and films add an artistic level to the exhibition. Multimedia terminals allow visitors to read the panels in other languages and gain information on various topics in more detail than presented in the exhibition.

The colors of the exhibition panels were selected from pigments produced personally by Georg Popp using Omani earth and minerals. The entire color palette of the exhibition panels is therefore authentically Omani. It is also unique, because this color set was digitalized and produced exclusively for the first time for use in this exhibition, and reflects the real and naturally-occurring colors of Oman.

The emblem of the exhibition project in the form of a glass sculpture was presented to UNESCO in November 2015 at an event held in conjunction with the 38th General Conference. Symbolizing the diversity of the world's religions and cultures, as it does, and exemplifying the Sultanate's role in establishing policies of tolerance, acceptance, and peaceful coexistence among peoples, it is now part of the permanent art collection at the UNESCO Headquarters in Paris.

The success of this Omani-German venture demonstrates that contrary to widespread opinion, constructive cooperation between East and West is quite possible even today. This is due mainly to the objective presentation of the content, free of blatant commercial interests, which helps to diffuse misgivings about Islam in Europe and elsewhere in the world.

Information on the exhibition "Tolerance, Understanding, Coexistence: Oman's Message of Islam" can be found at www.islam-in-oman.com

Kalligraphie - die Kunst des Schönschreibens – ist ein Teil des Ausstellungsprojekts.
Calligraphy - the art of writing – is part of the exhibition.

Tolerance, Understanding, Coexistence: Oman's message of Islam

SHAIKH ABDULLAH BIN MOHAMMED AL SALMI

RELIGIÖSE TOLERANZ
EINE VISION
RELIGIOUS TOLERANCE
A VISION

OLMS

PAPERBACK

Eine Sammlung von Reden in fünf Sprachen, die für gegenseitiges Verständnis werben.
A collection of speeches in five languages that promote mutual understanding.

Plädoyer für Frieden und Menschlichkeit

Plea for peace and humanity

Abdullah Bin Mohammed Al Salmi: „Religiöse Toleranz –
eine Vision für eine neue Welt"

Abdullah Bin Mohammed Al Salmi: "Religious Tolerance –
A Vision for a New World"

نداء للسلام والإنسانية
السالمي: "التقبل الديني: نظرة مستقبلية للعالم الجديد."

في زمن يغلب فيه حديث الناس عن صراع الحضارات والأديان وتظهر علامات عدم تقبل الأديان وزيادة التزمت الكراهية، فإننا بحاجة إلى ومضات للتعاون المشترك. بعض هذه الومضات للتفاهم المشترك بين الحضارات وأبتاع الديانات نجدها في خطابات معالي الشيخ عبد الله بن محمد السالمي، وزير الأوقاف والشؤون الإسلامية في سلطنة عُمان (2018). وقد تم نشر هذه الأفكار تحت عنوان "التقبل الديني: نظرة مستقبلية للعالم الجديد."

In Zeiten, in denen vom Kampf der Kulturen und Religionen gesprochen wird und die Zeichen auf religiöse Intoleranz und Fanatismus stehen, sind Impulse für ein konstruktives Miteinander gefragt. Anregungen zur Verständigung zwischen den Kulturen und Religionen liefern die Reden von Shaik Abdullah bin Mohammad Al Salmi, Minister für Stiftungen und religiöse Angelegenheiten im Sultanat Oman (2018).

Religiöse Konflikte werden zunehmend zu einer globalen Bedrohung. Fanatiker schüren Angst, Misstrauen und Hass und errichten Mauern zwischen westlichen Gesellschaften und der islamischen Welt. Gedanken zu einer weltweiten Verständigung, die ein Plädoyer für die gemeinsame Verantwortung für Frieden darstellen, finden sich in dem Buch „Religiöse Toleranz. Eine Vision". Der umfangreiche Band präsentiert sechs Reden von Shaik Abdullah bin Mohammad Al Salmi, Minister für Stiftungen und religiöse Angelegenheiten im Sultanat Oman.

Der Autor verleiht seiner Vision Ausdruck, dass alle Religionen über gemeinsame humanistische Werte verbunden sind und den Wunsch nach Freiheit, Gleichheit und Toleranz teilen. Daraus erwächst für ihn die Chance nach Verständigung und tragfähigen Lösungen. Al Salmi betont den friedliebenden Geist des Islam gegenüber dem Juden- und Christentum sowie den anderen Religionen und Kulturen der Welt. Kritisch hinterfragt er die Rolle von Politik und Religion in der heutigen Welt. In seinen Reden beruft er sich auf den Koran, den jüdischen Gelehrten Ibn Kammuna und den Dalai Lama. Den katholischen Theologen Hans Küng zitiert er unter anderem mit den Worten: „Frieden unter den Nationen ist nicht ohne Frieden unter den Religionen möglich."

Gehalten wurden die Reden zwischen 2005 und 2014 vor internationalem, hochrangigem Publikum – auf interreligiösen, wissenschaftlichen, sozialen oder kulturellen Konferenzen im Oman sowie an religiösen Einrichtungen und Universitäten in Europa und den USA. Der Band ist in fünf Sprachen angelegt: Deutsch, Englisch, Arabisch, Chinesisch, Hebräisch.

Abdullah Bin Mohammed Al Salmi; Religiöse Toleranz: Eine Vision für eine neue Welt / Religious Tolerance: A Vision for a new World. 29,80 Euro bzw 49,80 (hochwertige Ausgabe): ISBN: 978-3-487-08566-1 oder ISBN: 978-3-487-08564-7

In times when people speak of the battle between different cultures and religions and when the signs are pointing to religious intolerance and fanaticism, impulses are urgently needed for a constructive way of living together. Proposals for an understanding between different cultures and religions can be found in the speeches of Shaik Abdullah bin Mohammad Al Salmi, Minister of Endowments and Religious Affairs in the Sultanate Oman (2018).

Religious conflicts are becoming more and more of a global threat. Fanatics fuel fear, distrust and hatred and build walls between Western societies and the Islamic world. Reflections on global communication that represent a plea for a shared responsibility for peace can be found in the book Religious Tolerance: A Vision. The extensive volume presents six speeches of Shaik Abdullah bin Mohammad Al Salmi, Minister of Endowments and Religious Affairs in the Sultanate Oman.

The author expresses his vision for all religions to be connected because of their shared humanist values and the desire to achieve freedom, equality and tolerance. From this he sees arising a chance for mutual understanding and sustainable solutions.

Al Salmi stresses the peaceful spirit of Islam regarding Judaism and Christianity as well as other religions and cultures all over the world. He is critical of the role that politics and religion play in today's world. In his speeches he refers to the Quran, the Jewish scholar Ibn Kammuna and the Dalai Lama. Among the words he cites of the catholic theologian Hans Küng are, "Peace among the nations is impossible without peace among the religions."

The speeches were delivered between 2005 and 2014 to international audiences of high rank – at interreligious, scholarly, social or cultural conferences in Oman as well as at religious institutions and universities in Europe and the USA.

In order to address a broad readership, the volume encompasses five language: German, English, Arabic, Chinese, Hebrew.

Pius Schmidt aus München und Muadh Abdulmalik Al-Badaei aus Maskat.
Pius Schmidt from Munich and Muadh Abdulmalik Al-Badaei from Muscat.

Voneinander lernen

Learning from Each Other

Deutsche und omanische Schüler
leben und arbeiten miteinander

German and Omani students
living and working together

التعلم من بعضهم البعض – أحياناً في مسقط وأحياناً في ميونخ
يعيش الطلاب العُمانيون والألمان مع بعضهم البعض

هم يتعلمون كيف يستطيع الانسان في حياته اليومية الاستغناء عن البلاستيك و يستمعون إلى الموسيقى سوياً. يوجد بين الطلاب العُمانيين والألمان أشياء كثيرة مشتركة أكثر مما نراه في النظرة الأولى. منذ عام 2010م تقوم مدرستين خاصتين بتنظيم تبادل خاص بين الطلبة في ميونخ وفي مسقط وهذا التبادل هو الأول من نوعه بين المانيا ودولة عربية. يرافق السيد فلوريان شرودر هذا التبادل بصفته مدرس ألماني مع زملائه العُمانيين عبد الرحمن الهمامي وشريفة عمير الرواحي حيث ينظم سوياً معهم مشاريع مشتركة مضمون أحدها هو إيجاد طريقة يستطيع الإنسان من خلالها الاستغناء عن المواد الصناعية. كما تستضيف العائلات المضيفة الطلاب الوافدين ويعاملوهم كأنهم جزء من العائلة. وهنا يكتشفون تشابهات ويحترمون الاختلافات في العادت والتقاليد، حيث أن هذا مهم لنجاح هذا البرنامج على المدى الطويل.

Deutsche und omanische Schüler lernen im Team - etwa über das Vermeiden von Plastik.
German and Omani students learning together, including how to avoid using plastic.

Sie lernen, wie man im Alltag ohne Plastik auskommen kann und hören zusammen Musik: Deutsche und omanische Schüler haben mehr gemeinsam, als es auf den ersten Blick scheint. Seit 2010 organisieren zwei Privatschulen einen außergewöhnlichen Austausch zwischen München und Maskat – als ersten dieser Art zwischen Deutschland und einem arabischen Land.

Die beiden Jungen sind 16 Jahre alt. Doch während der eine unweit der Alpen mit ihren Blumenwiesen aufwächst, kommt der andere aus einem kargen Land, in dem die Familie morgens um fünf Uhr gemeinsam betet: Pius Schmidt aus München und Muadh Abdulmalik Al Badaei aus Maskat. Sie sind Freunde geworden – und wundern sich dennoch über manches, was sie vom anderen erfahren. „Erst habe ich befürchtet, kein Wort zu verstehen, wenn sich die Familie auf Arabisch unterhält. Aber es war cool, weil bei Muadh zuhause fast nur Englisch gesprochen wird. Und neben traditionellen Liedern laufen auch eine Menge neuer Songs aus den Charts", erzählt Pius nach seinem Besuch in Maskat. „Wir haben Fußball und Karten gespielt und beim Essen war's witzig – Muadh kann das prima mit den Händen, während ich immer gekleckert habe. Daran muss man sich erstmal gewöhnen." Schließlich kamen die beiden so gut miteinander klar, dass beim

They learn how to go through life without plastic, and they listen to music together. German and Omani students have more in common than you would first think. Since 2010, two private schools have been running a ground-breaking exchange programme between Munich and Muscat – the first of its kind between Germany and an Arab country.

The two boys in our story are 16 years old. One of them has grown up not far from the Alps with their fields of flowers, and the other comes from a barren country, where the family prays together at 5am: Pius Schmidt from Munich and Muadh Abdulmalik Al Badaei from Muscat. They have grown to be friends and are still surprised by some of the facts they learn about each other. "At first, I was afraid I wouldn't understand a single word when the family spoke in Arabic. But it was cool because Muadh almost always spoke English at home. And in addition to traditional songs, there are loads of new hit songs on the radio," Pius explains after his stay in Muscat. "We played soccer and cards, and eating was a funny experience. Muadh is great at eating with his hands, but I kept spilling food. That's something you have to get used to." In the end, they got along so well that their eyes were filled with tears when they said their goodbyes

Learning from Each Other

Abschied am Flughafen die Tränen flossen. Muadhs Mutter Asma meint noch Wochen später: „Wir vermissen Pius."

Pius und Muadh haben sich über einen Schüleraustausch zwischen der Münchner Sabel-Schule und der Ahmad bin Majid Private School in Maskat kennengelernt. Es ist der erste dieser Art zwischen Deutschland und einem arabischen Land. „Dahinter stehen eine private Initiative und die Tatsache, dass Privatschulen recht selbstständig unabhängig vom Staat agieren können", sagt Florian Schröder, der den Austausch als Lehrer begleitet. Gemeinsam mit seinem omanischen Kollegen Abdulrahman Al Hamumi und Sharifa Omair Al Rawahy organisiert er gemeinsame Projektarbeiten, in denen es zum Beispiel um Nachhaltigkeit und das Vermeiden von Kunststoff geht. Für die Omaner ein großes Thema: Im Land werden Plastikflaschen oft noch achtlos in die Landschaft geworfen, ein Bewusstsein für den Umweltschutz und seine Herausforderungen keimt gerade erst auf. Die Ahmad bin Majid Schule will hierbei Vorreiter sein und arbeitet zusammen mit anderen Partnern an der Ausweitung dieses Bewusstseins in der Schule und in der Gesellschaft insgesamt.

Dass die Zusammenarbeit der Schulen und aller Beteiligten so gut funktioniert, ist für Florian Schröder ohne Unterstützung nicht denkbar. „Vor allem haben uns Georg Popp und Juma Al Maskari von der Deutsch-Omanischen Gesellschaft unter die Arme gegriffen. Sie haben uns mit ihrem Know-how begleitet und auch finanzielle Mittel organisiert." Behörden wie die deutsche Botschaft und die Konferenz der Kultusminister legen keine Steine in den Weg, sondern helfen im Gegenteil mit Visa und Finanzen.

„Im Prinzip sind wir gleich, wir sprechen nur verschiedene Sprachen"

"Basically, we are alike, we only speak different languages"

at the airport. Weeks later, Muadh's mother Asma still says: "We miss Pius."

Pius and Muadh got to know each other through a student exchange programme between the Sabel School in Munich and Ahmad bin Majid Private School in Muscat. It is the first exchange programme of its kind between Germany and an Arab country. "It is backed by a private initiative because private schools can act quite independently from the state," says Florian Schröder, a teacher who monitors the exchange programme. Together with his Omani colleagues, Abdulrahman Al Hamumi and Sharifa Omair Al Rawahy, he organises joint projects that deal with topics such as sustainability and the avoidance of plastic. This is a major issue for the Omanis. In their country, plastic bottles are still carelessly tossed aside. An awareness of environmentalism and its challenges is only just starting to develop. Ahmad bin Majid School wants to be a trailblazer in this area and is working with other partners to raise awareness at the school and in Omani society in general.

For Schröder it is unthinkable that the collaboration between the schools and everyone involved could be so successful without additional support: "Georg Popp and Juma Al Maskari from the German-Omani Association have really helped us out. They've supported us with extensive know-how and have organised funding."

Instead of putting obstacles in their way, agencies such as the German Embassy and the Conference of Ministers of Education have helped them out with visas and financial support.

For two weeks a year, the Germans and the Omanis visit each other and live with their respective families. Schröder explains that these exchange visits usually run smoothly, apart from some homesickness and the occasional minor culture shock that comes from being in a foreign country. "It is wonderful to experience that we are basically the same, we just speak different languag-

Muadh Abdulmalik Al Badaei aus Maskat und Pius Schmidt aus München sind Freunde geworden.
Muadh Abdulmalik Al Badaei from Muscat and Pius Schmidt from Munich have become friends.

Voneinander lernen

Zwei Wochen im Jahr besuchen sich die Deutschen und die Omaner gegenseitig und leben in den jeweiligen Familien. Die Austauschbesuche gehen in der Regel reibungslos über die Bühne, meint Florian Schröder – abgesehen von ein wenig Heimweh und ab und zu einem kleinen Kulturschock im jeweils anderen Land. „Es ist eine wunderbare Erfahrung, dass wir im Prinzip gleich sind, nur andere Sprachen sprechen." Diskussionsbedarf gibt es höchstens, wenn's zum Beispiel um die Religion geht, die das Leben in Maskat stark bestimmt. Dann fragen die deutschen Schüler schon mal, ob sie auch früh aufstehen müssen, um zu beten. Abdulrahman Al Hamumi macht die Erfahrung, dass die Gastfamilie ihre tägliche Routine in der Regel ganz normal beibehält. „Zugleich kümmert sie sich aber auch darum, dass sich der Gastsohn als Teil der Familie fühlt. Sie geben sich viel Mühe, die kulturellen und religiösen Vorstellungen des Gastes richtig zu verstehen und zu respektieren – vor allem im Hinblick auf Mahlzeiten, Kleidung oder soziale Kontakte. Das ist wichtig für den langfristigen Erfolg des Austauschprogramms", sagt der Lehrer.

es." They only need to consider things such as whether religion could be an issue, because it is a highly relevant aspect of life in Muscat. Some German students may ask if they also have to get up early to pray. According to Al Hamumi, the host families usually just go about their daily routine. "At the same time, however, they also make sure that the visiting 'son' feels like part of the family. They go out of their way to understand the cultural and religious expectations of their guest and to respect them, particularly regarding meals, clothing and social interactions. This is extremely important for the long-term success of our exchange programme," the teacher says.

Dr Eva Schmidt, Pius's mother, and Asma Abdulmalik, Muadh's mother, wanted to avoid uncertainties caused by different lifestyles from the very start. That is why the two families got to know each other before Pius's journey to Muscat. "We sent them photos of us via WhatsApp and they sent us photos of them in traditional attire," Eva

Das Team der Lehrer, die den Austausch organisieren: Wilfried Hülser, Florian Schröder, Mr. Abu Ubaida El Neel , Aydin Davulcu, Abdulrahman Al Hamumi (v. l.).
The team of teachers: Wilfried Hülser, Florian Schröder, Mr. Abu Ubaida El Neel , Aydin Davulcu, Abdulrahman Al Hamumi (from left).

Voneinander lernen

Unsicherheiten durch unterschiedliche Lebensgewohnheiten wollten Dr. Eva Schmidt, die Mutter von Pius, und Asma Abdulmalik mit ihrem Sohn Muadh von Anfang an aus dem Weg gehen. Deshalb haben sich die Familien schon vor Pius' Reise nach Maskat miteinander bekannt gemacht. „Wir haben uns gegenseitig Bilder über WhatsApp geschickt – wir und die Omaner in ihrer Tracht", sagt Eva Schmidt. „So konnten wir sehen, zu wem Pius fliegt und dass zum Beispiel die Frauen nicht voll verschleiert sind." Asma überwand ihre anfänglichen Bedenken, einen fremden Jungen quasi als sechstes Kind für eine Zeit aufzunehmen, indem sie die Verantwortung für den Gast ihrem Sohn übertrug: „Er sollte ihm das Bett machen und sich auch sonst kümmern. Dafür habe ich keine Zeit." Die Mütter wurden von ihren Söhnen überzeugt, weil die Jungs unbedingt an dem Austausch teilnehmen. wollten. „Pius hat sich beworben. Er ist weltoffen, probiert gerne Gerichte aus aller Herren Länder", sagt Eva Schmidt. So war es entgegen Asmas Befürchtungen für den Jungen kein Problem, mit der arabischen Familie zu essen. „Wir haben unseren Tisch verkauft und nehmen alle Mahlzeiten auf dem Boden ein. Das lehrt uns Bescheidenheit", sagt Asma.

Über die App tauschten sich die Familien regelmäßig aus, während Pius in Oman weilte. Auf einem Foto sahen die Schmidts ihren Sohn plötzlich in omanischer Tracht, der so genannten Dishdasha. Derart gewandet durfte er die Gastfamilie in die Moschee zum Freitagsgebet begleiten – eine aufregende Erfahrung: „Die Größe der Moschee hat mich fasziniert, es gibt diesen riesigen farbigen Teppich und keine Möbel, das verstärkt den imposanten Eindruck noch. Besonders interessant war es, zu sehen, dass die Frauen in einem gesonderten Raum beten."

Die Schmidts haben Muadh im Gegenzug durch München geführt, wo er sich besonders über das schnelle Tempo wunderte, mit dem die Deutschen in der Stadt unterwegs sind. Besonderes Erlebnis an einem kühlen Morgen: Der Atem wurde als Hauch vor dem Mund sichtbar. Ein Besuch in Zell am See stand auch auf dem Programm von Muadhs Besuch – denn dieser Ort wird in Maskat als eine Art Paradies empfunden.

Unterdessen hofft Lehrer Florian Schröder, den Austausch mit weiteren Familien im Oman und in Deutsch-

says. "That way we could see who Pius was going to meet and that the women weren't completely veiled." Asma got over her initial concerns about taking a strange boy into her family for a long-term stay, effectively as a sixth child. She delegated the responsibility for their guest to her son. "My son had to prepare the bed and also take care of everything else. I didn't have time for that." The sons convinced their mothers that they wanted to take part in the exchange no matter what. "Pius applied. He is open-minded and loves to try food from all around the world," Eva says. Therefore, despite Asma's apprehension, Pius did not have any problem eating with the Arab family. "We sold our table and now we eat all our meals on the floor. That has taught us modesty," Asma says.

The two families regularly communicated via the app while Pius was staying in Oman. In one picture, the Schmidts suddenly saw their son in Omani clothing, the dishdasha. In this attire, he was allowed to accompany his host family to the mosque for Friday prayers – an exciting experience. "I was fascinated by the size of the mosque, there's a huge colourful carpet and no furniture which makes it seem even larger. It was really interesting to see that the women prayed in a separate room", says Pius.

In return, the Schmidts showed Muadh around Munich, where he was especially surprised by how fast Germans get around in the city. A particularly memorable experience one chilly morning was seeing his breath in the cold air. A visit to Zell am See was also on the agenda during Muadh's stay because this place is considered a sort of paradise in Muscat.

Meanwhile, Schröder is hoping to extend the exchange programme to include more families in Oman and Germany, as well as additional teachers. His counterpart, Abdulrahman Al Hamumi, is aiming to achieve the same goal in Oman. Over the years, the two of them have grown to be close friends, which is helping them to successfully expand the exchange program. Together, they are working hard to win over young students from the Sabel Schools in Germany and Ahman bin Majid School in Oman to participate in the programme by hosting and visiting each other with their families.

Learning from Each Other

land sowie zusätzlichen Lehrerkollegen ausbauen zu können. Sein Counterpart Abdulrahman Al Hamumi strebt im Oman die gleichen Ziele an. Beide sind über Jahre hinweg enge Freunde geworden – das hilft ihnen dabei, das Austauschprogramm erfolgreich weiter auszubauen.

„Das Austauschprogramm soll bald noch mehr Schüler zusammenbringen"

"The exchange program will soon bring together more students"

Wie alles begann

Die Familien bilden die Basis des Austauschprogramms. Das betont Najim M. Al Timami, Gründer der Ahmad bin Majid Privatschule in Maskat, die mit den Sabel Schulen in München zusammenarbeitet. Beide Institutionen unterstützen die Familien dabei, Ähnlichkeiten zu entdecken und zugleich Unterschiede zwischen den Kulturen, den Traditionen sowie den schulischen Bräuchen zu schätzen – auf dieser weltbürgerlichen Basis werden auch Probleme im Bildungskontext und globale Perspektiven diskutiert.

Das Konzept des Austauschprogramms wurde entwickelt, als Najim Al Timamis Familie 2009 einen deutschen Austauschschüler für ein Jahr aufnahm, damit er eine private Schule besuchen konnte. Seit 2010 hat der Austausch zwischen Maskat und München innerhalb von acht Jahren mehr als 240 Familien zusammengebracht. Über 240 Schüler wurden darauf vorbereitet, ein Leben lang Freunde in dieser globalen Gemeinschaft zu werden. Hamad N. Al Timami, der Direktor der Ahmad bin Majid Private School, hebt die Schwerpunkte des Austauschprogramms hervor: kulturelles Verständnis; Zusammenarbeit zwischen Jugendlichen, Familien und Schulen; Führung; globale Perspektiven; Toleranz, Verständnis und Koexistenz (TUC).

Weitere Informationen gibt es unter www.schueleraustausch-oman.de.

How everything began

"Families are the backbone of the exchange programme", stresses Najim M. Al Timami, the founder-chairman of Ahmad bin Majid Private School, which cooperates with the Sabel schools in Munich. Both schools help families to celebrate their similarities while also appreciating the differences between their cultures, traditions and school customs. This multicultural arena is also a place to discuss issues relating to education and global perspectives.

The concept of an exchange programme started in 2009 when Najim Al Timami's family hosted a German student for a one-year, cultural visit to study at a private school. That experience sowed the seeds for the broader exchange programme. The ABM-Sabel Student Exchange Programme followed in 2010, and over the next eight years, the ABM-Sabel School Exchange Programme brought together over 240 families from the two schools and, in the process, connected and prepared over 240 students for life-long friendships in this global community. Hamad N. Al Timami, the Principal of Ahmad bin Majid Private School, highlights that the key areas in the exchange program are: cultural understanding; collaboration between youths, families and the schools; leadership; global perspectives; and tolerance, understanding and co-existence.

Further information is available at www.schueleraustausch-oman.de.

Die Jungs erleben einen Sonnenuntergang über dem arabischen Golf.
The boys experience a sunset over the Arabian Gulf.

Learning from Each Other

Frische Temperaturen gegen die Hitze

Cool Temperatures to Counter the Heat

Ein deutsch-omanisches Geothermie-Projekt
mit erneuerbarer Energie

A German-Omani geothermal project
with renewable energy

درجات حرارة مقبولة مقابل درجات حرارة عالية
برنامج عُماني ألماني جغرافي-حراري مع مصادر طاقة
بديلة

ترتفع درجات الحرارة في عُمان أحياناً لتصل إلى 45 درجة مئوية. لذلك يأمل المواطنون أن تكون درجة الحرارة في منازلهم ومكاتبهم منخفضة وباردة. إن 50% من الطاقة الكهربائية المنتجة من النفط والغاز تذهب لهذا الغرض. لكن مصادر الطاقة لها نهاية. لذلك تحاول الدولة ابتكار طرق جديدة في مجال الطاقة البديلة و GFZ (مركز هيلم هولتز للأبحاث في بوتستدام — مركز الأبحاث الجغرافي الألماني) في بوتستدام سوف يقوم ببناء مشروع الطاقة البديلة ومشروع الطاقة الحرارية الشمسية الجغرافي في عام 2020م. حيث سيكون المركز الاجتماعي في مسقط هو المبنى الأول الذي يتم تبريده من خلال التقنية الجديدة.

Im Oman kann es draußen bis zu 45 Grad heiß werden. Deshalb wünschen sich die Einheimischen stark heruntergekühlte Häuser und Büros. Bis zu 50 Prozent der aus Öl und Gas gewonnenen Elektrizität wird dafür im Land verwendet. Doch die Energiequellen sind endlich, weswegen das Land auf innovative Konzepte im Bereich erneuerbarer Energien setzt.

Wer im Sultanat Oman in einem heißen Sommer bei Außentemperaturen bis um die 45 Grad unterwegs ist, freut sich auf Abkühlung in der Mall oder ein frisches Lüftchen aus der Air Condition des Lieblingsrestaurants. „Bis zu 50 Prozent der aus Öl und Gas gewonnenen Elektrizität wird in unserm Land für die Erzeugung von Kühlungsenergie aufgewendet" sagt Dr. Sausan Al Riyami vom IATI, Institute of Advanced Technology Integration, in Maskat. „Öl und Gas sind begrenzt, deshalb setzen wir verstärkt auf erneuerbare Energien wie Solar- und Erdwärme."

In Oman, outdoor temperatures can reach 45 degrees Celsius, which is why locals want to cool down their houses and office buildings. In the past, Omanis built eco-houses out of natural materials which eventually helped to cool their indoor temperatures. Up to 50 percent of the country's oil-based and gas-based electricity is used for cooling. However, these sources of energy are finite, so the country is focusing on innovative concepts in the field of renewable energies.

People who spend time outside during the summer in Oman, where temperatures can soar up to 45 degrees, are happy to cool down in a mall or in the comfortable air conditioning of their favourite restaurant. There is currently a lot of effort being put into reducing the energy used in cooling systems. As part of these efforts, the Oman Eco House Design Competition is one of the Research Council's initiatives to raise awareness of the possibilities and importance of environmentally-friendly buildings and eco-design in Oman.

Dr. Felina Schütz in Potsdam mit Khalid Al Hinai bei der Prüfung von Untersuchungsergebnissen.
Dr Felina Schütz in Potsdam with Khalid Al Hinai looking at test results.

Cool Temperatures to Counter the Heat

IATI ist eine 2014 gegründete Initiative des Forschungsrats (The Research Council) in der omanischen Hauptstadt. Seit 2015 werden gemeinsam mit vier deutschen Helmholtz-Zentren in drei Bereichen Projekte entwickelt: Wasser, erneuerbare Energien und Öl / Gas.

Neue Wege im Bereich erneuerbarer Energien beschreitet die omanische Wissenschaftlerin mit ihrer deutschen Kollegin Dr. Felina Schütz vom Deutsche GeoForschungsZentrum GFZ. Seit 2015 planen sie gemeinsam eine solarthermisch betriebene Anlage, die ab 2020 das erste Gebäude in Maskat, das Social Center, kühlen soll. Der Untergrund wird dabei für eine intelligente Rückkühlung des Systems benutzt.

Dr. Felina Schütz: „Gemeinsam mit IATI möchten wir neue Lösungen zur Produktion von Kälteenergie erarbeiten. Wir übertragen dabei nicht einfach schon bekannte Konzepte, sondern entwickeln gemeinsam Ideen, die für das Sultanat passen."

Die Zusammenarbeit mit dem GFZ hat Modellcharakter für das junge omanische Institut. „Anwendungsorientierte wissenschaftliche Institute wie das GFZ existieren bislang im Oman nicht", so Dr. Al Riyami. „Der Knowhow-Transfer stellt entscheidende Weichen für die zukünftige Ausrichtung unserer Arbeit."

An dem Projekt arbeiten etwa 15 omanische und zirka zehn deutsche Teilnehmer zusammen. Für Workshops, Seminare oder ganze Studiengänge reisen die jungen Omaner für Wochen oder sogar Jahre nach Deutschland. Einer davon ist Khalid Al Hinai. Der 27-Jährige kam 2016 nach Deutschland und absolvierte seinen Master-Studiengang Energietechnik (Energy Engineering) an der Technischen Universität Berlin. „Ich schätze sehr, dass wir im Team so kollegial zusammenarbeiten", sagt er.

Khalid Al Hinai pendelt zwischen dem GFZ Potsdam und IATI in Maskat hin und her. „Ich hoffe, auch bei zukünftigen spannenden Projekten der Institute mit dabei zu sein", sagt er und lacht. „Vielleicht lerne ich noch so gut Deutsch, dass ich mich mit meinen Kollegen in ihrer Muttersprache unterhalten kann."

"Up to 50 percent of our country's oil and gas-based electricity is used for cooling," says Dr Sausan Al Riyami from IATI, the Institute of Advanced Technology Integration in Muscat. "There is a limited supply of oil and gas, so we are focusing more on renewable energies, such as solar and geothermal heat."

IATI, founded in 2014, is an initiative of the Research Council in Oman's capital. Since 2015, it has cooperated with four German Helmholtz centres to develop projects in three areas: water, renewable energies and oil/gas.

Dr Al Riyami is exploring new opportunities in the field of renewable energies with her German colleague, Dr Felina Schütz from Deutsche GeoForschungsZentrum GFZ Potsdam. In 2015, they began working on plans for a plant run on solar thermal energy that will provide cooling for a pilot building in Muscat, the Social Center, in 2020. The substrate will be used for intelligent return-cooling of the system.

Dr Schütz: "In cooperation with IATI, we want to develop new solutions for the production of cooling energy. We aren't just applying known concepts, but developing ideas that are appropriate for the Sultanate."

The collaboration with GFZ serves as a model for the young Omani institute. "Up until now, there haven't been any applied science institutes like GFZ in Oman," Dr Al Riyami explains. "This transfer of know-how truly sets the course for the future direction of our work."

Around 15 Omani and ten German participants are working together on this project. Young Omanis travel to Germany for weeks or even years to attend workshops, seminars and long-term university courses. One of them is Khalid Al Hinai. The 27-year-old came to Germany in 2016 and received his Master's degree in Energy Engineering at the Technische Universtität Berlin. "I really appreciate the team spirit on this project," he says.
Khalid divides his time between GFZ Potsdam and IATI in Muscat. "I hope to be involved in exciting future projects run by the Institute," he says with a smile. "Maybe someday I'll speak German so well that I can talk to my colleagues in their mother tongue."

Frische Temperaturen gegen die Hitze

Das deutsch-omanische Team in Maskat.
The German-Omani team in Muscat.

Aus Wärme wird Kälte – das Prinzip der Geothermie

Die geplante Anlage der Teams um Dr. Sausan Al Riyami und Dr. Felina Schütz ist eines von drei Pilot-projekten im Rahmen einer langfristig angelegten Kooperation zwischen der Helmholtz-Gemeinschaft und dem Sultanat Oman.

Im Prinzip arbeitet das System wie ein Kühlschrank, nur dass statt Elektrizität Wärmeenergie verwendet wird. Grob skizziert funktioniert die innovative Tech-nik so: In einem geschlossenen Kreislauf wird Wasser verdampft, absorbiert, erneut verdampft und kon-densiert anschließend wieder zu Wasser. Die Anlage besteht aus zwei Zylindern mit mehreren Kreisläu-fen. In einem Verdampfer wird Wasser bei niedrigem Druck und niedriger Temperatur verdampft. Durch diesen Prozess wird dem Gebäude Wärme entzogen. Der Wasserdampf wird dann von einer Salzlösung absorbiert und in einen weiteren Verdampfer ge-pumpt. Dort wird die Wärmeenergie der Solaranlage genutzt, um das Wasser von der Lösung zu trennen. Die Salzlösung fließt anschließend zurück zum Absorber, während sich der Wasserdampf in einem Kondensator verflüssigt, bevor der gesamte Prozess von neuem beginnt.

Nähere Infos zum Projekt unter:
IATI Institute of Advanced Technology Integration,
Innovation Park Muscat; www.iati.om
GFZ Geoforschungszentrum am Helmholtz-Zentrum,
Potsdam; www.gfz-potsdam.de

Using heat to chill – the geothermal principle

The plant that Dr Al Riyami and Dr Schütz's team are planning to construct is one of three pilot projects within the framework of a long-term collaboration between the Helmholtz Association and the Sultan-ate of Oman.

Basically, the system works like a refrigerator, but instead of electricity, thermal energy is used. This innovative technology works roughly as follows: in a closed circuit, water is evaporated, absorbed, evap-orated again and then condensed back to water. The plant consists of two cylinders with several circuits. The water is evaporated at low pressure and at a low temperature. This process drains heat from the building. The water vapour is then absorbed by a saline solution and pumped into another evaporator. There, the thermal energy of the solar plant is used to separate the water from the solution. Afterwards, the saline solution flows back to the absorber and the vapour is liquefied in a condenser, before the whole process starts again.

Further information on this project:
IATI Institute of Advanced Technology Integration,
Innovation Park Muscat; www.iati.om
GFZ Geoforschungszentrum am Helmholtz-Zentrum,
Potsdam; www.gfz-potsdam.de

Cool Temperatures to Counter the Heat

Jahrhunderte alte Grafittis in Al Khashbah zeigen berittene Menschen
Centuries-old Grafittis in Al Khashbah show mounted people.

Auf dem Weg zurück in die Bronzezeit

Return to the Bronze Age

Zu Besuch bei den Archäologen
aus Tübingen in Al Khashbah

Visiting Tübingen archaeologists
in Al Khashbah

في طريق العودة إلى العصر البرونزي
زيارة علماء الآثار من توبنغن إلى الخشبة

هم يعملون مثل بدو عصريين في طريق العودة إلى العصر البرونزي: د. كونراد شميدت من معهد الثقافات للشرق الأدنى القديم (IANES) في جامعة توبنغن وطلابها قضوا أربع سنوات في الحفر والبحث في قرية الخشبة على حافة جبال الحجر لمعرفة المزيد عن المستوطنات التي يعود تاريخها إلى الألفية الثالثة والرابعة قبل الميلاد. وقد عثروا على أقدم دليل حتى الآن لمعالجة النحاس في عُمان: آلاف الشظايا من الفرن والبوتقة. بالإضافة إلى ذلك، عثر الأخصائيون، خلال أعمال التنقيب، على أدلة نادرة على أن الحرفيين في عُمان قد استخدموا أدوات حجرية. هذا، ويتعلم الطلاب أيضًا كيفية التضامن والتعامل مع بعضهم البعض في بيئة قاحلة، حيث يبذل الجيران العُمانيون في ذلك قصارى جهدهم للمساعدة.

Der staubige Boden wird durchsiebt, um Kupferstäbchen oder Muschelperlen zu finden.
The dusty ground is sieved to find copper rods or shell pearls.

Sie arbeiten wie neuzeitliche Nomaden, die auf dem Weg zurück in die Bronzezeit sind: Dr. Conrad Schmidt vom Institut für die Kulturen des Alten Orients (IANES) der Universität Tübingen und seine Studierenden haben drei Jahre lang im Ort Al Kashbah am Rande des Hajar-Gebirges gegraben und geforscht, um mehr über Siedlungen aus dem vierten und dritten Jahrtausend vor Christus zu erfahren. Sie fanden den bisher ältesten Nachweis für die Verarbeitung von Kupfer im Oman: einen Brennofen. Außerdem entdeckten die Spezialisten Beweise dafür, dass Handwerker bereits mit Steinwerkzeugen gearbeitet haben. Die Studierenden erfahren während der Grabungsarbeiten auch, wie man in einer kargen Umgebung zusammenhält und miteinander auskommt. Dabei helfen die omanischen Nachbarn nach Kräften.

Wir sind irgendwo am Rande des Hadschar-Gebirges verabredet. Conrad Schmidt hat mir einen Landkarten-

They work like modern-day nomads heading back to the Bronze Age: Dr Conrad Schmidt from Tübingen University's Institute for Ancient Near Eastern Studies (IANES) and his students have conducted excavations and research for three years at Al Kashbah, on the edge of the Al Hajar Mountains. They are there to learn more about the settlements from the fourth and third millennia BC. They found the as-yet oldest evidence of copper processing in Oman – a kiln. In addition, they discovered proof that craftsmen were already working with stone tools back then. During the excavations, the students also learned to work together in barren surroundings and to get along with each other. Their Omani neighbours helped as best they could.

We had decided to meet somewhere on the edge of the Al Hajar Mountains. Conrad Schmidt had sent me part of a map via email where a red cross indicated the lo-

ausschnitt gemalt, auf dem ein rotes Kreuzchen bei den Orten Sinaw und Mukhtru den Ort Al Khashbah markiert. Dort soll ich ihn und seine 20 Studierenden finden. Vor dem inneren Auge wachsen Siedlungen aus der Bronzezeit empor, zwischen deren Häusern die Archäologen aus Tübingen wie neuzeitliche Nomaden durchs Land wandeln. Doch als ich mich mit meinem weißen Leih-Toyota der beschriebenen Stelle nähere, stehen dort nur einige windzerzauste Bäume in einer weiten, von Steinen bedeckten Landschaft. Verstreut liegen Häuschen wie hingewürfelt vor mir, in der Ferne die Silhouette der Berge. Ich zücke mein Smartphone mit der omanischen Simkarte, doch der Archäologie-Experte ist unter seiner dortigen Nummer nicht erreichbar. Inshallah (so Gott will) werde ich ihn treffen, so würden die Einheimischen wohl sagen - das gleiche denke auch ich, fahre auf gut Glück weiter und dann sehe ich sie unweit der Straße: Junge Menschen mit heller, teils geröteter Haut, auf einem Hügel hockend, die blonden und brünetten Schöpfe mit Hüten oder Tüchern gegen die sengende Sonne vermummt, auf ihren Knien Karten und Listen für Dokumentationen. Ein Mann mit grau meliertem Zopf löst sich aus der Gruppe, kommt zu mir und sagt durchs heruntergekurbelte Autofenster: „Na, haben Sie's gut gefunden?"

cation of Al Khashbah, near Sinaw and Mukhtru. That was where I was to find him and his 20 students. I pictured settlements from the Bronze Age emerging from the sands, and the archaeologists from Tübingen strolling around the houses like modern-day nomads. But as I drove closer to the described spot in my white rental Toyota, there were only a few wind-blown trees in an expansive landscape covered with stones. Little houses were scattered in front of me like rolled dice, in the far distance was the silhouette of the mountains. I pulled out my smartphone with an Omani sim card but the archaeology expert could not be reached under his local number. Inshallah (God willing) I will meet him, the locals would probably say. I thought the same and journeyed on. And then I saw them, not far from the road. Young people with fair, slightly-burnt skin, were crouching on a hill, protecting their blonde and brunette hair from the scorching sun with hats or scarfs; maps and lists for documentation on their laps. A man with plaited grey hair stepped out of the group, came over to me and addressed me through the wound-down window: "So, did you have any trouble finding your way?"

Etwa 70 Türme aus der Bronzezeit sind im Oman bekannt

About 70 towers from the Bronze Age are known in Oman

Diskussion an der Fundstelle: Conrad Schmidt und Stephanie Döpper (hinten von links) mit zwei Studierenden.
Discussion at the excavation site: Dr Conrad Schmidt and Stephanie Döpper (top left to right) with two students.

Conrad Schmidt befasst sich mit vorderasiatischer Archäologie - will heißen mit den vorchristlichen Jahrtausenden in einem großen Gebiet. Dazu gehören die Türkei, Syrien, der Libanon, Jordanien, Iraq, Iran, Kuwait, Saudi Arabien, Qatar, Bahrain, die Vereinigten Arabischen Emirate und Oman, das frühere Mesopotamien, um die wichtigsten Länder zu nennen. Seit Syrien kein sicheres Grabungsland mehr ist, sucht Schmidt nach Alternativen - und hat sie im Oman gefunden. „Wir möchten wissen, wie die Menschen hier vor 3000 Jahren gelebt haben. Waren sie sesshaft oder Nomaden? Was haben sie gegessen, wie sah die Landschaft aus? Wuchsen schon Palmen oder wurde Getreide angebaut?", erklärt der Experte, während ich neben ihm her über den trockenen Boden stolpere. Stephanie Döpper, die mit ihm die Grabung leitet, begleitet uns zu zwei Studenten, die neben einem Kreis aus Steinen die Erde wegfegen. „Diese Anordnung nennen wir Archäologen ‚tower', also Turm", sagt Schmidt. „Wir vermuten, dass es ein kommunales Gebäude war, vielleicht ein Versammlungsort. Und in der näheren Umgebung finden wir zum Beispiel Schlacke oder einzelne Kupfer-Objekte. Das heißt: Hier wurde intensiv Kupfer verarbeitet."

Etwa 70 solcher Türme aus der Zeit 3000 bis 2000 vor Christus sind bekannt, erfahre ich. Entdeckt hat sie unter anderem die dänische Archäologin Karen Frifelt, als sie in den 1970er Jahren auf der Suche nach Fundorten durch den Oman fuhr. Damals hat sie bestimmt auch ein Kreuzchen auf der Landkarte gemacht und gehofft, dass irgendwann jemand wie Conrad Schmidt mit seinen Studierenden vorbeikommt und mehr über den besonderen Ort herausfindet. Immerhin gibt es hier zehn Türme und einer davon wurde sogar (sehr selten!) quadratisch angelegt. Unbekannte haben vor ein paar hundert Jahren kleine Bilder von Pferden und Menschen in die Steine gemeißelt, eine Art frühe Graffitis. „Um Wissen über die alten Kulturen im Lande zu sammeln, unterstützen Ausländer die Omaner. Aber die Menschen im Dorf helfen uns. Wir haben bei Grabungen schon erlebt, dass die jungen Mädchen Fundstücke wie etwa Knochen sortieren – nachdem wir ihnen versicherten, dass wir nur forschen und sie nicht ihrer Familienandenken berauben wollen", sagt Stephanie Döpper und fügt an: „Daran kann man sehen, welche schlechten Erfahrungen man hier mit sogenannten Antiquitätenhändlern gemacht hat, die

Conrad Schmidt deals with Near Eastern archaeology (i.e. the pre-Christian millennia), covering a huge geographical area, including Turkey, Syria, Lebanon, Jordan, Iraq, Iran, Kuwait, Saudi Arabia, Qatar, Bahrain, the United Arab Emirates and Oman, formerly Mesopotamia. When Syria stopped being a safe excavation country, Schmidt started looking for alternatives, and found it in Oman. "We want to know how people lived here 3000 years ago. Were they settlers or nomads? What did they eat? What did the landscape look like? Did palm trees already grow back then or was grain cultivated?" the expert explains, as I stumble next to him over the dry ground. Stephanie Döpper, who leads the excavation with Schmidt, accompanies us to two students who are brushing away the earth next to a circle made of stones. "We archaeologists call this arrangement a 'tower'," Schmidt says. "We believe that it was a communal building, maybe a meeting place. And in the immediate vicinity we've found slag and the occasional copper object, which means that copper was processed here."

I learn that around 70 towers of this kind, dating from between 3000 and 2000 BC, have been identified. One of their discoverers is Danish archaeologist Karen Frifelt, who first found some in the 1970's when she was driving through Oman looking for excavation sites. Back then, she carefully marked the spot on the map and hoped that one day someone like Conrad Schmidt would come along with his students and find out more about this special place. There are actually ten towers here, and one of them was even laid out in a square shape, which is extremely unusual. Several hundred years ago, unknown people carved small horses and humans into the stones, a kind of early graffiti. "Omanis receive a lot of foreign support when it comes to gathering knowledge about the ancient cultures in the country. But local villagers also help us. After we assured the locals that we only wanted to do research and not rob them of their family keepsakes, we saw young girls sorting out finds such as bones at excavation sites," Döpper says. She adds, "This shows how bad previous experiences with antique dealers must have been. Treasure hunters who were presumably looking for precious objects, such as historic carved silver daggers."

165

vermutlich hinter lukrativen Objekten wie historischen, silbernen Krummdolchen her waren."

Zehn Jahre lang hat die Archäologin gemeinsam mit Conrad Schmidt den Plan verfolgt, den Boden bei Al Khashbah unter die Lupe zu nehmen. Gemeinsam haben die beiden Anträge bei der Deutschen Forschungsgemeinschaft und beim omanischen Ministry for Heritage and Culture (Ministerium für kulturelles Erbe) gestellt. Mit Erfolg: Das Projekt wurde über vier Jahre gefördert und brachte wichtige Erkenntnisse über Siedlungen aus dem vierten und dritten Jahrtausend vor Christus, der so genannten Hafit-Zeit. Die Archäologen fanden den bisher ältesten Nachweis für die Verarbeitung von Kupfer im Oman. Außerdem entdeckten sie seltene Beweise dafür, dass die Handwerker mit Steinwerkzeugen gearbeitet haben. Weil auf dem Gebiet um Al Khashbah so viele Gebäude und andere archäologische Fundstücke locken, steht eine Fortsetzung der Arbeiten an. Immer wieder sind Conrad Schmidt und Stephanie Döpper mit Studierenden vor Ort, graben und machen Fotos sowie dreidimensionale Bilder mit Drohnen aus der Luft, um die Stellen zu finden, an denen vor Jahrtausenden Menschen ihre Spuren hinterlassen haben. Neben einem versuchsweise angelegten Schacht, der Strukturen in der Erde erkennen lässt, kniet Susanne Maier und misst den Testschnitt aus. Die Tübingerin hat auf ihre Buchhändlerlehre noch ein Archäologiestudium gesattelt. Bei einer Pause im Schatten eines Baumes wird sie nachher sagen, wie sehr sie es schätzt, bei einer solchen Grabung selbstständig arbeiten zu können. „Allein schon um alle Arbeitsschritte kennenzulernen", ergänzt Michaela Balluff, eine zarte junge Frau, die ebenso wie Susanne Maier noch nicht weiß, ob sie den Beruf des Archäologen später einmal tatsächlich ergreifen möchte.

Doch darauf kommt es im Moment nicht an, eher auf die kleinen, alltäglichen Erlebnisse: „Ich freue mich über Funde wie ein Kupferstäbchen oder eine Muschelperle, die früher bestimmt mal zu einem Schmuckstück gehört hat", sagt Susanne Maier. Mancher ihrer Kommilitonen muss erstmal den Boden durchsieben, um solche Schätze zu entdecken. Eine staubige Angelegenheit, bei der es genau hinzuschauen gilt, um das Alter der einzelnen Erdschichten richtig zu beurteilen. Dokumentiert wird das Ganze am Computer im „Gra-

For ten years, the archaeologists followed their the plan to carefully examine the ground around Al Khashbah. Together, they applied for funding requests from the German Research Foundation and the Omani Ministry for Heritage and Culture. They were successful and the project was funded for four years, gaining relevant insight into settlements from the fourth and third millennia BC, known as the Hafit period. They found the oldest piece of evidence so far for the processing of copper in Oman. In addition, they found rare proof for the theory that craftsmen worked with stone tools. As there are so many fascinating buildings and other archaeological finds in the area around Al Khashbah, the project is set to continue. Schmidt and Döpper are continuously on site with their students. They dig and take photos, including three-dimensional pictures taken with airborne drones, in order to find human traces from many millennia ago. Next to a tentatively constructed shaft that enables identification of structures in the soil, Susanne Maier is on her knees measuring the test section. Maier, from Tübingen, supplemented her apprenticeship in bookselling with a degree in archaeology. Later, when she spends her break in the shade of a tree, she tells me how much she appreciates being able to work autonomously at this kind of excavation. Michaela Balluff, a delicate young woman, adds that "For starters, you learn all the work processes." Balluff and Maier are still unsure whether they will actually take up a profession in archaeology one day.

But for now, that's not so important. The focus is on the small, every-day experiences. "I'm happy finding artefacts such as a copper rod or a pearl that must have been part of a trinket at some time," Maier says. Some of her fellow students have to sift the earth to find gems like that. This is dusty work, and it's important to look very closely in order to correctly estimate the age of the different strata. The whole project is documented on a computer in the "excavation house", which Conrad Schmidt is very proud of. The house is a small Omani villa that the owner and his family only use for holidays. The students are using it as their temporary home, and you can't be prudish there because everyone sleeps on the floor next to one another, presumably not too different from the Bronze-Age nomads. Back then, however, there were no bathrooms

Conrad Schmidt erläutert omanischen Besuchern die Ausgrabungsergebnisse in Al Khashbah.
Conrad Schmidt explains the excavation results in Al Khashbah to Omani visitors.

bungshaus", auf das Conrad Schmidt richtig stolz ist: eine kleine omanische Villa, die der Besitzer mit seiner Familie nur an Feiertagen besucht. Die Studierenden haben sie als Wohngemeinschaft auf Zeit in Beschlag genommen. Zimperlich darf man da nicht sein: Alle schlafen dicht an dicht auf dem Boden, nicht viel anders vermutlich als die Nomaden in der Bronzezeit. Die hatten allerdings kein Badezimmer, in dem Hautcreme- und Zahnpastatuben fein säuberlich nebeneinander liegen. Und die jungen Archäologen können sich im Gegensatz zu den früheren Bewohnern der Gegend auch eine erfrischende Dusche gönnen, für die nach der Grabung eine strenge Reihenfolge unter den Beteiligten gilt. Wer fertig ist, bringt sich und den anderen einen Teller Suppe mit. Schweigend löffeln die Studierenden und schöpfen Kraft für die nächste Grabung zwischen den steinernen Türmen des Oman. Es wirkt so, als lernten sie nicht nur viel über das Leben im Vorderasien der Bronzezeit, sondern auch darüber, wie Menschen in einer so kargen Umgebung zusammenhalten und miteinander auskommen müssen.

with neatly-placed tubes of lotion and toothpaste. And, unlike those who lived in this area in earlier days, the young archaeologists can treat themselves to a refreshing shower. There is a set routine among the group after an excavation. Whoever is finished, organises a bowl of soup for the group. Eating without a single word, the students gather their strength for the next excavation among the stone towers of Oman. It appears that they are not only learning a lot about life in the Middle East in the Bronze-Age, but also about sticking together and getting along in barren surroundings.

More on the Middle Eastern archaeological projects, with a focus on Oman, can be found on the information platform ArchaeOman at www.archaeoman.de.

Return to the Bronze Age

Mehr über die Projekte der Vorderasiatischen Archäologie mit dem Schwerpunkt Oman erfährt man auf der Informationsplattform ArchaeOman www.archaeoman.de.

Die Spur antiker Hehler verfolgen

Manchmal bringen Touristen die Archäologen auf eine Spur, die eine spannende Grabung nach sich zieht: So geschehen mitten in der Wüste des „Empty Quarter": Im Jahr 2012 dachten Reisende, sie hätten dort die Überreste eines alten Schlachtfeldes gefunden. In Wirklichkeit entdeckten sie den Standort einer historischen Metallschmelze, der kriminalistischen Spürsinn erforderte: Es gab Waffen aus Kupferlegierungen, vor allem Dolche, aber offensichtlich auch Grabbeigaben, die von einem benachbarten früheisenzeitlichen Friedhof (um 800 v. Chr.) gestohlen wurden. Eine ungewöhnliche Entdeckung an einem Ort mit besonderem Namen: Uqdat al-Bakrah bedeutet „Der Hals des Kamels". Um herauszufinden, wie die Fundstücke in die Wüste gekommen waren, wurde ein internationales Team zusammengestellt, dessen Mitglieder aus Oman, Italien, Frankreich, der Tschechischen Republik und Deutschland kamen. Die Ergebnisse dieser Zusammenarbeit sind als Buch erschienen. Mitherausgeber Paul A. Yule: „Statt eines prähistorischen Schlachtfeldes entdeckten wir eine antike Hehler-Station aus der Zeit von zirka 800 v. Chr. Anscheinend wurden wertvolle Beigaben aus prähistorischen Gräbern geplündert und für den Wiederverkauf so verschmolzen, dass ihr Originalform – also Dolch oder Metallgefäß - nicht mehr erkennbar war. Es handelte sich eine Art prähistorische Geldwäsche."

Paul A. Yule and Guillaume Gernez (editors), Early Iron Age Metal-Working Workshop in the Empty Quarter, Sultanate of Oman, Universitätsforschungen zur prähistorischen Archäologie, Band 316, Bonn, Habelt, ISBN 978-3-7749-4112-0

On the trail of ancient stolen artefacts

Sometimes tourists lead the archaeologists on a trail that results in an exciting excavation. That happened in the middle of the desert of the "Empty Quarter": In 2012, travellers thought they had found the remains of an old battlefield. They had actually discovered the site of a historical metal smelter, which ended up requiring some crime-solving skills. There were weapons made from copper alloys, mostly daggers, and also funerary goods that had been stolen from a neighbouring graveyard in the early Iron Age (around 800 BC). This was an unusual discovery at this location, which is called Uqdat al-Bakrah, meaning "The Camel's Neck". In order to learn how these objects ended up in the desert, an international team was put together, whose members came from Oman, Italy, France, the Czech Republic and Germany. The results of this collaboration have been published in a book. Co-editor Paul A. Yule states "Instead of a prehistoric battlefield, we discovered an ancient site where stolen goods were traded in around 800 BC. Apparently, funerary goods were looted from prehistoric graves, then melted for resale. They were altered in such a way that the original object, such as a dagger or metal vessel, could no longer be recognised. This was a form of prehistoric money laundering."

Paul A. Yule and Guillaume Gernez (editors), Early Iron Age Metal-Working Workshop in the Empty Quarter, Sultanate of Oman, Universitätsforschungen zur prähistorischen Archäologie, Band 316, Bonn, Habelt, ISBN 978-3-7749-4112-0

Auf dem Weg zurück in die Bronzezeit

Return to the Bronze Age

Gesundheit ist Reichtum

Health is Wealth

Mediziner sammeln Erfahrungen
in Deutschland und dem Oman

Medical practitioners gain experience
in Germany and Oman

الصحة هي ثروة
يجمع الأطباء في المانيا وفي عُمان خبراتهم الطبية

إن مرض السكري الشائع في المجتمع يصاب به أهل عُمان وسكان المانيا. هذا هو مثال على التشابه بين البلدين والتحديات الطبية التي يواجهانها. يوجد منذ سنوات عديدة تبادل طبي في الخبرات بين عُمان وألمانيا حيث إن الدكتور يورغ لوكس هو المسؤول عن برنامج التبادل لطلاب دراسة الطب في مدينة دوسلدورف. كما يعمل الدكتور يوسف الهنائي كطبيب اختصاصي في أمراض العيون في المشفى الجامعي في ميونيخ. وقد اكتشف هذان الطبيبان تشابه كبير بين النظام الصحي في البلدين.

Dr. Jörg Lux betreut ein Austauschprogramm von omanischen Medizinstudierenden in Düsseldorf. Dr. Yousuf Al Hinai arbeitet als Augenarzt am Universitätsklinikum München. Beide Fachärzte stellen fest: Es gibt viele Parallelen zwischen den Gesundheitssystemen beider Länder.

Alles fing mit Khalil an. Er kam 2009 per Zufall als omanischer Medizinstudent nach Düsseldorf, um dort an der Uniklinik sein Praktikum zu absolvieren – und war begeistert. Der Düsseldorfer Gynäkologe Dr. Jörg Lux nahm den jungen Omani unter seine Fittiche, nicht ahnend, dass dadurch ein reger Austausch entstehen würde. „Nach seiner Rückkehr hat Khalil in Maskat von seinen Erfahrungen berichtet und es kamen erste offizielle Anfragen, wie eine Kooperation aussehen könnte", erinnert sich Lux.

In den Curricula für Medizinstudierende im Sultanat ist festgeschrieben, dass die angehenden Mediziner einige Wochen im Ausland verbringen. „Die meisten gehen in englischsprachige Länder", sagt der Düsseldorfer Gynäkologe. „Aber mancher möchte Deutschland kennen lernen, schon allein, weil der Sultan regelmäßig hier ist." Seit 2011 kommen zwei Mal jährlich etwa sechs oder sieben Studierende von der arabischen Halbinsel nach Düsseldorf – immer in der vorlesungsfreien Zeit. „Neben dem Klinikalltag und den Vorlesungsverpflichtungen wäre das sonst nicht zu schaffen", erklärt Lux. „Allein wegen der Sprachprobleme brauchen die Praktikanten eine intensive Begleitung. Das fängt an, wo man ein Ticket für Bus oder Straßenbahn kauft und geht bis zu fachlichen Fragen, welche Behandlungen bei welchen Diagnosen bei uns üblich sind".

Für viele der jungen Nachwuchs-Mediziner ist es der erste Aufenthalt in Europa. „Sie stürzen hier oft bildlich gesprochen ins kalte Wasser, da sie sich vorher meistens kaum mit ihrem Gastgeberland auf Zeit beschäftigt haben", so Jörg Lux. Für alle Fälle hat jeder der Austauschstudenten seine Telefonnummer in der Tasche.

Der Frauenarzt mit über 30jähriger Erfahrung im Klinikbetrieb hat auch schon erlebt, wie Mentalitätsunterschiede in der Praxis zu Hürden werden können. Wer etwa als Praktikant bei einer Operation dabei sein will, muss die hygienischen Vorschriften einer Klinik akzep-

Dr Jörg Lux is in charge of an exchange programme for Omani medical students in Germany. Dr Yousuf Al Hinai works at Munich University Hospital as an ophthalmologist. Both specialists firmly believe that there are many parallels between the health systems of the two countries.

It all started with Khalil, an Omani medical student who came to Düsseldorf in order to do an internship at the university hospital. He really enjoyed his time there. Local gynaecologist, Dr Jörg Lux, took the young Omani under his wings, not knowing that this would lead to a dynamic exchange programme. "After his return, Khalil told people in Muscat about his experiences, and soon the first official requests arrived for a more formal collaboration," Dr Lux recalls.

The curriculum for medical students in the Sultanate requires prospective physicians to spend a few weeks abroad. "Most go to countries where English is spoken," Dr Lux says. "But some want to learn more about Germany, not least because the Sultan is here on a regular basis." Since 2011, around six or seven students from the Arabian Peninsula have come to Düsseldorf twice a year, always during their semester breaks. "It simply wouldn't be manageable in addition to the daily hospital routine and the mandatory lectures," Dr Lux explains. "Because of the language barrier, the interns need a great deal of support. Issues range from where to buy bus and tram tickets to subject-related questions, such as which treatments are common for which diagnoses."

For many young prospective physicians, this is their first visit to Europe. "They are thrown in at the deep end because they have usually had very little dealings with their temporary host country before," Dr Lux says. To be on the safe side, every exchange student has Lux's telephone number in their pocket.

Lux has more than 30 years' experience working in hospitals and he has witnessed how different mentalities can put up obstacles when practicing medicine. If an intern wants to attend a surgery, they must accept the sanitary rules of the clinic, such as wearing a surgical cap. "There have been instances where female Omani students didn't attend a surgery because they didn't want to take off their headscarves," Dr Lux says. "Some

tieren. Und dazu zählt, eine OP-Haube aufzusetzen. „Es ist schon vorgekommen, dass omanische Studentinnen nicht dabei waren, weil sie ihr Kopftuch nicht ablegen wollten", so Lux. „Manche brauchen auch besondere Betreuung, weil sie extrem schüchtern sind und sich nicht trauen, Fragen zu stellen."

Die Studierenden bleiben drei bis sechs Wochen, aber der Kontakt hält zuweilen über viele Jahre. „Ich bekomme heute noch von einem ehemaligen Praktikanten, der heute Professor in Kanada ist, jedes Jahr im Dezember einen Weihnachtsgruß", so Lux. Auch wenn die Omaner von Deutschland begeistert sind und schon mehr als 100 Studierende nach Düsseldorf kamen – die hiesigen angehenden Mediziner müssen zu Gegenbesuchen noch motiviert werden: Bislang entschieden sich nur zwei Deutsche für ein Praktikum im Oman. „Da geht noch was", meint Dr. Lux, der sich sehr für sein kultur- und generationenübergreifendes Projekt engagiert. „Der Oman wird unterschätzt, es ist noch eine Menge Aufklärungsarbeit zu leisten."

Lux selbst war zwei Mal im Oman. „Mich hat die High-Level-Medizin im Sultan Qaboos University Hospital beeindruckt", erläutert er. „Modernste Technik in den Fachabteilungen, gut ausgebildete Ärzte, professionelle Betreuung. Ich hätte Lust, dort einmal zu praktizieren."

Dr. Yousuf Al Hinai praktiziert in Deutschland
Augenarzt Dr. Yousuf Al Hinai aus dem Oman hat im Gegenzug den Sprung gewagt: Er kam nach erfolgreichem Medizinstudium an der Sultan Qaboos University 2011 nach Deutschland und arbeitet am Universitätsklinikum München.

Wenn Al Hinai das omanische Gesundheitssystem beschreiben soll, dann gebraucht er ein Sprichwort: „Health is wealth and an ounce of prevention is better than a pound of cure" – also: Gesundheit bedeutet Reichtum; und ein Quäntchen Prävention ist besser als ein Pfund Behandlung. „Der Mediziner fügt hinzu: "Weil das Thema Gesundheit für uns so wichtig ist, besitzen wir im Sultanat auch ein effektives Gesundheitssystem auf einem hohen Standard. Um nur ein Beispiel zu nennen: Regelmäßige Gesundheitsuntersuchungen in Schulen nehmen deutlich zu. Damit wird überprüft, ob alle notwendigen Impfungen erfolgen."

Im Oman hat jeder Einwohner Anspruch auf kostenfreie Gesundheitsleistungen. Spezialkliniken wie das Krebs-

also need special attention because they are extremely shy and are too scared to ask questions."

The students stay for three to six weeks, but sometimes remain in contact for many years. "One former intern, who is now a professor in Canada, has been sending me a Christmas card every December since we first met," Dr Lux says. Although the Omanis really enjoy their time in Germany, the German doctors-to-be need to be motivated more to visit Oman. So far, more than 100 Omani students have come to Düsseldorf, but only two Germans have interned in Oman. "There is definitely room for improvement," says Dr Lux, who is highly committed to his cross-cultural and cross-generational projects. "People underestimate Oman, we still have a lot of awareness raising to do."

Lux himself has been to Oman twice. "I was impressed by the high-level medical facility at the Sultan Qaboos University Hospital," he explains. "They have state-of-the-art technical equipment in the specialty departments, well-educated physicians, and professional care. I would love to practice there some time."

Dr Yousuf Al Hinai practices in Germany
Omani ophthalmologist Yousuf Al Hinai took a different path. After successfully graduating in medicine at the Sultan Qaboos University, he came to Germany in 2011 to work at Munich University Hospital.

When Al Hinai is asked to describe the Omani healthcare system, he quotes a proverb: "Health is wealth, and an ounce of prevention is better than a pound of cure." The physician adds that "as the topic of health is so important for us, we have an effective, high-standard healthcare system in the Sultanate. For example, there is a clear increase in regular health checks at schools. This is done to ensure that children have received all necessary vaccinations."

In Oman, every citizen is entitled to free healthcare. Specialised clinics such as the Cancer Care Centre and the Cardiac Disease Centre show that the Sultanate is rapidly expanding its medical system. Many of the hospitals, especially the larger and specialised ones, such as the Royal Hospital of Oman and the Sultan Qaboos University Hospital, are still located in the capital Mus-

Studierende aus dem Oman bleiben zwischen drei und sechs Wochen in Düsseldorf.
Students from Oman stay in Düsseldorf for between three and six weeks.

zentrum (Cancer Care Center) und das Zentrum für Herz- und Gefäßerkrankungen (Cardic Disease Center) zeigen, dass das Sultanat im Eiltempo medizinisch aufstockt.

Noch sind viele vor allem größere und spezialisierte Kliniken wie das Royal Hospital of Oman und das Sultan Qaboos University Hospital in der Hauptstadt Maskat angesiedelt. „Hier werden aktuell Anstrengungen unternommen, die medizinischen Angebote mehr in die Regionen zu bringen und dafür zu sorgen, dass Termine bei Fachärzten noch schneller möglich werden", so Dr. Al Hinai.

Wohlstandserkrankungen wie Diabetes betreffen Omaner und Deutsche gleichermaßen. In 2015 waren im Sultanat rund 87.000 Diabetiker registriert. Bei einer Bevölkerung von etwa drei Millionen Omanis waren demnach 14,8 Prozent betroffen. In der Ausgabe des Diabetes-Atlas der International Diabetes Federation (IDF) lag Deutschland 2015 im europäischen Vergleich mit 6,5 Millionen Menschen mit Diabetes mellitus an

cat. "Efforts are currently underway to make medical care more accessible to more regions, and to ensure that appointments with specialists are faster to obtain," Dr Al Hinai explains.

Diseases of affluence, such as diabetes, affect both Omanis and Germans. In 2015, around 87,000 diabetics were registered in the Sultanate. This means that 14.8 percent of the Omani population of roughly three million were affected. In the 2015 issue of the Diabetes Atlas, published by the International Diabetes Federation (IDF), Germany came in second of all European countries with 6.5 million citizens diagnosed with diabetes mellitus. That equates to 9.9 percent of the German population.

"There are extensive public campaigns to increase awareness of having a healthy diet and the importance of exercise," Dr Al Hinai says. "Traditional Omani meals consisting of fish, salad and dates, which are rich in vitamins, are healthy and contain only a small amount of

Health is Wealth

zweiter Stelle. Das entspricht 9,9 Prozent der Gesamtbevölkerung – Tendenz steigend.

Es gibt große öffentliche Kampagnen, um das Bewusstsein für gesunde Ernährung und die Bedeutung von Bewegung zu erhöhen", so Dr. Al Hinai. „Das traditionelle omanische Essen mit Fisch, Salaten, vitaminreichen Datteln enthält wenig Fett und ist gesund. Aber immer mehr Menschen ernähren sich nicht ausgewogen, essen Chips und andere fettreiche Lebensmittel, und sind körperlich zu wenig aktiv."

Seit 1986 können Omaner im eigenen Land Medizin studieren. Aktuell dauert ein Studium sieben Jahre. Für viele Nachwuchsmediziner ist es selbstverständlich einige Jahre im Ausland zu praktizieren – zum Beispiel in Großbritannien, Amerika, Australien, Neuseeland oder eben auch Deutschland.

Im Vergleich der Gesundheitssysteme beider Länder sieht der omanische Facharzt keine großen Unterschiede – weder im Klinikalltag noch bei den Untersuchungen oder im Operationsbetrieb. „Allerdings ist das Spektrum an Krankheiten, das ich hier behandle, größer als im Oman."

Besonders gefällt ihm die enge Verknüpfung von Forschung und Hochleistungsmedizin in Deutschland. „Am Klinikum München ist ein Forschungszentrum integriert. Dort beschäftigt man sich mit wichtigen Fragen: Wie entstehen Krankheiten, welche neuen Diagnosemethoden werden gebraucht, welche medikamentösen und nicht-medikamentösen Behandlungen können helfen und mit welchen Strategien können Krankheiten vermieden werden? Da die Wege kurz sind, finden aktuelle Erkenntnisse schnell den Weg in den klinischen Alltag."

Seine Zukunft sieht Yousuf Al Hinai im Oman: „In ein paar Jahren gehe ich zurück ins Sultanat. Ich bin aber sicher, dass der fachliche Austausch und die guten Kontakte mit meinen deutschen Kollegen erhalten bleiben." Um sich selbst fit zu halten, spielt der 38-Jährige regelmäßig Tischtennis oder schwingt sich aufs Surfbrett. Will er es sportlich eher gemütlich angehen, dann macht er es wie viele Deutsche und Omaner – er schaut Fußball. Und drückt nicht nur für die omanische Nationalelf die Daumen, sondern auch für Bayern München.

fat. But more and more people do not follow a balanced diet. They eat chips and other fatty food, and don't exercise enough."

Since 1986, it has been possible for Omanis to study medicine in their own country. It currently takes seven years to graduate. Many prospective doctors consider it an obvious choice to practice medicine abroad for a few years – for example, in Great Britain, America, Australia, New Zealand or Germany.

When comparing the healthcare systems of both countries, Dr Al Hinai does not see significant differences in either the everyday routine in the hospitals or in examinations and surgeries. "However, the range of diseases I treat here is larger than in Oman."

He particularly enjoys the strong bond between research and high-performance medicine in Germany. "A research centre is integrated into Munich University Hospital. It deals with important research questions – How do diseases originate? What new diagnosis methods are needed? Which treatments, with or without medication, can help, and which strategies can prevent diseases? Because communication paths are short, new findings can quickly be applied at the hospital."

Dr Al Hinai sees his future in Oman. "In a few years, I will return to the Sultanate. I am sure, however, that I will stay in touch with my German colleagues, both privately and for subject-related issues."

Kostenfreie Gesundheitsleistungen für alle Omaner

Free health services for all Omanis

In order to stay fit, the 38-year-old regularly plays table tennis or jumps onto his surfboard. If he wants to enjoy sport in a more relaxed way, he does what many Germans or Omanis do, he watches soccer. And he not only supports the Omani national team, but Bayern Munich as well.

Weihrauch – wohlduftend und gesund

Natürliche Heilmittel spielen sowohl in Deutschland als auch auf der arabischen Halbinsel eine Rolle. Zu den Geschenken der Natur Omans gehört der Weihrauch – mit einem erstaunlich breiten Wirkungsspektrum.

Boswellia ist der lateinische Name des Weihrauchbaums. Einige der weltweit besten Sorten wachsen im Süden Omans, in der Region Dhofar. Den luftgetrockneten Gummiharz gibt es als große Körner von weißlich-gelb bis rötlich-braun. Das Harz minderer Qualität in dunkleren Tönen dient geräuchert dem guten Geruch, die besseren fast weißen Qualitäten werden gekaut oder in Wasser aufgelöst. Die positiven Wirkungen zum Beispiel bei Magenschmerzen sind in Studien bewiesen. Wird das Harz äußerlich angewendet, soll es wund- und geschwürheilend wirken, Entzündungen im Augenbereich lindern und bei Brustdrüsenschwellungen stillender Frauen helfen. Innerlich angewendet soll er bei Gedächtnisschwäche, Migräne und Kopfschmerzen sowie Entzündungen im Bereich der Atemwege helfen.

Incense – fragrant and healthy

Natural remedies play a role both in Germany and on the Arabian Peninsula. One of the gifts of Oman's flora is incense, which has an impressive range of applications.

Boswellia is the Latin name for incense. Some of the world's best varieties grow in South Oman, in the Dhofar region. The air-dried gum resin is available as large grains ranging in colour from white-yellow to red-brown. If burned, the darker, lower-quality resins provide a lovely scent. The higher-quality resins, that are almost white, are chewed or dissolved in water. Studies have proven positive effects; for example, for stomach aches. If the resin is applied externally, it is said to heal wounds or ulcers, ease inflammations in the eye area and alleviate mastitis in breastfeeding women. Taken internally, it helps with poor memory, migraines and headaches, as well as inflammations of the respiratory tract.

Samtnasige und sanfte Wüstentiere

Gentle Desert Animals with Velvety Noses

Die beliebtesten Tiere der Omaner
werden auch in Deutschland gezüchtet

The most popular animals among the Omanis
are now also being bred in Germany

الحيوانات ذوات الأنف الحريري والصحراوية والناعمة هي أحب الحيوانات عند العُمانيين يمكن تربيتها في المانيا أيضاً

الهجن هي الحيوانات المحبوبة عند أهل عُمان. ولكي تكون تربية الجمال جيدة، فإنه يتم مراقبة مربي الجمال من قبل الجهات المسؤولة العليا بشكل دائم. حيث يكون سباق الهجن أحياناً في الأعراس وبعض المناسبات وأحياناً مسابقات الهجن. لقد بدأت تربية الأبل تصل إلى المانيا حيث يوجد أول اسطبل ومزرعة لتربية الأبل في المانيا تحت إشراف عائلة بيكي مراكوارد في مدينة فيسيلهوفيدي-هيسينغين والتي تقع تقريباً على مسافة ساعة بالسيارة شرق مدينة بريمن.

Kamelwettrennen gehören zu traditionellen omanischen Hochzeiten dazu.
Camel races are part of traditional Omani weddings.

Omaner lieben ihre Kamele. Um möglichst rein-rassige Zuchtlinien zu erhalten, werden Züchter von oberster Stelle offiziell überwacht. In Rennen, bei Schauläufen anlässlich von Hochzeiten oder auf Schönheitswettbewerben treten die Tiere gegeneinander an. Auch in Deutschland gibt es inzwischen erste Kamelfarmen.

Sanft schwankt der Sattel von links nach rechts und wieder zurück. Im Takt der Schritte hebt und senkt sich der Horizont hinter den Dünen der Sharqia Sands im Osten des Omans. Auch wer, wie hier die meisten an diesem Morgen, zum ersten Mal im Leben auf einem Kamel sitzt, fühlt sich schon nach wenigen Minuten in eine andere Ära versetzt. In eine Zeit vor den Geländewagen, als man allein mit diesen belastbaren Tieren wochenlang durch die Wüste ziehen konnte. Ohne Kamelkarawanen war Fernhandel durch Weltgegenden wie diese lange unmöglich. Doch was fasziniert Kamelhalter bis heute an den Wüstentieren?

Saif bin Sultan bin Rashid Albadi fällt da einiges ein. Sein ganzes Leben hat der Beduine den Kamelen gewidmet. Er

Omanis love their camels. In order to maintain the purest breeding lines, breeders are monitored by the highest levels of authority. The animals compete against each other at races, show events and pageants. There are now also camel farms in Germany.

The saddle gently swings back and forth, in time with eat step, and the horizon rises and falls behind the dunes of the Sharqia Sands in the Eastern Part of Oman. After only a few minutes sitting on a camel, riders are transported to another era; to a time before SUVs, when you only had these resilient animals for transport and it took weeks to cross the desert. For a long time, without the availability of camel caravans, long-distance trade was impossible in areas like this. But what is it about these desert animals that still fascinates camel owners today?

Saif bin Sultan bin Rashid Albadi can think of many things. The Bedouin has dedicated his whole life to camels. He lives in Saham, a village around 200 kilometres to the West of Muscat. Thanks to agriculture, Oman is greener here in late summer than almost anywhere else. The irrigation systems constantly spray water between

Gentle Desert Animals with Velvety Noses

lebt in Saham, einem Dorf rund 200 Kilometer westlich von Maskat. Dank Landwirtschaft ist der Oman hier im Spätsommer so grün wie an kaum einem anderen Ort. Unablässig sprühen die Bewässerungsanlagen zwischen die Bananenpalmen und auf das Gras, das auch Albadis Kamele ab und an zu fressen bekommen. 20 Tiere stehen hinter einer halbhohen Steinmauer in zwei langen, offenen Unterständen, vier weitere auf dem Platz dazwischen, mit locker zusammengebundenen Vorderläufen am Davonlaufen gehindert.

Es ist später Nachmittag. „Abendessenszeit für die Kamele", sagt Albadi. Während Helfer Zweige herbeitragen, kniet der Endfünfziger im Sand zwischen den Stallungen und zählt auf, wofür die Tiere gezüchtet werden: Als Rennkamele, zur Milchproduktion, für Schönheitswettbewerbe oder Schaulaufen. „Es ist mir eine Herzensangelegenheit, die verschiedenen Zuchtlinien zu erhalten", sagt Albadi. Seit einigen Jahren wird dies auch von höchster Stelle unterstützt. Nach Saudi-Arabien ist der Oman auf der Arabischen Halbinsel das Land mit den zweitmeisten Kamelzüchtern. Sie werden vom Royal Camel Corps überwacht, das genau Buch über die Abstammung der einzelnen Tiere führt und auf möglichst reinrassige Zuchtlinien achtet.

Doch das Kamel ist längst auch über seine Heimatländer hinaus beliebt. „Es war der Jugendtraum meines Mannes, mit Kamelen zu arbeiten", erzählt Beke Marquard. Mit ihrer Familie leitet sie eine Kamelfarm in Visselhövede-Hiddingen rund eine Stunde Autofahrt östlich von Bremen. Fernab der Wüste verfiel Andreas Marquard hier schon als Kind den Höckertieren. Mit 25 machte er seinen Traum wahr und kaufte sich das erste Kamel. Inzwischen kümmern er, Beke und ihre beiden Kinder sich um etwa 70 Tiere.

Abendessen im Kamelstall von Saif bin Sultan bin Rashid Albadi.
Dinner in the camel stable of Saif bin Sultan bin Rashid Albadi.

the banana palm trees and on the grass that Albadi's camels are also allowed to eat sometimes. Twenty animals are kept behind a low stone wall in two long, roofless shelters; four more in the space between. There is no danger of them running away because their front legs are loosely bound together.

It is late afternoon. "Dinner time for the camels," Albadi says. While helpers bring twigs, the man in his late fifties kneels down in the sand between the stables and talks about the reasons why the animals are bred: for races, for the production of milk, for pageants or for show. "It is an issue close to my heart to preserve the various breeding lines," Albadi says. For several years now, this has also been supported by the highest levels of authority. After Saudi Arabia, Oman has the second highest number of camel breeders on the Arabian Peninsula. They are monitored by the Royal Camel Corps, which keeps close tabs on the pedigree of every single animal and aims to ensure the purest possible breeding lines.

Camels have long been popular outside their countries of origin. "It was my husband's childhood dream to work

„Kamele haben einen ausgeglichenen Charakter"

"Camels have a balanced character"

Samtnasige und sanfte Wüstentiere

Ob im norddeutschen Tiefland oder der Batina-Ebene, die Kamelhalter schwärmen von den besonderen Eigenschaften ihrer Tiere. „Sie haben einfach einen tollen Charakter", sagt Beke Marquard. „Sie sind so ruhig und ausgeglichen." Ähnlich geht es Saif bin Sultan bin Rashid Albadi. Auch er schätzt seine Tiere für ihre sanfte Art. Seine Familie hat schon immer Kamele gezüchtet. Früher waren es hauptsächlich ihre eigenen, heute züchtet Albadi überwiegend für andere Halter. Nur drei der Tiere auf seinem Hof gehören ihm. Die übrigen Stuten wurden von ihren Besitzern zu Albadi gebracht, damit er die Zuchthengste auswählt und die Fohlen in den ersten Monaten für ihre jeweiligen Aufgaben ausbildet.

Die ideale Zuchtzeit beginne im September und ende im Frühjahr, erklärt er. So kämen die Fohlen in der kühleren Phase des Jahres auf die Welt. „Die Kleinen sind dann kräftiger", sagt er. Auch Familie Marquard züchtet Kamele und bildet Fohlen aus. Anders als im heißen Klima des Omans kommt der Kamelnachwuchs in Deutschland gerade rechtzeitig im Frühjahr zur Welt, um die wärmeren Monate des Jahres zu genießen. Auf der Kamelfarm leben die Tiere in einem offenen Stall mit ausgedehnten

with camels," Beke Marquard says. She and her family run a camel farm in Visselhövede-Hissingen, about a one-hour drive east from Bremen. Far from the desert, Andreas Marquard first became fascinated by the humped animals as a young child. At the age of 25, he fulfilled his dream and bought his first camel. Now, he, Beke and their two children take care of around 70 camels.

Whether in the North German lowlands or the Batinah plateau, camel owners gush over the special characteristics of the animals. "They simply have a great personality," Beke says. "They are so calm and even tempered," agrees Albadi. He also appreciates his animals' gentle nature. His family has always bred camels. Formerly, they mainly bred their own, but today Albadi breeds them predominantly for other owners. Only three of the animals on his farm belong to him. The other mares were brought to Albadi by their owners in order to choose breeding stallions for them and to train the calves for their respective tasks.

He explains that the ideal breeding season begins in September and ends in spring. That way, the calves are

Gentle Desert Animals with Velvety Noses

Weiden. Gelegentlich kommen dort auch Besucher vorbei, um sich die Tiere anzuschauen und auf ihnen zu reiten. „Viele sind anfangs ein bisschen skeptisch, wenn sie zum ersten Mal auf einem Kamel sitzen", sagt Beke Marquard. „Aber es dauert gar nicht lange, dann sind die meisten schwer begeistert."

Auch auf den Dünen des Omans genießen Urlauber die Aussicht vom Kamelrücken. Doch die Tiere haben noch eine Menge anderer Aufgaben, außer Touristen durch die Wüste zu schaukeln. Besonders der prestigeträchtige Rennsport gewinnt an Bedeutung. 2003 investierte Sultan Qaboos eine Million Rial, umgerechnet mehr als zwei Millionen Euro, in den Bau von Rennstrecken im ganzen Land. Seither veranstaltet die Omaner Camel Racing Federation Rennen und trägt damit zur Ausbreitung des Kamelsports bei.

Bei einem der Schaulaufen lässt sich beobachten, wie die Kamele Tempo aufnehmen. Das Rennen ist Teil einer traditionellen omanischen Hochzeit. Die gesamte männliche Festgesellschaft hat sich an einer gut 500 Meter langen Laufstrecke versammelt, die mit angehäuften Sandwällen links und rechts begrenzt ist. Alle zehn Minuten rennen zwei prächtig herausgeputzte Kamele um die Wette, bunte Quasten zieren das Geschirrzeug. Die Schaulaufen sind ein großes Spektakel, auch wenn es anders als bei den richtigen Rennen, bei denen oft 100 Kamele gleichzeitig antreten, nur darum geht, zu sehen und gesehen zu werden.

Als Lastentier mag das Kamel weitgehend überflüssig geworden sein. Doch die Liebe zu den belastbaren Tieren hält an. Nicht zuletzt auch deshalb, weil das Kamel für viele Araber einen kulturellen Anker darstellt. Die traditionelle beduinische Lebensform ist praktisch ausgestorben, doch das Kamel als eines ihrer Kernelemente ist immer noch da. So wie sich viele Touristen einen kurzen Ritt gönnen, um den Bräuchen der Wüstenvölker nachzuspüren, schlägt das Kamel für einige Araber eine ganz reale Brücke zu den Traditionen ihrer Vorfahren. Und selbst dort, wo Kamele ursprünglich nicht beheimatet sind – wie in der Nähe von Bremen – bringen die Tiere einen Charme mit, den kein Geländewagen ersetzen könnte.

born in the cooler months of the year. "The little ones are stronger then," he says. The Marquard family also breeds camels and trains calves. In contrast, the camel offspring in Germany are born in spring, just in time to enjoy the warmer months of the year. On the camel farm, the animals live in an open stable with enormous pastures. Sometimes visitors come by to look at the animals and ride on them. "Many people are sceptical when they sit on a camel for the first time," says Beke. "However, it doesn't take long for most people to be won over."

In the dunes of Oman, tourists also enjoy the view from atop a camel's back. However, the animals perform a multitude of other tasks besides gently rocking tourists through the desert. The prestigious sport of camel racing is especially gaining in importance. In 2003, Sultan Qaboos invested one million rial, the equivalent of more than 2 million euros, into the construction of racing tracks all over the country. The Omani Camel Racing Federation has hosted races ever since, contributing to the uptake of camel racing. This has been so successful that the UN just added the Omani horse and camel races, known as Al Ardhah, to the UNESCO list of intangible cultural heritage.

At a show race, you can see how the animals pick up speed. The race is part of a traditional Omani wedding ceremony. All of the male attendees have gathered at a racing track roughly 500 meters long, which is bordered on each side by sand banks. Every ten minutes, two splendidly attired camels race against each other, with colourful tassels decorating their harnesses. These show races are great spectacles, even if the only thing important here, unlike in a real race, is to see and be seen.

Camels have become almost redundant as beasts of burden. However, the love for these sturdy animals remains strong, not least because the camels represent a cultural anchor for many Arabs. The traditional Bedouin way of life is all but extinct, but the camel, one of its key elements, lives on. Just as many tourists treat themselves to a short ride in order to experience the customs of the desert peoples, for some Arabs the camel signifies a real link to the traditions of their ancestors. Even places that camels do not usually call home, such as the North German lowlands, are brightened by the charming nature of these animals which no SUV could ever replace.

Samtnasige und sanfte Wüstentiere

Gentle Desert Animals with Velvety Noses

ﺕ ﻭﺍﻻﺳـﺘﻔﺎﺩﺓ ﻣﻨﻪ ﻓﻲ ﺍﻟﺘﺼﺎﻣﻴﻢ ﺍﻟﺠﺪﻳﺪﺓ

ﺟﻤﻌﺔ ﺍﻟﻤﺴﻜﺮﻱ	ﺟﻮﺭﺝ ﺑﻮﺏ

ﻫﺬﻩ ﺍﻟﺰﺧﺎﺭﻑ ﻣﻦ ﺟﻤﻴﻊ
ﻟﻄﻨﺔ ﻋﻠﻰ ﺷﻜﻞ ﺻﻮﺭ
ﻟﻬﺬﻩ ﺍﻟﺰﺧﺮﻓﺔ ﺍﻟﺠﻤﻴﻠﺔ ،
ﺍﻥ ﻳﺴﺘﻔﻴﺪ ﻣﻨﻪ ﻃﻠﺒﺔ
ﻗﺴﺎﻡ ﺍﻟﺘﺮﺑﻴﺔ ﺍﻟﻔﻨﻴﺔ ﻓﻲ
ﻛﻴﻔﻴﺔ ﺗﺼﻤﻴﻢ ﻣﺜﻞ
ﻟﺘﻲ ﺭﺳﻤﻬﺎ ﺍﺟﺪﺍﺩﻫﻢ ،
ﺑﺪ ﺍﻟﻤﻜﺎﺗﺐ ﺍﻻﺳﺘﺸﺎﺭﻳﺔ
ﻟﺘﻌﺮﻳﻒ ﺍﻟﻤﻮﺍﻃﻦ ﺍﻟﻌﻤﺎﻧﻲ
ﻑ ﺍﻟﻘﺪﻳﻤﺔ ﻭﻳﺨﺘﺎﺭ ﻣﺎ
ﺎ ﻓﻲ ﺑﻨﺎﺀ ﻣﻨﺰﻟﻪ ، ﻭﻛﺬﻟﻚ
ﺩ ﺑﺎﻟﻜﻤﺒﻴﻮﺗﺮ ﺑﺤﻴﺚ ﻳﻜﻮﻥ
ﻣﻦ ﺍﻟﺰﺧﺮﻓﺔ ﺍﻟﻌﻤﺎﻧﻴﺔ ،
ﻫﻨﺎﻙ ﺧﻄﻮﻃﺎ ﺑﻐﺪﺍﺩﻳﺔ ،
ﺭﻏﺒﻨﺎ ﺍﻥ ﻳﻜﻮﻥ ﻫﻨﺎﻙ ﺧﻂ
ﻊ ﻣﻦ ﻫﺬﻩ ﺍﻟﺰﺧﺮﻓﺔ .

ﺗﻨﻈﻴﻤﻪ ﻟﻠﻤﻌﺮﺽ ﻭﻗﺎﻝ
ﺗﻌﺮﻑ ﺍﻟﺸﺒﺎﺏ ﺍﻟﻌﻤﺎﻧﻲ ﻥ
ﺍﻟﺘﻲ ﺗﻮﺟﺪ ﺑﺎﻷﺑﻮﺍﺏ
ﻘﺪﻳﻤﺔ ﻛﻨﺰ ﻳﺠﺐ ﺍﺳﺘﺜﻤﺎﺭﻩ
ﻳﻪ ﻣﻦ ﺍﻻﻧﺪﺛﺎﺭ ﻭﺍﻻﺳﺘﻔﺎﺩﺓ
ﻳﺮﻩ ﻭﺍﻟﺘﺠﺪﻳﺪ ﻓﻴﻪ ﺑﻤﺎ
ﺤﻴﺎﺓ ﺍﻟﻤﻌﺎﺻﺮﺓ ، ﻭﻟﻜﻲ
ﻓﻜﺎﺭ ﺍﻻﺟﺪﺍﺩ ﻟﻤﺌﺎﺕ ﺍﻟﺴﻨﻴﻦ
ﻥ ﺗﻀﻴﻊ ﺑﻬﺬﻩ ﺍﻟﺴﺮﻋﺔ .
ﺟﻮﺭﺝ ﺑﻮﺏ ﺣﻮﻝ ﺍﻫﻤﻴﺔ
ﺍﻟﻤﻘﺘﺮﺡ ﺍﻥ ﻫﺬﺍ ﺍﻟﻤﺸﺮﻭﻉ
ﺍﻫﺘﻤﺎﻣﺎﺕ ﺟﻼﻟﺔ ﺍﻟﺴﻠﻄﺎﻥ
ﺳﻌﻴﺪ ﺍﻟﻤﻌﻈﻢ ﺑﺎﻟﺘﺮﺍﺙ
ﻭﺍﻟﺪﻟﻴﻞ ﻋﻠﻰ ﺫﻟﻚ ﻭﺟﻮﺩ
ﺻﺔ ﺑﺬﻟﻚ ـ ﻭﺯﺍﺭﺓ ﺍﻟﺘﺮﺍﺙ
ﺍﻟﺜﻘﺎﻓﺔ ـ ﻭﻧﺄﺧﺬ ﺍﻓﻜﺎﺭ

ﺗﺼﻤﻴﻢ ﻫﺬﻩ ﺍﻟﺰﺧﺮﻓﺔ ﻣﻦ ﺍﻻﻫﺎﻟﻲ
ﻭﺍﻻﺟﺪﺍﺩ ﺍﻟﻤﻬﺘﻤﻴﻦ ﺑﺎﻟﺰﺧﺮﻓﺔ ﻭﻧﻌﻤﻞ
ﺍﺭﺷﻴﻔﺎ ﻧﺠﻤﻊ ﻓﻴﻪ ﻛﻞ ﻣﺎ ﻳﺘﻢ ﺗﺤﺼﻴﻠﻪ
ﻣﻦ ﺻﻮﺭ ﺍﻭ ﺭﺳﻮﻣﺎﺕ ﻭﻳﻌﺪ ﺗﺤﻠﻴﻞ
ﻫﺬﻩ ﺍﻟﺰﺧﺎﺭﻑ ﻭﺗﺒﻮﻳﺒﻬﺎ ﻭﺗﺼﻨﻴﻔﻬﺎ
ﻣﺮﺟﻌﺎ ﺍﺳﺎﺳﻴﺎ ﻟﻠﺰﺧﺎﺭﻑ ﺍﻟﻌﻤﺎﻧﻴﺔ ،
ﻭﺍﺷﺎﺭ ﺍﻧﻪ ﻟﻴﺲ ﻫﻨﺎﻙ ﻣﺸﺮﻭﻉ ﺳﺎﺑﻖ
ﻟﻠﻤﺤﺎﻓﻈﺔ ﻋﻠﻰ ﺍﻟﺰﺧﺎﺭﻑ ﻓﻲ ﺍﻟﺴﻠﻄﻨﺔ ،
ﻭﺍﺿﺎﻑ : ﻳﺠﺐ ﺍﻥ ﻧﻌﻤﻞ ﺑﺎﻗﺼﻰ
ﺳﺮﻋﺔ ﻟﻠﺤﻔﺎﻅ ﻋﻠﻰ ﻫﺬﺍ ﺍﻟﺘﺮﺍﺙ ﻻﻥ
ﺍﻓﻜﺎﺭ ﺍﻟﻌﻤﺎﻧﻴﻴﻦ ﻓﻲ ﻫﺬﺍ ﺍﻟﻤﺠﺎﻝ ﺍﻟﻬﺎﻡ
ﻳﻤﻜﻦ ﺍﻥ ﺗﻀﻴﻊ ﻓﻲ ﻭﻗﺖ ﻗﺼﻴﺮ .
ﻭﻋﻦ ﺍﻫﺘﻤﺎﻣﻪ ﺑﻬﺬﻩ ﺍﻟﺰﺧﺎﺭﻑ ﻗﺎﻝ :
ﻟﻘﺪ ﺟﺬﺑﺖ ﺍﻧﺘﺒﺎﻫﻲ ﻻﻧﻬﺎ ﺗﺨﺘﻠﻒ ﻛﺜﻴﺮﺍ
ﻋﻦ ﺍﻟﺰﺧﺎﺭﻑ ﻓﻲ ﺩﻭﻝ ﺍﺳﻴﺎ ﻭﺍﻟﺪﻭﻝ
ﺍﻟﻌﺮﺑﻴﺔ ﻭﺍﻻﻭﺭﻭﺑﻴﺔ ، ﺣﻴﺚ ﺗﻤﺘﺎﺯ

ﺑﺎﻟﺴﻬﻮﻟﺔ ﻭﺍﻟﺘﻌﻘﻴﺪ ﺍﻟﺮﻳﺎﺿﻲ ﻭﺍﻥ
ﺍﻟﻤﺤﺎﻓﻈﺔ ﻋﻠﻰ ﺍﻟﺘﺮﺍﺙ ﻭﺣﺪﻩ ﻻ ﻳﻜﻔﻲ ،
ﺍﻧﻤﺎ ﺗﻘﺪﻳﻢ ﻫﺬﺍ ﺍﻟﺘﺮﺍﺙ ﻟﻼﺟﻴﺎﻝ
ﺍﻟﻨﺎﻫﻀﺔ ﺳﻮﺍﺀ ﻓﻲ ﺍﻟﻤﺪﺍﺭﺱ ﺍﻭ ﺍﻻﻧﺪﻳﺔ
ﻭﺍﻟﻤﺮﺍﺳﻢ ، ﻭﺍﺷﺎﺭ ﺍﻟﻰ ﺍﻧﻪ ﻳﻤﻜﻦ ﺍﻥ
ﺗﻌﻤﻞ ﻣﺴﺎﺑﻘﺎﺕ ﺣﻮﻝ ﺍﺟﻤﻞ ﺍﻟﺰﺧﺎﺭﻑ
ﺍﻟﻌﻤﺎﻧﻴﺔ .

ﻭﺍﻫﺎﺏ ﺍﻥ ﺗﻮﻟﻲ ﺍﻟﺰﺧﺮﻓـﺔ ﻓﻲ
ﺍﻟﺴﻠﻄﻨﺔ ﺍﻫﺘﻤﺎﻣﺎ ﻣﻤﺎﺛﻼ ﻟﻼﻫﺘﻤﺎﻡ
ﺑﺎﻟﺘﺮﺍﺙ ﻓﻲ ﺍﻟﺴﻠﻄﻨﺔ ﺑﺸﻜﻞ ﻋﺎﻡ ،
ﻭﻻﺣﻈﺖ ﺑﻤﺮﺳﻢ ﺍﻟﺸﺒﺎﺏ ﻋﻠﻰ ﺳﺒﻴﻞ
ﺍﻟﻤﺜﺎﻝ ﺷﺒﺎﺑﺎ ﻳﺮﺳﻤﻮﻥ ﻟﻮﺣﺎﺕ ﻭﻟﻜﻦ
ﺗﻨﻘﺼﻬﻢ ﺍﻟﻤﺰﺍﻭﺟﺔ ﺑﻴﻦ ﺍﻟﻘﺪﻳﻢ
ﻭﺍﻟﺤﺪﻳﺚ ﺍﻟﺬﻱ ﺗﺘﻤﻴﺰ ﺑﻪ ﺑﻼﺩﻩ .

ﻭﺣﻮﻝ ﺍﺷﻴﺎﺀ ﺍﺧﺮﻯ ﺟﺬﺑﺖ ﺍﻧﺘﺒﺎﻩ
ﺟﻮﺭﺝ ﺑﻮﺏ ﻭﻳﻤﻜﻦ ﺗﺒﻨﻴﻬﺎ ﻗﺎﻝ : ﻳﻤﻜﻦ
ﺍﻥ ﻧﺤﺎﻓﻆ ﻋﻠﻰ ﺍﻻﻟﻮﺍﻥ ﺍﻟﻌﻤﺎﻧﻴﺔ
ﻭﺍﻟﺴﻠﻄﻨﺔ ﺯﺍﺧﺮﺓ ﺑﺎﻻﻟﻮﺍﻥ ﻓﻲ ﺍﻟﺼﺨﻮﺭ
ﻭﺍﻟﺠﺒﺎﻝ ﻭﺍﻟﺴﻬﻮﻝ ﻭﺍﻟﺒﺮﺍﺭﻱ ﻭﺫﻟﻚ
ﺑﻌﻤﻞ ﻣﺮﻛﺰ ﻟﻼﻟﻮﺍﻥ ﻭﺑﺬﻟﻚ ﻳﻤﻜﻦ
ﺍﻻﺳﺘﻐﻨﺎﺀ ﻋﻦ ﺍﻻﻟﻮﺍﻥ ﻣﻦ ﺍﻟﺨﺎﺭﺝ .

ﻭﺍﺷﺎﺭ ﺍﻟﻰ ﺍﻥ ﺍﻟﻤﺮﻛﺰ ﻋﻠﻰ ﺳﺒﻴﻞ
ﺍﻟﻤﺜﺎﻝ ﻳﻌﻤﻞ ﺑﻪ ﺟﻴﻮﻟﻮﺟﻴﻮﻥ ﻭﺭﺳﺎﻣﻮﻥ

Zeitungsbericht über die erste gemeinsame Ausstellung von Juma Al Maskari und Georg Popp 1993 in Maskat.
Newspaper report about the first joint exhibition in 1993 in Muscat.

Juma und Georg: Freunde fürs Leben

Juma und Georg: Friends for Life

Seit über 35 Jahren vertrauen sie einander –
schreiben, organisieren und filmen zusammen

For more than 35 years they have shared a deep friendship –
They write, organise and make films together

**جمعة المسكري وجورج بوب: أصدقاء لطول العمر
يثقون ببعضهم البعض منذ أكثر من 35 سنة ويكتبون
وينظمون ويصورون أفلام سوياُ**

التقيا لأول مرة عن طريق الصدفة في مسكن الطلبة في عام
1983م – الشاب العُماني جمعة المسكري وطالب الفن
الألماني جورج بوب. وبما أنه لم تكن هناك جامعات في
السلطنة في ذلك الوقت، فإن معظم الطلاب العُمانيين ذهبوا
إلى البلدان الناطقة باللغة الإنجليزية. وقد قرر جمعة كأحد
القلائل الذهاب إلى ميونخ. اليوم، جمعة وجورج صديقان منذ
أكثر من 35 عامًا. من خلال عيون صديقه، تعرّف جورج
على بلده بأعين مختلفة – وكان مهتماً بالعودة إلى عُمان، التي
كانت غير معروفة تماماً في ألمانيا في بداية التسعينات. وفي
أثناء الرحلات المشتركة لهما، اكتشف ألوان الصحراء
والصخور والوديان الفاتنة. في عام 1993م، نظم كليهما أول
معرض مشترك للصور والأعمال الفنية في مسقط. تبع ذلك
العديد من المشاريع الأخرى، بما في ذلك الكتب والأفلام. لا
تنضب الأفكار الخاصة بالأنشطة من رؤوس الصديقين حتى
يومنا هذا.

Juma Al Maskari (li.) und Georg Popp haben gemeinsam noch viel vor.
Juma Al Maskari (left) and Georg Popp still have a lot of plans together.

Sie trafen sich 1983 das erste Mal im Münchner Studentenwohnheim – der junge Omaner Juma Al Maskari und der deutsche Kunststudent Georg Popp. Eine intensive Freundschaft entwickelte sich. 1993 organisierten beide ihre erste Ausstellung in Maskat, in der die Fotos von Juma und die Objekte Georgs die Wahrnehmung der jeweils anderen Kultur spiegelten. Viele weitere Projekte, auch Bücher und Filme, folgten. Die Ideen für Aktivitäten gehen den Freunden bis heute nicht aus. Georg Popp erzählt:

„Meine erste Reise nach Oman unternahm ich 1992. In jener Zeit konnte man sich schwerlich ein Land vorstellen, das abgeschiedener war als das Sultanat. Es erwies sich schon als Abenteuer, überhaupt einen Flug zu buchen. Der Mitarbeiter im Reisebüro bestand darauf, mir ein Ticket nach Amman in Jordanien zu verkaufen. Niemand kannte den Buchungscode für Maskat. Im Rückblick scheint es mir, als wäre meine Ankunft im Land das Ergebnis eines Zusammenspiels von Vorhersehung und omanischer Politik. Vielleicht war es aber auch der Wille Allahs.

In 1983, a young Omani, Juma Al Maskari, and a German art student, Georg Popp, met by accident for the first time in a student home. Because there were no universities in the Sultanate at that time, Omani students usually went to countries where English was spoken. Juma was one of the few to choose Munich. Juma and Georg have now been friends for more than 35 years. Through his friend's eyes, Georg saw a different perspective of his home country. At the same time, he developed an interest in Oman, which was totally unknown in Germany at the beginning of the 1990s. On trips they took together, he was fascinated by the colours of the desert, the rocks and the wadis. In 1993, they organised their first exhibition of pictures and artistic works in Muscat. Many projects followed, including books and films. The two friends have never been short of ideas for new activities.

"My first trip to the Sultanate took place in 1992. At that time, it was difficult to think of a more remote corner of the world. Just booking a flight proved to be an ad-

189

Juma Al Maskari and Georg Popp – Friends for Life

Falaj-Systeme – typische Wasserstraßen im Oman.
Falaj systems – typical waterways in Oman.

venture. The travel agent obstinately insisted on trying to sell me a ticket to Amman in Jordan. No one knew what the booking code for Muscat was. Looking back, it seems that my landing there was a result of a mix of personal luck and Omani politics; or maybe it was the will of Allah.

My personal journey to Oman began back in 1983 and was entirely accidental. My girlfriend was looking for a room in a student home. The only place on offer with a waiting time of less than a year was the 'International House'. When she moved in, she was warmly welcomed by an Arab in nickel-framed glasses, an Omani named Juma Al Maskari. There was no university in the Sultanate at that time, so students were all sent abroad to study. For personal reasons, most opted to study in Arabic-speaking or English-speaking countries. In those days, only four Omanis chose the more challenging option of Germany.

Juma had had an interest in physics since his school days. The development of physics in the 1920s saw a significant growth in Germany, thanks to German physicists, and continued to increase over the following decades. This is why he chose to study for his degree in Germany. Another influence was his love of classical music.

The initially casual contact turned into a close and strong friendship between us. I answered many questions that he and the other Omanis put to me regarding German culture, and this forced me to reflect more critically on my own personal preferences and on our local customs and religion. They were deeply shocked, when first visiting a south German baroque church, to be confronted by bones laid out as relics in side altars and lovingly detailed depictions of saints being tortured. 'So you pray to old bones? How can your children sleep after going to church? Is this the religion of brotherly love?' And on weekends there was always the Omanis' wish to visit a river with a waterfall and simply to stand and look into the raging waters. Juma's numerous photos gave me another way of looking at our everyday life.

When I finished my studies at the Academy of Fine Arts, Oman had just issued the first tourist visas. Now was

1983 führte eine zufällige Begegnung dazu, dass ich mit Oman in Berührung kam. Damals suchte meine Freundin ein Zimmer in einem Studentenwohnheim. Das einzige Angebot mit einer Wartezeit von unter einem Jahr gab es im ‚International House'. Als sie einzog, wurde sie herzlich von einem Araber mit Nickelbrille willkommen geheißen: Es war Juma Al Maskari aus Oman. Weil es damals noch keine Universität im Sultanat gab, wurden alle Studierenden ins Ausland geschickt. Aus persönlichen Gründen zog es die meisten in Länder, in denen Arabisch oder Englisch gesprochen wurde. Nur vier Omaner wählten die deutlich schwierigere Option Deutschland. Einer von ihnen war Juma.

Er interessierte sich seit seiner Schulzeit für Physik – ein Fachgebiet, das in Deutschland seit den 1920er Jahren einen Aufschwung erlebt hatte. So kam es, dass Juma seinen Hochschulabschluss in Deutschland machen wollte. Hinzu kam seine Liebe zur klassischen Musik.

Nach ersten lockeren Kontakten entwickelte sich eine tiefe Freundschaft zwischen uns. Viele Fragen, die er und die anderen Omaner zu der Kultur ihres Gastgeberlandes

Juma Al Maskari and Georg Popp: Freunde fürs Leben

stellten, brachten mich zum Nachdenken – über meine persönlichen Ansichten, unsere Gewohnheiten und unsere Religion.

Die Omaner waren regelrecht geschockt, als sie das erste Mal in einer süddeutschen Barockkirche in einem Nebenaltar Knochen von Heiligen als Reliquien entdeckten, und dazu detailgetreue Schilderungen der Folterqualen, die die heiligen Männer erlitten hatten. Ihre Kommentare: ‚Ihr betet alte Knochen an? Wie können eure Kinder nach dem Besuch einer Kirche schlafen? Ist dies eine Religion der brüderlichen Liebe?'

Jedes Wochenende wollten die omanischen Studierenden einen Fluss oder einen Wasserfall besuchen. Dann standen sie da und schauten einfach in das tosende Wasser. Jumas zahlreiche Fotos eröffneten mir zusätzlich eine ganz neue Perspektive auf unseren Alltag.

In der Zeit, als ich mein Studium an der Kunstakademie beendete, stellte Oman die ersten Touristenvisa aus. Das war meine Chance, eine neue Welt zu entdecken. Was ursprünglich als eine dreiwöchige Ferienreise geplant war, entwickelte sich zu einem Projekt, das noch immer andauert.

Meine Versuche, mich auf die Reise vorzubereiten, scheiterten: Es gab einfach keine ernstzunehmende Reiseliteratur. Ich begann, Arabisch zu lernen. Am ersten Tag der Reise musste ich allerdings feststellen, dass Jumas Familie bevorzugt Suaheli sprach – die Familie stammte aus Sansibar. Sobald wir eingetroffen waren, packte uns Jumas Bruder Salim, der Geologe ist, in sein Auto und chauffierte uns durch Wüsten und Wadis. Ich war sofort fasziniert und gefesselt von den Farben Omans und begann, Pigmente zu suchen. Salim war Kenner der Steine und Felsarten Omans, hatte diese aber niemals aus der Perspektive eines Künstlers betrachtet. Zusammen gingen wir auf Farbentdeckungsreise – wir machten Exkursionen in Regionen mit roten, violetten, schwarzen, weißen und gelben Gesteinen. So wie Juma Deutschland erforscht hatte, so wollte ich mehr und mehr über dieses faszinierende Land mit seinen liebenswerten Menschen wissen.

1993 organisierte ich mit Juma eine große Ausstellung in Maskat: ‚Blick auf Deutschland – Blick auf Oman'. Juma zeigte seine persönlichen Eindrücke von Deutschland in

my chance to discover a new world. What was originally planned as a three-week holiday turned into a project, which, years later, has shown no sign of coming to an end. Preparing for my initial journey was very difficult because of the complete lack of travel literature. So I set about learning Arabic, only to find out on the first day that Juma's family preferred to speak Swahili; the family came from Zanzibar. Almost as soon as we arrived, Juma's brother Salim, a field geologist, loaded us into his car and drove us through deserts and wadis. I was immediately captivated by the colours of Oman and began to look for pigments. Salim had a thorough knowledge of all the stones and rocks in Oman but had never viewed them from the point of view of an artist. Together, we explored the country according to colour, making expeditions to regions of red, violet, black, white and yellow. Just as Juma had set about thoroughly investigating Germany, I began to want to know more and more about this fascinating new land with its endearing people.

In 1993, we organised a large exhibition in Muscat – "Views of Germany – Views of Oman". Juma showed his personal impressions of Germany in photographs depicting bones in churches, dogs wearing "clothes", jet trails in the sky, Jehovah's Witnesses standing on corners, and everyday life in German families. I concentrated on artistic works, created with colours obtained

Auf Forschungsreise in der Heimat des Freundes

On a research trip to the friend's home country

Juma Al Maskari and Georg Popp – Friends for Life

Fotos. Zu sehen waren unter anderem Reliquienknochen in Kirchen, ‚Kleider' tragende Hunde, Kondensstreifen von Flugzeugen am Himmel, an Kreuzungen stehende Zeugen Jehovas, aber auch Szenen aus dem Alltagsleben deutscher Familien. Ich konzentrierte mich auf künstlerische Arbeiten, die mit Hilfe von Farben aus omanischer Erde entstanden und auf textile Drucke mit typischen omanischen Mustern, wie man sie an alten Türen findet. Dann wurde ich eingeladen, den ersten Reiseführer über Oman in deutscher Sprache zu schreiben. Illustriert wurde er mit Fotos von Juma und mir. Dass ich diese Aufgabe erfüllen konnte, verdanke ich vor allem Juma, seinem Bruder Salim und den Familien Al Maskari und Al Harthi. Alle unterstützten meine Arbeit und standen mir mit Ratschlägen und praktischer Hilfe zur Seite. Weder Juma noch ich hätten damals gedacht, dass nach mehr als 25 Jahren und diversen Neuauflagen das Buch immer noch im Umlauf ist.

Auf das Buch folgten viele weitere Herausforderungen, die wir gemeinsam annahmen und meisterten. Dazu zählt die Produktion von Dokumentarfilmen über Oman – ‚Religiöse Toleranz in Oman' und ‚Islamische Kunst in Oman' in Kooperation mit dem Filmemacher Wolfgang Ettlich. Dann die dreiteilige Dokumentarserie ‚Die Söhne Sindbads' über die Geschichte der omanischen Seefahrer mit dem Regisseur Friedrich Klütsch (Seite 90). Das jüngste Projekt widmet sich der Suche nach den historischen Wurzeln und dem Austausch zwischen Oman und Ostafrika; ein Thema, das besonders Juma am Herzen liegt, da er in Sansibar geboren wurde.

Unsere vertrauensvolle persönliche Beziehung war auch das Fundament, auf dem viele Aktivitäten der Deutsch-Omanischen-Gesellschaft gründeten. Das bedeutendste Projekt war sicher der Aufbau eines Schüleraustauschs zwischen Deutschland und Oman (Seite 144). Zusammen haben wir vor deutschen Schülern und ihren Eltern gesprochen – und dabei ein lebendes Beispiel abgegeben, wie diese beiden Länder und Kulturen kooperieren. Dadurch wurden Bedenken zerstreut und Sorgen darüber, ob der Besuch einer Welt, die so anders erschien als die eigene, überhaupt machbar war. Jumas und meine Freundschaft zeigte, wie ein Austausch den Schleier des Unbekannten lüften kann.

from Omani soil, and textile prints with ornaments from Omani doors.

Following this, I was invited to write the first German travel guide on Oman, illustrated with photos by Juma and me. I was able to complete this task thanks above all to Juma, his brother Salim, and the whole Al Maskari and Al Harthi families, who all supported my work and gave advice and practical assistance. Neither of us expected that now, more than 25 years and many editions and updates later, this book would still be in circulation.

But the book turned out to be merely a starting point for many more joint challenges over the following years. We produced documentary films relating to Oman: 'Religious Tolerance in Oman' and 'Islamic Art in Oman', in collaboration with filmmaker Wolfgang Ettlich. We worked with filmmaker Friedrich Kluetsch on a three-part documentary, 'Sons of Sinbad', about the history of Omani seafaring. And now, we have a new project searching for the historic trade roots between Oman and East Africa, a subject very dear to Juma, having been born in Zanzibar.

Our very trusting personal relationship was the foundation on which many of the German-Omani Association's activities were built. The most significant of these was the establishment of an ongoing school exchange programme between Germany and Oman. Speaking together in front of German students and their anxious parents is a way of presenting a living example of collaboration between the two countries and cultures and sweeping away their concerns about a visit to a world perceived to be so very different. We reassure them that a visit is exactly what will remove it from the realm of the unknown.

This successful collaboration, and exchange of thoughts and views, which started in 1983, has been very inspiring for us both, and we are keen to see what the coming years have in store for us."

Juma Al Maskari and Georg Popp: Freunde fürs Leben

Eine erfolgreiche und ausgesprochen fruchtbare Zusammenarbeit, ein Austausch von Gedanken und Ansichten – all das,
was 1983 begann, war und ist weiterhin sehr inspirierend für
uns beide. Und wir sind neugierig, was die kommenden
Jahre für uns noch bereithalten."

Georg Popp

Der Künstler und Fotograf Georg Popp beschäftigt
sich seit über 25 Jahren auf sehr intensive und
persönliche Weise mit dem Sultanat Oman und
seinen Menschen. Durch seine seit Studientagen
bestehende Freundschaft mit dem Omani Juma Al
Maskari hat er über die Jahre intensive Einblicke in
das Sultanat Oman gewonnen.

Seit 1992 ist das Sultanat Oman mit künstlerischen
Arbeiten, Publikationen, Ausstellungen und Projekten der Arbeitsschwerpunkt von Georg Popp.

Um seinen verschiedenen Aktivitäten ein gemeinsames Dach zu geben, gründete er 1999 die Arabia
Felix Synform GmbH (www.oman.de), deren Ge-
schäftsführer er ist.

Er veröffentlichte mehrere Artikel und Bücher über
das Sultanat, darunter den ersten umfassenden
deutschsprachigen Reiseführer über das Land, der
inzwischen in der 7. Auflage erschienen ist und 2010
auch in englischer Sprache veröffentlicht wurde.

Von 2001 bis 2009 war er Beirat für Kultur der
Deutsch-Omanischen Gesellschaft e.V. Von 2009
bis Ende 2018 war er Generalsekretär dieser offiziel-
len bilateralen Gesellschaft.

Reiseführer von Georg Popp und Juma Al Maskari:
Oman – Juwel am Arabischen Golf. 7. überarbeitete
Ausgabe vom 26.8.18, Edition Temmen, Edition Erde
Reiseführer, 19,90 Euro, ISBN 978-3-8378-3009-5

Georg Popp

The artist and photographer Georg Popp employs
for more than 25 years on very intensive and personal way with the Sultanate of Oman and his people.
By his since study days existing friendship with
the Omani Juma Al Maskari, he has over the years
gained intensive insights into the the Sultanate of
Oman.

Since 1992, the Sultanate of Oman has been the
focus of Georg Popp's work - in cultural projects,
publications, exhibitions and projects.

In order to achieve a common understanding of his
various activities
roof, he founded in 1999 the Arabis Felix Synform
GmbH (www.oman.de), whose managing director
he is.

He has published several articles and books on the
Sultanate, including the first comprehensive Ger-
man-speaking travel guide about the country, the
has now been published in its 7th edition and was
also published in English in 2010.

From 2001 to 2009 he was an adviser for culture of
the German-Omani Society e.V.. From 2009
until the end of 2018 he was Secretary General of
this official bilateral company.

Travel guide: Oman – Jewel of the Arabian Gulf
ISBN-13: 978-9622178137, 416 pages

Maßanzüge im Geschäft von Uwe Sengele in Garmisch-Partenkirchen – bereit für ihren großen Auftritt.
Made-to-measure suits in the shop of Uwe Sengele in Garmisch-Partenkirchen – ready for her big appearance.

„The Garmish" und der Hofschneider des Sultans

"The Garmish" and the Court Tailor of the sultanate

Wo der Sultan wohnt
und Uwe Sengele Maß für omanische Smokings nimmt

Where the Sultan lives
Uwe Sengele takes measurements for Omani tuxedos

"غارميش" وخياط البلاط السلطاني
حيث يعيش السلطان ويأخذ أوفي سنغيلي القياس لبدلة عُمانية رسمية

في السبعينيات، اختار السلطان قابوس غارميش-بارتنكيرشن كمركز إقامة له أثناء تواجده في المانيا. ويعرف السكان المحليون: أنه يأتي كل ثلاث سنوات إلى هنا لقضاء بضعة أسابيع. حيث يسير المزيد والمزيد من أبناء وطنه على خطى السلطان ويقضون عطلة الصيف في بافاريا العليا. ويعيش أوفي سنغيلي، خياط البلاط السلطاني، في غارمش – بارتنكيرشين. لقد اختار هذا اللقب الذي يستحقه بنفسه ذلك أنه لا تسافر أية شركة أخرى من شركات خياطة الملابس الرجالية الألمانية إلى عُمان من أجل تقديم البدلات الأنيقة الرسمية والقمصان الأنيقة والمناسبة. إن شخصاً مثل سنغيلي، والذي يفهم زبونه ويعرف رغباته ثم يخيط له ملابس تكون على قياسهم بالضبط، لديه جمهور من الزبائن المخلصين. إلا أن هذا الخياط لا يريد أن يتباهى بهذا الشيء أمام كل الناس. ويتناسب أسلوبه الخاص المتواضع بشكل جيد مع طبيعة العُمانيين وحاكمهم، الذي يتصرف ومن وراء الكواليس كرجل عمل خيري دبلوماسي – على سبيل المثال كداعم لمشفى الأطفال هاونرشين في ميونيخ.

Viele Omaner genießen vor allem den Sommer in Garmisch-Partenkirchen.
Many Omani enjoy especially the summer in Garmisch-Partenkirchen.

In den 1970er Jahren hat Sultan Qaboos bin Said Garmisch-Partenkirchen als sein deutsches Zuhause gewählt. Die Einheimischen wissen: Ungefähr alle drei Jahre kommt er für einige Wochen hierher. Immer mehr seiner Landsleute folgen den Spuren des Sultans und bleiben den Sommer über in Oberbayern. In Garmisch-Partenkirchen lebt auch Uwe Sengele, der Hofschneider des Sultanats. Ein selbst gewählter Titel, der ihm gebührt, denn schließlich reist kein anderer deutscher Herrenausstatter in den Oman, um persönlich elegante Anzüge, Smokings und dazu passende feine Hemden abzuliefern.

In munterem Tempo geht es bergauf, links und rechts der Straße türmt sich der vereiste Schnee der vergangenen Woche hüfthoch. Thomas Heinzinger trägt auch im Taxi eine gestreifte Strickmütze und steuert den Wagen lässig durch die Kurven oberhalb von Garmisch-Partenkirchen. Die Schilder zeigen Richtung Tierheim und Wildfütterung, kaum ein Mensch würde vermuten, dass wir hier mitten in Oberbayern gleich einen Landsitz von Sultan Qaboos erreichen. „Da war früher die Almhütte, ich kann mich gut erinnern. Ich war ein Bub und wir machten dorthin Ausflüge, um Waldkauz und Marder zu beobachten", erzählt der Fahrer, während wir einen Zaun mit geschlossenen Toren erreichen, über dem man weiß bedeckte Dächer herauslugen sieht. Kameras halten Wacht. Denn in der ehemaligen Almhütte und ihren umliegenden Gebäuden lebt der Sultan mit seinem Gefolge, wenn er in Deutschland ist. Was für einen Blick hat er auf die Kette der Berge in der Ferne! Die Zugspitze ist auch darunter. Und die Garmischer haben eine neue

In the 1970's, the Sultan chose Garmisch-Partenkirchen as his German home. It is well known that he spends a few weeks here every three years or so. More and more of his compatriots have followed his example and spend their summers in Upper Bavaria. Another man who lives in Garmisch-Partenkirchen is Uwe Sengele, the "Court Tailor of the Sultanate". He chose the title himself, and he deserves it. No other German men's outfitter travels to Oman in person to deliver elegant suits, tuxedos, and finely tailored shirts.

We drive at a brisk pace up the mountain; to the left and right of the road, the snow that has fallen in the past few weeks has frozen over and lies in waist-high piles. In the cab, Thomas Heinzinger, our driver, is wearing a striped knitted cap and casually drives along the windy road above Garmisch-Partenkirchen. We see signs pointing to an animal shelter and wildlife feeding area. Very few people would suspect that right here, in the middle of Upper Bavaria, they would also find Sultan Qaboos' country estate. "There used to be an Alpine cabin and I remember it well. I was a boy and we took trips here to observe brown owls and martens," the driver recounts, as we reach a fence and locked gate behind which are snow-covered roofs. Cameras monitor everything. The Sultan and his entourage live in the former "cabin" and the surrounding buildings when he is in Germany. The view of the distant mountain ranges, including the mighty Zugspitze, is breath-taking. The people of Garmisch got a new cabin for their outings, with a beer garden that is only a few hundred meters from the original site.

The Garmish and the Court Tailor of the Sultanate

Uwe Sengele (li.)mit seinem Bruder Simon zu Besuch in Maskat - neue Anzüge müssen ausgeliefert werden.
Uwe Sengele with his brother Simon visiting Muscat - new suits have to be delivered.

Hütte für ihre Ausflüge bekommen - mit einem Biergarten, ein paar hundert Meter vom ursprünglichen Standort entfernt.

In den 1970er Jahren hat sich der Sultan Garmisch-Partenkirchen als sein deutsches Zuhause gewählt. Die Einheimischen wissen: Etwa alle drei Jahre reist er für einige Wochen hierher. Um die Jahreswende 2014/15 war er sogar für neun Monate während einer medizinischen Behandlung da. Mit ihm kommt jedes Mal sein Hofstaat - 700 Menschen, die für die Zeit des Aufenthaltes in den Alpen leben. Täglich wird dann die Milch seiner Ziegen aus Maskat eingeflogen. So heißt es jedenfalls in Garmisch und Taxifahrer Thomas Heinzinger versteht das: „Unsere Ziegenmilch ist viel fettreicher als diejenige von dort, die Tiere bekommen ja ganz anderes Futter."

Seit Jahren folgten immer mehr seiner Landsleute den Spuren von Sultan Qaboos Al Said. Man könnte sagen: Jeder in Oman träumt davon, „the Garmish" zu sehen. Wer dorthin gelangt, isst gern wie am Golf das omanische Reis-Leibgericht Biryani im Akrams, einem von zwei arabischen Restaurants. Bestaunt den ewigen Schnee auf der Zugspitze und geht in die Partnachklamm, um

The Sultan chose Garmisch-Partenkirchen as his German home in the 1970s. The locals know that he spends a few weeks here every three years or so. At the end of 2014 and start of 2015, he spent nine months here for medical treatment. He is always accompanied by his entourage – 700 people who live in the Alps as long as he is there. During his stay, goat's milk is flown in daily from Muscat, or so the rumour goes. Heinzinger can understand the rumour well. "Our goat's milk is much higher in fat than theirs, the animals are fed differently," he explains.

For years now, more and more of Sultan Quaboos Al Said's fellow countrymen have followed his example. You could say that everyone in Oman dreams of seeing "the Garmish." Omanis who visit like to keep their local tradition of eating Biryani, Oman's favourite rice dish, at Akrams, one of two Arab restaurants in the area. They marvel at the perpetually snow-covered Zugspitze and enjoy visiting the Partnachklamm Canyon to hear the rush of the waterfall. The Omanis take their summer in Upper Bavaria and hope for rain, while the thermometer rises above 40 degrees Celsius at home. In Garmisch, on the Maxhöhe, people can practically pass right by

„The Garmish" und der Hofschneider des Sultans

the Sultan's front door. In Muscat, he lives behind a wall of sandstone more than a kilometre long.

A man who has seen both residences up close is Uwe Sengele. He knows that there is a small mosque on the Alpine estate and has also been inside the palace's fitting-rooms in Muscat to take the measurements of many Omanis. After all, he is the Court Tailor of the Sultanate. He chose the well-deserved title himself, because no other German men's outfitter travels to Oman to personally deliver elegant suits, tuxedos, and finely tailored shirts.

Simone Wassmer and Uwe Sengele's shop is located in the pedestrian zone of Garmisch-Partenkirchen. One spring day in 2011, the men's outfitter opened its doors early because two friends, a father and son, were coming to be fitted out. They talked on the first floor of the shop, where suits hang neatly lined up and customers can pick from a range of glittering buttons. Suddenly the doorbell rang downstairs in the sales room and an Arab man with a well-groomed beard stood there. Would it be possible for Sengele to measure him up for a tuxedo? Father and son let the guest go first – a stroke of luck for the tailor. When he delivered the tailor-made tuxedo to Muscat a few months later, the unknown client was so pleased that he immediately placed another order. Sengele thought nonchalantly: "Well, maybe eleven outfits will be ordered, like for a football team."

Some time later, the fax started chattering in the shop: a large number of suits and tuxedos with spare trousers, shirts and belts were to be delivered. Even the hairdressers of the generous Omani were to receive a suitable alternative to the classic Omani Dishdasha for trips to Europe. „When everything was ready, it took three days to distribute the suits," says Uwe Sengele, the strong Bavarian with the frizzy grey curls. His eyes flash at the thought of this operation. The client from Muscat had not only shown himself to be a man of honour, but had also turned out to be a high-ranking civil servant. Since then, the two have been sending each other funny messages via WhatsApp, meeting each other in Germany and Oman, and going to the football together – not only to Bayern Munich matches, but also to a match to cheer on the Omanis against Jordan.

den Wasserfall rauschen zu hören. Die Omaner übersommern sozusagen in Oberbayern und hoffen auf Regen, während zuhause das Thermometer über 40 Grad klettert. Eins bleibt aber gleich: Sie können quasi vor der Haustür ihres Sultans vorbeifahren – in Maskat lebt er hinter einer kilometerlangen Sandsteinmauer, in Garmisch auf der Maxhöhe.

Einer, der schon bei beiden Wohnsitzen hinter die Kulissen geschaut hat, ist Uwe Sengele. Er weiß, dass auf dem Grundstück in den Alpen auch eine kleine Moschee steht und hat in Maskat schon die Anproberäume des Palastes betreten, um dort bei vielen Omanern Maß zu nehmen. Denn er ist der Hofschneider des Sultanats. Ein selbst gewählter Titel, der ihm gebührt, denn schließlich reist kein anderer deutscher Herrenausstatter in den Oman, um persönlich elegante Anzüge, Smokings und dazu passende feine Hemden abzuliefern.

In der Fußgängerzone von Garmisch-Partenkirchen liegt das Geschäft von Simone Wassmer und Uwe Sengele. Eines Frühlingstages im Jahr 2011 hatte der Herrenausstatter die Tür schon früh aufgesperrt, weil befreundete

The Garmish and the Court Tailor of the Sultanate

Kunden kamen, Vater und Sohn. Man besprach sich im ersten Stock des Ladenlokals, wo Anzüge fein säuberlich aufgereiht hängen und blitzende Knöpfe in Reih und Glied zur Auswahl stehen. Plötzlich ging unten im Verkaufsraum die Klingel und ein arabischer Mann mit gepflegtem Bart stand da. Ob es möglich sei, dass Sengele bei ihm Maß für einen Smoking nehme? Vater und Sohn gaben dem Gast den Vortritt – ein Glück für den Maßschneider. Denn als dieser wenige Monate später den passenden Smoking nach Maskat brachte, freute sich der unbekannte Auftraggeber so sehr, dass er gleich einen weiteren Auftrag ankündigte. Sengele dachte unbekümmert: Naja, da werden vielleicht elf Outfits bestellt werden, wie für eine Fußballmannschaft.

Nach einiger Zeit begann das Fax im Ladenlokal zu rattern: eine große Anzahl Anzüge und Smokings mit Ersatzhosen, Hemden und Gürteln sollte geliefert werden. Selbst die Friseure des generösen Omaners sollten für Reisen nach Europa die passende Alternative zur klassischen omanischen Dishdasha erhalten. „Als alles fertig war, hat es drei Tage gedauert, die Anzüge zu verteilen", erzählt Uwe Sengele, der kräftige Bayer mit den wuscheligen grauen Locken. Seine Augen blitzen bei dem Gedanken an diesen Einsatz. Der Auftraggeber aus Maskat hatte sich nicht nur als Ehrenmann gezeigt, sondern auch als hochrangiger Staatsbediensteter entpuppt. Seitdem schicken sich die beiden gegenseitig amüsante Nachrichten über WhatsApp, treffen sich hüben wie drüben, gehen zusammen zum Fußball – nicht nur zu Spielen von Bayern München, sondern auch zu einem Match, bei dem es galt, die Omaner im Spiel gegen Jordanien anzufeuern.

Uwe Sengele fand seine Bestimmung als Maßschneider auf Umwegen: Der Mann aus Oberbayern hat Holzbearbeitung gelernt, dann suchte er andere Herausforderungen und fand sie bei der Bundeswehr: Alle Berggipfel rund um Garmisch hat er damals mit einem Militärhubschrauber erkundet. Doch wie sollte es weitergehen? Ein Erlebnis mit Lebensgefährtin Simone wies Mitte der 1990er Jahre den Weg: „Ich wollte sie elegant ins Ballett in München einladen und hatte keine Krawatte. Schließlich haben wir eine an der Theatinerstraße erstanden – für den gleichen Preis wie die beiden Ballett-Tickets ", erzählt Uwe Sengele. Die Idee, Krawatten zu verkaufen, war geboren. Noch lukrativer wurde das Geschäft, als maßgeschneiderte Hemden, Anzüge, aber auch Blusen und Kostüme für die Damen dazukamen.

Sengele's journey to becoming a tailor was somewhat indirect. The Bavarian first finished an apprenticeship in woodworking and was then on the lookout for a new challenge. He found it with the Bundeswehr, the German armed forces. He explored all the mountain tops surrounding Garmisch by military helicopter. But what next? An experience in the middle of the 1990s with his partner Simone paved the way. "I wanted to treat her to an elegant evening at the ballet in Munich, but I didn't own a tie. In the end, we bought one on Theatinerstraße for the same price as the two tickets to the ballet," Sengele recounts. The idea of selling ties was born that day. The business became even more successful when custom-made shirts, ties, and also blouses and suits for women, were added to the line.

Sengele attributes the success of his small, high-quality tailor business "Die Krawatte" (The Tie) to his motto: "Listen carefully to what people want. One person may want a tight-fitting shirt, the next one may prefer it looser. There are no standard sizes, and physiques change over time". A person like Sengele, who understands his clients and provides clothes that fit like a second skin, easily attracts a loyal clientele. His clients recommend him to others, which is why an Omani princess is now among his customers. However, the tailor has no desire to shout this from the rooftops. His demeanour, which is both assertive and restrained, suits

**Viele Omaner
‚übersommern'
in Garmisch**

*Many Omani
spend the summer
in Garmisch*

„The Garmish" und der Hofschneider des Sultans

Abgeschieden liegt der Wohnsitz von Sultan Qaboos bin Said in Garmisch-Partenkirchen – mit grandiosem Ausblick auf die Berge.
The secluded residence of Sultan Qaboos bin Said in Garmisch-Partenkirchen – with a magnificent view of the mountains.

Dass der kleine, feine Herrenausstatterladen „Die Krawatte" so gut floriert, führt Uwe Sengele auf sein Motto zurück: Genau hinhören, was die Leute wollen. Der eine mag das Hemd eng sitzen haben, der nächste lieber locker. Einheitsgrößen gibt es nicht und der Körperbau verändert sich im Lauf der Zeit. Einer wie Sengele, der sich in seine Kunden einfühlt und ihnen Kleider verschafft, die wie angegossen sitzen, hat ein treues Stammpublikum. Das empfiehlt ihn weiter und so kommt es, dass inzwischen auch eine Prinzessin aus Oman bei ihm einkauft. Das möchte der Maßschneider aber nicht an die große Glocke hängen. Sein bestimmtes, dennoch zurückhaltendes Auftreten passt zu den Omanern und ihrem Herrscher, der auch am liebsten als diplomatischer Wohltäter im Hintergrund agiert: So ist es ein offenes Geheimnis, dass Sultan Qaboos den Neubau der Haunerschen Kinderklinik an der Münchner Uniklinik mit einer Millionensumme unterstützt – ganz ohne spektakuläre Spendenübergabe.

the Omanis and their ruler well. The Sultan himself prefers to remain in the background as a diplomatic benefactor. It is an open secret that Sultan Qaboos has quietly donated a seven-figure sum to help with the reconstruction of the Haunersche Kinderklinik, a children's hospital at the Munich University Hospital.

The Garmish and the Court Tailor of the Sultanate

Vom Dorf ins deutsche Großstadtgewühl

From Mountain Village to the Bustle of a German City

Khalid Alfahdi lebte und studierte
sieben Jahre lang in Deutschland

Khalid Alfahdi lived and studied
in Germany for seven years

من قرية جبلية إلى مدينة كبيرة صاخبة في المانيا
عاش خالد الفهدي ودرس سبع سنوات في المانيا

لم يكُ التباين بين الوطن القديم والوطن الجديد يوماً ما أكبر من ذلك. فقد غادر الشاب خالد الفهدي والبالغ من العمر سن الثامنة عشرة قريته الصغيرة في الجبل المشهور "الجبل الأخضر" إلى مدينة فرانكفورت الكبيرة الصاخبة في ألمانيا بغرض الدراسة. وكان خالد سعيداً جداً عندما حزم حقيبته بعد سنة وغادر إلى مدينة أصغر اسمها ماربورغ لكي يدرس علوم الصحافة. عاش هذا الشاب العُماني سبع سنوات في المانيا. وعند رجوعه إلى عُمان أصبح يروي للناس هناك كيف استطاع التعرف على الشعب الألماني، ولماذا كان مهماً جداً بالنسبة له الإلمام باللغة الألمانية والحصول على الثقة، حيث سجل كل هذا في رواية قصة شخصية له. بعد الرجوع إلى عُمان بدأ البناء بثقة في مهاراته الشخصية الجديدة والمهارات التي اكتسبها أثناء فترة إقامته في المانيا. ومن ضمن ذلك القدرة على العمل مع فريق ضمن مشروع وإدارة جيدة متعددة الجوانب والاهتمامات.

Aus dem beschaulichen Dorf Saiq, direkt am bekannten Berg Jebel Akhdar gelegen, kam der damals 18-jährige Khalid Alfahdi mit einem Stipendium ins pulsierende, hektische Frankfurt / Main. Nach einem Jahr ging es weiter in die gemütliche Universitätsstadt Marburg. Hier lebte er in einer Studentenverbindung mit neuen Freunden aus aller Welt. Wie er die Deutschen empfindet und warum für ihn gute Sprachkenntnisse und Vertrauen so wichtig sind, erzählt er im Gespräch.

„Der Kontrast hätte nicht größer sein können: Aus dem mit rund 25 Grad warmen und beschaulichen Oman kam ich im Oktober 2011 ins herbstlich kühle, von Menschen wimmelnde Frankfurt am Main.

Ich stamme aus dem beschaulichen Dorf Saiq, direkt am bekannten Berg Jebel Akhdar und in der Nähe von Nizwa gelegen. Dort kennt jeder jeden. In Frankfurt lag meine Wohnung mitten in einem bekannten Vergnügungsviertel. Ein Kommen und Gehen, laute Musik und auch immer wieder Streitereien auf der Straße, die die Polizei schlichten musste. Das war anfangs ein Schock für mich, den ich erst einmal verdauen musste.

Die Stadt war einfach zu groß für mich. Es leben dort so viele Menschen, dass man kaum eine Chance hat, ein bekanntes Gesicht jemals wieder zu treffen Dadurch war es für mich sehr schwer, Kontakte zu knüpfen. Ich konnte mich ja auch anfangs kaum verständigen.

Schon als Schüler habe ich davon geträumt, im Ausland zu studieren und die Welt kennen zu lernen. Meine Sehnsuchtsorte waren die USA oder auch Großbritannien. Aber meine Abiturnoten waren nicht so gut, dass meine Wünsche bei der Vergabe von Studienplätzen bevorzugt behandelt wurden.

Ich kam mit einem Stipendium des DAAD, des Deutschen Akademischen Austauschdienstes. Zur Wahl standen mir Österreich oder Deutschland. Entschieden habe ich mich für Deutschland.

Zuerst besuchte ich Sprachkurse im Goethe-Institut und büffelte eifrig Vokabeln und Grammatik. Ich wollte wirklich schnell Deutsch lernen, denn ich rede gerne mit Menschen. Die Sprache brauchte ich außerdem,

A scholarship brought the 18-year-old Khalid Alfahdi from the tranquil village of Saiq, directly on the well-known mountain Jebel Akhdar, to the hustle and bustle of Frankfurt am Main. After one year, he moved on to Marburg, a more relaxed university town. He lived in a student house, making new friends from all over the world. He talks about what he thinks of the German people and why good language skills and trust are so important to him.

"The contrast could not have been greater. In October 2011, I left tranquil Oman when it was a warm 25 degrees Celsius and arrived in the frantic hustle and bustle of Frankfurt when the chill of autumn had set in.

I am originally from a little village, Saiq, which is located directly in the mountain area of Jebel Akhdar, close to Nizwa. Everybody knows everyone else there. In Frankfurt, my apartment was in the middle of a popular entertainment district. People were coming and going, there was loud music everywhere, and the police were always coming to break up fights on the street. At first that was a shock for me, but I got used to it.

However, the city was simply too huge for me. There are so many people there that it is highly unlikely that you'll encounter the same person twice. That made it very hard for me to make new contacts. And, in the beginning, I could hardly communicate.

When I was in school, I dreamed of studying abroad and exploring the world. I longed to go to the United States, or maybe Great Britain. However, I didn't finish school with particularly good grades, so my preferences were not prioritised by those who made the decisions about study locations.

I received a German Academic Exchange Service (DAAD) scholarship, and I had the choice of Austria or Germany. I picked Germany.

At the beginning, I attended a language course at the Goethe Institute and diligently learned new words and grammar. I really wanted to learn German quickly, because I like to talk to people. I needed the language in order to begin my studies as soon as possible, and to make friends. I am convinced that language is what brings

From Mountain Village to the Bustle of a German City

Khalid Alfahdi (re.) im Kreis von Freunden und Studienkollegen.
Khalid Alfahdi (right) surrounded by friends and fellow students.

um zügig mit dem Studium beginnen zu können und auch Freunde zu finden. Meine Überzeugung ist, dass man nur über die Sprache zusammenkommt und die ist notwendig, um Vertrauen und damit Freundschaften aufzubauen.

Adieu Frankfurt – nach einem Jahr hatte ich genug von der quirligen Stadt, packte meine Koffer und zog nach Marburg. In der traditionsreichen, überschaubaren Universitätsstadt im Bundesland Hessen habe ich mich gleich viel wohler gefühlt. Wegen der vielen Studenten aus aller Welt ist man dort offen und oft ganz unkompliziert, ich konnte leichter Menschen kennenlernen.

Mehrere Jahre war die Studentenverbindung des Corps Suevia-Straßburg mein Zuhause. Wir waren dort insgesamt etwa 130 Mitglieder und es hat einfach Spaß gemacht, mit so vielen jungen Leuten aus verschiedenen Ländern zusammen zu kommen, zu reden oder etwas zu unternehmen. Wir haben ein echtes Multikulti-Leben geführt. Meine Freunde kamen natürlich zum Teil aus Deutschland, aber auch zum Beispiel aus Südkorea, Kasachstan oder der Ukraine.

An der Philipps-Universität habe ich mit großer Begeisterung Medienwissenschaft studiert. Auf welchen

people together, and it is necessary for building trust and friendships.

Goodbye Frankfurt: After a year, I'd had enough of the busy city, and I packed my bags and moved to Marburg. From the very start, I felt much more at home in the smaller Hessian university town, which is steeped in tradition. Because of the large number of students from all over the world, people are more open-minded there and are usually very uncomplicated, so it was easier for me to meet people.

For several years the Corps Suevia-Strasbourg student house was my home. There were roughly 130 of us. It was fun to get together with so many young people from different countries, and to talk to each other and to hang out. It was a very multicultural life. Some of my friends were German, of course, but others were from South Korea, Kazakhstan, Ukraine, and many other places.

At Philipps University, I enthusiastically undertook media studies. What are the different channels for communicating with people? How does the press work? How is a radio station organised? I learned the answers to all these questions.

Vom Dorf ins deutsche Großstadtgewühl

verschiedenen Kanälen kann man mit Menschen kommunizieren, wie arbeitet die Presse, wie ist ein Rundfunksender organisiert? All das waren Fragen, auf die ich Antworten erhalten habe.

Man sagt ja manchmal den Deutschen nach, sie seien nicht gastfreundlich. Ich kann dieses Vorurteil nicht bestätigen. Wenn erst einmal Vertrauen da ist und wenn man ehrlich miteinander umgeht, dann sind die Deutschen sehr gastfreundlich und großzügig. Ich war während meiner sieben Jahre in Marburg oft bei deutschen Freunden zu Gast und habe bestimmt dreimal mit deutschen Familien Weihnachten gefeiert. Und Weihnachten ist ja schließlich ein ganzes besonderes Fest, zu dem man nur Verwandte oder nahestehende Menschen einlädt.

Was mir immer gut gefallen hat, sind die unterschiedlichen Gesichter der Städte. Ich war in Hamburg, Bremen oder München – und jede Stadt hier hat ihren ganz eigenen Charakter. Mal durch einen Hafen, eine Altstadt oder wie in München durch einen Fluss wie die Isar geprägt. Das gefällt mir sehr.

Gewöhnungsbedürftig war es für mich anfangs, gemeinsam mit Frauen Seminare zu besuchen. In meiner Kindheit und auch in der Schule waren wir nur unter Jungs. Erst in den letzten Jahren werden bei uns im Oman Jungen und Mädchen auch in gemischten Klassen unterrichtet. Den Kontakt mit Mädchen musste ich erst lernen und war anfangs sehr unsicher. Um das zu überbrücken, habe ich meine Kommilitoninnen erst so behandelt wie meine besten Freunde. Mit diesem kleinen Trick bin ich ganz gut klargekommen. Heute ist mir der Kontakt und sind mir auch Freundschaften mit Frauen in meinem Alter ganz selbstverständlich.

Wenn ich darüber nachdenke, was „typisch deutsch" ist, fallen mir die Pünktlichkeit und das Wetter ein. Ich musste mich schon daran gewöhnen, dass in Deutschland so streng nach Terminen gelebt wird. Bei uns im Oman hat keiner über Monate im Voraus Termine im Kalender, wir sind da wesentlich spontaner und entspannter. Ja, und das feucht-kalte Wetter vor allem im Winter hat mir am Anfang schon zu schaffen gemacht.

You sometimes hear that Germans aren't considered to be that friendly or hospitable. I can confirm that this is not the case. As soon as they trust you, and you can be honest with each other, the Germans are very hospitable and generous. During my seven years in Marburg, I frequently visited German friends, and I spent three Christmases with German families. Christmas is a special festivity that you usually only want to celebrate with relatives or people you are close to. I always liked to experience the differences between the various cities. I visited Hamburg, Bremen and Munich. Each city has its unique characteristics – sometimes it's a harbour, sometimes a historical city centre, or sometimes a river, such as the Isar in Munich. I really like the diversity.

At first, I had to get used to attending classes with women. In my childhood, and also in school, there were only boys. Only in recent years have boys and girls been taught together in co-ed classes in Oman. I had to learn how to interact with girls, and I was really insecure in the beginning. In order to overcome that, I treated my female classmates as if they were my best friends. This approach helped me. Today, interacting with women my

> *„Ich habe die Deutschen als gastfreundlich und großzügig erlebt"*
>
> *"I have found Germans to be hospitable and generous"*

own age, and being friends with them, is natural to me. If I think about what is 'typically German'. I think of punctuality and the weather. I had to get used to the fact that in Germany, appointments are a big part of life. No one in Oman has appointments in their calendar months in advance. We are far more spontaneous and relaxed. And the weather. It's damp and cold in Germany, especially in winter, which really got to me in the beginning.

From Mountain Village to the Bustle of a German City

Manchmal werde ich gefragt, wie ich mich durch mein Leben im Ausland verändert habe. Ich bin bestimmt durch den Kontakt mit Menschen aus verschiedenen Kulturen offener geworden. Es ist auch ganz normal für mich geworden, mit anderen über persönliche Meinungen zu diskutieren. Das mache ich natürlich jetzt auch, wenn ich bei meiner Familie bin. Das ist für meine Eltern bestimmt nicht immer ganz einfach. Aber so bin ich jetzt nun einmal.

Was kommt nach dem Abschluss – diese Frage habe ich mir immer wieder gestellt. Ich schwankte zwischen einer Karriere in meiner neuen Heimat in Europa und dem Land, mit dem ich mich fest verwurzelt fühle – dem Sultanat Oman.

Deutschland ist schon schön mit seinen grünen Wäldern und Wiesen, seiner vielseitigen Kultur und seinen schier unendlichen Möglichkeiten, seine Interessen zu leben. Aber letztlich kenne ich kein Land, das an den Oman heranreicht – fast 1500 Kilometer Küste, viel Sonne, die wunderbare Wüste und nie haben wir es weit bis zum Meer. Was braucht man mehr? Deshalb habe ich mich entschieden, nach Abschluss meines Studiums zurück in den Oman zu gehen.

Ich nehme viel Positives mit zurück in meine Heimat. Heute kann ich zielorientiert Ideen verwirklichen. Es ist für mich ganz selbstverständlich, zusammen mit anderen im Team zu arbeiten. Unterschiedliche Menschen und Interessen zusammen zu bringen – das ist mir wichtig. Dabei spielt für mich eine gute Kommunikation eine ganz wichtige Rolle.

Ich wünsche mir sehr, dass ich meine Erfahrungen in Deutschland im Oman nutzen kann, um die Beziehung zwischen beiden Ländern weiter zu vertiefen. Beide Kulturen verbindet eine langjährige Freundschaft und ich bin davon überzeugt, dass wir in Zukunft noch viele Projekte gemeinsam erfolgreich auf den Weg bringen werden – ob auf wirtschaftlicher, kultureller oder bildungspolitischer Ebene. Dabei würde ich gerne meinen Beitrag leisten."

Sometimes people ask me how I have changed having lived abroad. I am sure that I grew to be more open-minded as a result of having contact with people from different cultures. It's also now very normal for me to discuss personal opinions. Of course, these days, I do that all the time when I spend time with my family. It's probably not easy for my parents, but it's the way I am now.

What will happen after graduation? I asked myself this very question over and over again. I was torn between a career in my new home in Europe or in the country of my roots – the Sultanate of Oman.

Sure, Germany is beautiful with its green forests and meadows, its multifaceted culture and its endless opportunities to live out your interests. But in the end, I can't think of any country to rival Oman. It has almost 1,500 kilometres of coastline, lots of sunshine, an amazing desert, and you are never too far from the sea. What more could you ask for? That's why I decided to return to Oman after I graduated.

There are many positive things I took with me when I went home. Today, I am very goal-oriented when implementing my ideas. Working in a team is essential for me. It is important to bring different people and interests together, and effective communication is particularly important.

I sincerely hope that my experience in Germany can be useful to Oman, and can strengthen the relationship between the two countries. Both cultures are connected by many years of friendship, and I am sure that we will successfully work on many joint projects – economic, cultural or educational – in the future. I would love to contribute to that."

Gruppenfoto bei einem Empfang der Botschaft Omans in Berlin, rechts im Bild: Khalid Alfahdi.
Group photo at a reception at Oman's embassy in Berlin, on the right: Khalid Alfahdi.

Über den DAAD

Der DAAD (Deutscher Akademischer Austausch-dienst) bietet Studierenden und Wissenschaftlern aus dem Oman insgesamt 76 Fördermöglichkeiten – von Research Fellowship Programmen über Forschungsaufenthalte bis zu Hochschulsommerkursen in Deutschland.

Weitere Informationen unter
www.daad.de

On the DAAD

The DAAD (German Academic Exchange Service) offers a total of 76 types of sponsorship to students, scholars and scientists from Oman, ranging from research fellowship programmes and research stays, to summer schools in Germany.

For more information, visit
www.daad.de.

Zeltstoff statt Plastik

Tent Fabric
instead of Plastic

Frauen aus Sidab: Ein soziales Projekt
bringt Frauen Unterstützung – mit deutscher Unterstützung

A social project provides income for women,
with support from Germany

قماش خيمة بدلاً من البلاستيك
برنامج اجتماعي يساعد النساء في الحصول على دخل –
بمساعدة ألمانية

إن نساء صيادي السمك في سداب هن سيدات يحصلن على
دخل مادي من خلال مشروع "سيدات سداب" وذلك منذ
خمسة عشرة عام. هن يصنعن ويبعن حقائب ذات ألوان
زاهية ذات التطريز العُماني والمساطر البراقة، وأيضاً ذات
رسوم يدوية للزبائن الفضوليين. تقديم الوجبات المحضرة من
قبلهن كالحمص والفتوش والسلطة. إن الضيوف والسواح
الأجانب ومنهم كثير من المانيا يأتون إلى هذا المنزل في
قرية سداب جنوب مطرح، حيث يطبخون ويتبادلون
الأحاديث مع النساء. تدير السيدة لميس منذ فترة وجيزة
مشروع "مجموعة نساء سداب للخياطة". إن هدفهن هو
تعميم هذا المشروع بشكل واسع في جميع أرجاء سلطنة
عُمان لتقوية النساء وتأمين دخل لهن يساعدهن في حياتهن.

Dank der Aufträge verdienen vielen der Frauen das erste Mal in ihrem Leben eigenes Geld.
Thanks to the demand for their products many of the women are earning their own money for the first time in their lives.

Bei ihnen gibt es farbenfrohe Taschen mit traditionellen Omani-Mustern oder glitzernden Troddeln, auf Wunsch dekorative Handbemalung für neugierige Gäste oder leckere hausgemachte Gerichte wie Hummus und Fattoush Salad: Die Fischerfrauen von Sidab verdienen dank des sozialen Projektes „Sidab Women" ihr eigenes Geld – seit rund 15 Jahren, Lamis Al Kiyumi ist ihre Managerin und erzählt im Interview, wie ihre Arbeit das Selbstbewusstsein der Frauen stärkt.

Lamis, was zeichnet die Sidab Women Sewing Group aus?
Lamis Al Kiyumi: Zu uns kommen Frauen aus einfachen Verhältnissen. Wir helfen ihnen, mit Näharbeiten oder Kochen ihr eigenes Geld zu verdienen. Das Projekt wurde 2004 von Badriya Al Siyabi gegründet. Viele der Frauen verfügen dank der Arbeit bei uns das erste Mal über selbst verdientes Geld. Das macht sie stolz und stärkt ihr Selbstbewusstsein. Sie können ihre Familie unterstützen. Manche sind auch einfach glücklich darüber, sich selbst etwas Schönes leisten oder andere mit kleinen Geschenken bedenken zu können. Außerdem lernen sie

They make colourful bags with traditional Omani patterns and shiny tassels. On request, they do henna painting on the hands of curious tourists or prepare tasty home-made dishes such as hummus or fattoush salad. For around 15 years, the fisherwomen of Sidab have been earning their own income thanks to the "Sidab Women" social project. Lamis Al Kiyumi is its manager, and in this interview, she talks about how the project has strengthened the women's self-confidence.

Lamis, what makes the Sidab Women's Sewing Group special?
Lamis Al Kiyumi: The women who come to us are from modest backgrounds. We help them earn their own money by sewing or cooking. The project was launched in 2004 by Badriya Al Siyabi. Thanks to the work they do with us, many of these women have their own incomes for the first time. They're very proud of this and it strengthens their self-confidence. They can support their families. Some are just happy to be able to afford

Tent Fabric instead of Plastic

unter Anleitung neue Fähigkeiten, was sie in ihrer persönlichen Entwicklung voranbringt.

Was war die Ausgangsidee des Projekts?

Am Anfang stand die Idee, Einkaufstaschen aus strapazierfähigem Zeltstoff als Alternative zu Plastikbeuteln zu nähen – robust, immer wieder verwendbar und dekorativ. Im Laufe der Zeit kamen neue Produkte wie Überzüge für Wasserflaschen, Kissenbezüge, Handtaschen, Clutches oder Rucksäcke dazu. Für unsere unterschiedlichen Artikel verwenden wir ausschließlich Materialien aus der Region. Manche Designs sind schlicht und klassisch, andere modern. Neu im Sortiment sind Netze, die zum Einkauf von Obst und Gemüse gedacht sind. Sie sind leicht, können unendlich oft genutzt werden und sollen auch dazu beitragen, Plastiktüten zu reduzieren. Die Produkte können an den traditionellen Verzierungen erkannt werden. Alle Frauen sind eingeladen, eigene Vorschläge für neue Produkte einzubringen.

Wo ist das Projekt zu Hause?

In Sidab haben wir ein gemütliches Haus, in dem die Frauen an den Nähmaschinen arbeiten. Manche tun dies auch zu Hause. Die Frauen, die kochen können, bieten Cateringservice an. Alle Gerichte werden nach typischen Landesrezepten frisch zubereitet. Im Haus ist Platz für

something nice for themselves or to give little presents to others. They are also taught new skills, which furthers their personal growth.

What was the starting point of the project?

At first, we had the idea to sew some shopping bags from durable tent fabric to serve as an alternative to plastic bags. They were sturdy, reusable and decorative. Over time, new products were added, such as covers for water bottles, pillowcases, handbags, clutches and backpacks. We use only locally sourced materials for all these different articles. Some designs are simple and traditional, others are modern. The newest addition to our assortment are string bags for when you buy fruit or vegetables. They are light-weight, long-lasting, and reduce the use of plastic bags.

Where is the project's home?

We have a comfortable house in Sidab, where the women work on sewing machines. Some also do the work at home. Women who are able to cook offer catering services. All meals are freshly prepared following typical, traditional recipes. The building can accommodate up to 20 guests who want to learn about Omani traditions. German tourist groups are continuously among them. When they arrive at the house, visitors are greeted by

Gäste nehmen gerne eine Erinnerung an ihren Besuch in Sidab mit nach Hause – hier eine Tunika.
Guests are happy to take home a souvenir of their visit to Sidab, such as a tunic.

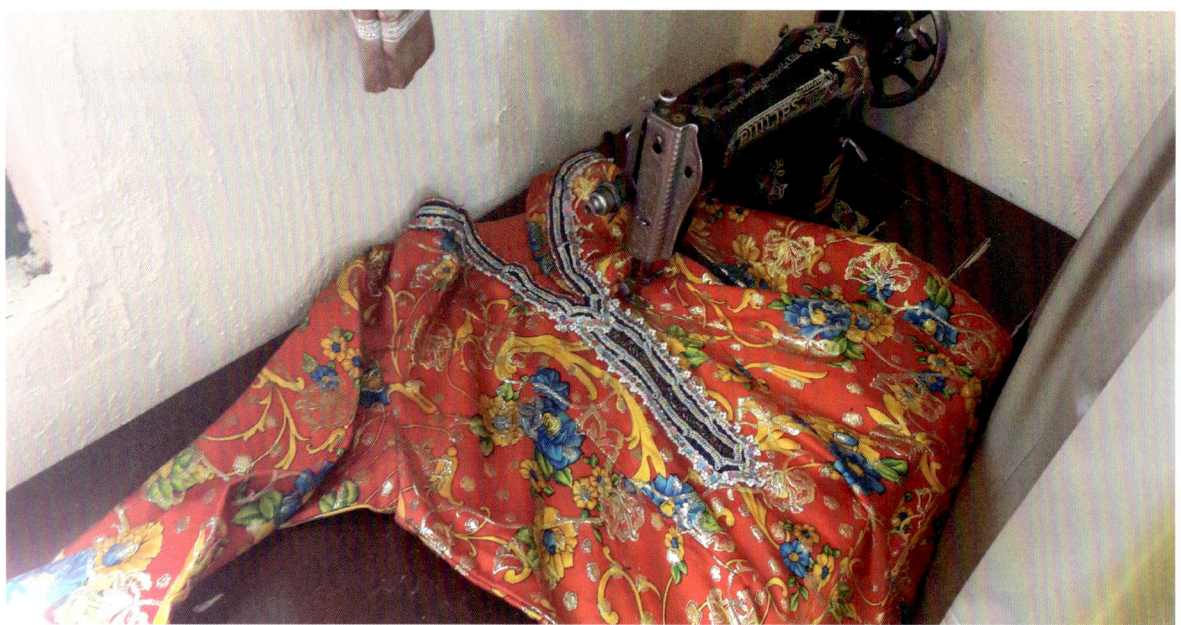

Zeltstoff statt Plastik

bis zu 20 Gäste, die omanische Traditionen kennenlernen möchten. Darunter sind auch immer wieder deutsche Reisegruppen. Wenn sie kommen, duftet unser Haus einladend nach Weihrauch. Wir sitzen dann zusammen – natürlich nach Landessitte auf Bodenkissen, reden miteinander und die Kinder tollen herum. Und natürlich gibt es omanischen Kaffee, den wir gemeinsam zubereiten. Manchmal laden wir auch eine Künstlerin ein, die feine Muster mit Hennafarbe auf Hände zaubert. Unsere deutschen Besucher genießen es immer sehr, einen so lebendigen Eindruck von der überlieferten Lebensweise zu bekommen.

Feiern Sie auch Feste?
Ja, eines der traditionellen omanischen Feste ist Hoal Hoal. Das wird gefeiert, wenn ein Kind ein Jahr alt wird. Es wird mit Münzen und Süßigkeiten beschenkt und andere Kinder tanzen ausgelassen herum.

Wie wird das Projekt finanziert?
Wir haben Sponsoren wie die Oman Oil Company, die uns unterstützen. Auch die Bank of Maskat und Shell haben uns finanziell schon geholfen.

Bleibt das Projekt in Sidab oder sind ähnliche Initiativen in anderen Orten geplant?
Wir werden an anderen Standorten ähnliche Projekte aufbauen – zum Beispiel im Süden in Salalah oder in Duqm. Wir möchten noch mehr Frauen stärken und auch die Idee weitertragen, dass wiederverwendbare Taschen viel besser sind als die Unmengen von Plastiktüten, die unserer Umwelt schaden.

the inviting aroma of incense. We then sit together on floor cushions, as is the local custom. We talk and the children play around us. Of course, we also serve Omani coffee, which we prepare together. In addition, we sometimes invite an artist who paints elaborate henna decorations on our hands. Our German visitors always enjoy experiencing our traditional way of life.

Do you also have celebrations?
Yes, one of the traditional Omani celebrations is Hoal Hoal. It takes place when a child turns one. The child receives coins and sweets, and the other children have fun dancing around.

How is the project funded?
We have sponsors who support us, such as Oman Oil. The Bank of Muscat and Shell have also provided financial assistance.

Will the project remain only in Sidab or are there plans for similar initiatives at other locations?
We want to set up similar projects at other locations; for example, in the south in Salalah or in Duqm. We want to empower even more women and spread the idea that reusable bags are much better than the vast quantities of environmentally-unfriendly plastic bags currently in use.

Sidab Women's Sewing Group, House 101,
Line 8905, Sidab
Sidabwomen.om@gmail.com
Infos zum Projekt auf instagram@sidab_women

Sidab Women's Sewing Group, House 101,
Line 8905, Sidab.
Sidabwomen.om@gmail.com.
Info on the project at instagram@sidab_women

Tent Fabric instead of Plastic

Epilog

Was fasziniert euch so sehr am Oman? Das wurden und werden wir immer wieder gefragt, wenn wir unser Buch vorstellen. Erst langsam rückt das Sultanat ins Bewusstsein der Deutschen. Kaum jemand weiß, dass die beiden Länder eine über 50-jährige konsularische Beziehung pflegen.

Wir, die beiden Herausgeberinnen, haben den Oman gemeinsam per Zufall entdeckt – als wir uns einen Traum erfüllten und in zwei Monaten in großen Schritten einmal um die ganze Welt reisten. Oman war 2015 das erste Land auf unserer Route; von unserem auf Weltreisen spezialisierten Reisebüro als sicherstes Land im arabischen Raum empfohlen. Wir blieben weniger als eine Woche – und verliebten uns am zweiten Tag.

Mit allen Sinnen tasteten wir uns in diese für uns neue Welt, die wir zunächst vor allem als spannenden und exotischen Orient wahrnahmen. Der allseits präsente Weihrauchduft, das farbenprächtige Getümmel im Souk Matrahs, die offenen und zuvorkommenden Einheimischen, die sandfarbene Weite des Hinterlandes, die rauen Bergketten und die scheinbar unendlichen Strände am türkisfarbenen Meer – all das hinterließ einen bleibenden Eindruck und wir wollten mehr über dieses Stückchen Erde und seine Menschen erfahren.

Nach unserer Rückkehr beschäftigten wir uns intensiver mit dem Oman, reisten immer wieder dorthin. Wir lernten mehr und mehr Menschen, Unternehmen und Organisationen kennen und staunten, wie viele Beziehungen zwischen Deutschland und dem Oman existieren: Ein langjähriger Austausch zwischen Schulen und jede Menge Know-how-Transfer in den Bereichen Wirtschaft, Wissenschaft, Gesundheit, Kultur und Medien, in Deutschland studierende Omaner und Deutsche, die sich im Oman beruflich neu orientieren – es gab da noch viel mehr, da waren wir uns sicher. Als Journalistinnen wollten wir diese persönlichen Erfolgsgeschichten erzählen.

Oman ist ein Land, das in Deutschland in den Medien so gut wie nie auftaucht. Die politischen Schlagzeilen werden beherrscht von den Konfliktherden dieser Welt. Wir hörten von den friedensstiftenden Vermittlungen des Sultans bei Krisen in der arabischen Welt. Eine Haltung, die unserer Einschätzung nach weltweit Nachahmer finden sollte.
Als Menschen, die bewusst am politischen Leben teilnehmen, waren für uns persönlich die vielen konkreten Projekte ein Zeichen, dass Menschen unterschiedlicher Kulturen mit unterschiedlichen Religionen friedlich zusammenleben und erfolgreich zusammenarbeiten können, wenn das Miteinander geprägt ist von Respekt und der Bereitschaft, voneinander zu lernen.

Wir brauchen weltweit neue konstruktive Ansätze, um unserer gemeinsamen Heimat, der verletzlichen Erde, eine Zukunft zu ermöglichen. Politische Analysen, Diskussionen, wissenschaftliche Analysen, Aufklärung und moralische Appelle – all das ist wichtig, um das Bewusstsein der Menschen weiterzuentwickeln.

Wir als Journalistinnen glauben aber auch an die Kraft von Kommunikation und die Wirkung von guten Vorbildern. Geschichten aus dem Leben können als Beispiele Impulse geben und erklären, wie es gehen kann. Ganz real, ganz einfach, ganz nachvollziehbar – so entstand die Idee eines Lesebuchs.

Dafür haben wir 25 Geschichten aus einem breiten Themenspektrum zusammengetragen. Sie erzählen in Worten und Bildern von Aufbruch und Neubeginn, Vertrauen und Aufmerksamkeit, von Innovation und beständigen Werten – und der Bereitschaft, die Hürden des Lebens als Aufforderung zu neuen Lösungen zu begreifen. Auf unserer Website www.omani-german-coop.com kommen die bewegten Bilder hinzu – denn die Geschichten gehen ja weiter, und das wollen wir auch zeigen.

Wir wünschen Ihnen viel Lese- und Sehvergnügen!

G. Brähler   N. Plankermann

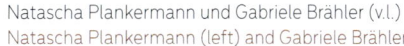

Natascha Plankermann und Gabriele Brähler (v.l.)
Natascha Plankermann (left) and Gabriele Brähler

Why are you so fascinated with Oman? That's the question we've been asked time and time again whenever we tell people about our book. Awareness of the Sultanate is only growing slowly here in Germany. Hardly anyone knows that the two countries have nurtured diplomatic relations for more than 50 years.

We, the two editors, discovered Oman together by chance when we fulfilled a dream and travelled around the world in leaps and bounds over two months. Oman was the first country on our itinerary in 2015. Our travel agent, a specialist in world travel, told us it is the safest country in the Arab world. We stayed less than a week and fell in love on the second day.

We dove into this new world of the Orient with all our senses; at first, it was exciting and exotic. The ever-present smell of incense, the vibrant hustle and bustle in Mutrah's souk, the open and obliging locals, the sandy expanse of the hinterland, the rugged mountain ranges and the seemingly endless beaches lining the turquoise sea. This all left a lasting impression and we wanted to learn more about this corner of the earth and its people.

After our return to Germany, we occupied ourselves more extensively with Oman, travelling there repeatedly. We got to know more and more people, companies and organisations, and were amazed how many relationships exist between Germany and Oman: a long-standing school exchange programme; lots of knowledge transfer in the fields of economics, science, health, culture and media; Omanis studying in Germany and Germans looking for a new professional direction in Oman. There was much more, we were sure of that. As journalists, we wanted to tell these personal stories of success.

Oman is a country that hardly ever appears in the German media. Political headlines are dominated by the world's hotbeds of conflict. We heard about the Sultan's peace-making efforts in times of crisis in the Arab world. An attitude that we believe should be emulated worldwide.

As people who make a concerted effort to participate in political life, we personally see the many German-Omani projects as real proof that people of different cultures with different religions can live together peacefully and work together successfully if there is mutual respect and a willingness to learn from each other.

We need new constructive approaches worldwide in order to make a future possible for our shared home, the vulnerable Planet Earth. Political analyses, discussions, scientific analyses, enlightenment and moral appeals – all of this is important in order to further develop people's awareness and understanding.

As journalists, we also believe in the power of communication and the influence of good role models. True life stories can serve as examples to inspire and explain how things can work. Totally real, totally simple, totally understandable – this is how the idea of a book came about.

We have put together 25 stories covering a wide range of topics. In words and pictures, they describe new beginnings, trust and consideration, innovations and enduring values, and the willingness to see life's hurdles as a chance for innovative solutions. There are also videos on our website www.omani-german-coop.com because the stories go on and that's what we want to show.

We hope you enjoy reading and watching!

BOSCH
Invented for life

Invented
for life

Simply.
Connected.

Autoren/Fotos Authors/Photos

Die meisten Geschichten in diesem Lesebuch „1001 Freundschaft" stammen aus der Feder der beiden Herausgeberinnen. Wir sind sicher, dass viele deutsch-omanische Beispiele erfolgreicher Begegnungen noch darauf warten, erzählt zu werden. Inshallah werden wir von diesen in einem weiteren Band berichten – oder in bewegten Bilder auf www.omani-german-coop.com.

Most of the stories in this book '1001 Friendships' were written by the two editors. We're certain there's still many stories about frutiful German-Omani encounters waiting to be told. Inshallah, we can tell them in another volume – or on www.omani-german-coop.com.

Gabriele Brähler, gebürtige Rheinländerin und seit rund 30 Jahre in Berlin zu Hause, wollte in jungen Jahren ursprünglich als Piratin die Welt bereisen. Da sich diese Laufbahn allerdings nur schwer umsetzen ließ, entschied sie sich für die Welt der Kommunikation. Heute arbeitet sie als Kommunikations- und Marketingberaterin sowie als Dozentin für Verbände, Organisationen und Unternehmen vor allem in der Gesundheitsbranche. Seit rund 16 Jahren steht sie zudem regelmäßig bei regionalen, nationalen und internationalen Redewettbewerben auf der Bühne. Als Präsentationscoach gibt sie ihre Erfahrungen an Menschen weiter, die aus privaten oder beruflichen Gründen in der Öffentlichkeit sprechen wollen.

Gabriele Brähler is a native oft he Rhineland bus has lived in Berlin for about 30 years. At a young age, she wanted to travel the world as a pirate. However, since this career choice was difficult to take, she chose the world of communication instead. Today, she works as a communications and marketing consultant as well as a lecturer for associations, organisations ans companies, especially in the healthcare sector. For about 16 years, she has also regularly appeared on stage at regional, national and international speaking competitions. As a presentation coach, she passes on her experience to people who want to speak in public for personal or professional reasons.

Texte ab S. 22, 36, 76, 90, 100, 120, 125, 140, 154, 170, 202, 210

Natascha Plankermann, geboren in Wuppertal, verlässt das Rheinland regelmäßig für ihre vielen Reisen – sie wohnt in Düsseldorf und arbeitet dort als Journalistin, Herausgeberin, Moderatorin sowie als Buchautorin und für verschiedene Medien. Wichtige Schwerpunkte: Medizin und Wissenschaftsthemen, Öffentlichkeitsarbeit für die Bundesarbeitsgemeinschaft Gesundheit und Sicherheit bei der Arbeit, Basi. Natascha Plankermann hat eine Fachzeitschrift für Inklusion (Praxis Fördern) verantwortet sowie ein Patientenmagazin ins Leben gerufen. Sie ist Chefredakteurin des „Rhein-Ruhr-Magazins", was sie jedoch nicht daran hindert, aus dem „melting pot" (Schmelztiegel unterschiedlichster Menschen) in Nordrhein-Westfalen in die Ferne zu schweifen, Neues zu entdecken und Pläne zu schmieden.

Natascha Plankermann was born in Wuppertal, but regularly leaves the Rhineland to go on one of her many journeys. She lives in Düsseldorf and works there as a journalist, editor, presenter and book author for various media. Her work focuses on medical and scientific topics, as well as public relations for the Federal Association for Occupational Safety and Health. Natascha was responsible for a journal on inclusion (Praxis Fördern) and launched a patient magazine. She is editor-in-chief of Rhein-Ruhr-Magazin, but this doesn't stop her from leaving the melting pot of North Rhine-Westphalia to go wandering in far-off places, discover new things and to forge new plans.

Texte ab S. 12, 22, 50, 58, 66, 82, 90, 144, 160, 194

UNFORGETTABLE MEMORIES AWAIT YOU.

Oman – a truly spectacular country
where you find authentic arabic experience
in a peaceful surrounding.

Allow Mark Tours to weave together a memorable holiday in Oman – a country
where you seldom need a reason to smile. Oman is diverse in nature, beautiful,
tempestuous and exhilarating. Make a date with nature. Discover something
spectacular at every step. Touch the untouched places. Unleash the adventure in
you. Experience the unique hospitality of a country, revered by the world. Go on,
find what you seek. To get a glimpse of this proud country, call Mark Tours. It's
sure to be an enlightening experience.

Tel: +968 24 786803 / 92886484 | www.mark-oman.com

Autoren/Fotos Authors/Photos

Wir freuen uns, dass unsere Gastautoren weitere Erfahrungen und spannende Perspektiven beigesteuert haben.

We are very grateful for the contributions made by our guest authors on their own fascinating experiences and perspectives.

Joachim Blum, Autor von „Preisgekrönt und am Puls der Zeit" (ab 112).

Joachim Blum, Author of 'Award-winning and with a finger on the pulse of time' (from 112).

Joachim Blum ist internationaler Medienberater und Honorarprofessor im Fach Medienwissenschaft an der Universität Trier.

Joachim Blum, international media consultant and Honorary Professor of Media Studies at the University of Trier.

Rebecca Hahn, Autorin von „Samtnasige und sanfte Wüstentiere" (ab 178).

Rebecca Hahn, Author of 'Gentle Desert Animals with Velvety Noses' (from 178).

Rebecca Hahn reiste Ende 2017 das erste Mal in den Oman, um mehr über Rennkamele, die Wüste und die arabische Kultur zu lernen. Nach zwei Monaten hatte sie Land und Leute so ins Herz geschlossen, dass sie am liebsten gar nicht mehr weggegangen wäre. Kaum zurück in Deutschland zählte sie bereits die Wochen bis zu ihrer Rückkehr in den Oman: Rund ein Jahr später besuchte sie ihre Gastfamilie dort erneut und fühlte sich schon wie zuhause. Seitdem freut sich die 25-Jährige darauf, ihre omanischen Freunde auch einmal in Deutschland willkommen zu heißen. Dort macht sie ihren Master in Physischer Geographie in Frankfurt am Main und arbeitet als freiberufliche Wissenschaftsjournalistin.

Rebecca Hahn travelled to Oman for the first time in late 2017 to learn more about race camels, the desert and Arab culture. After two months, the country and its people had become so close to her heart that she didn't want to leave. As soon as she was back in Germany, she started counting the weeks until her return to Oman. About a year later, she visited her host family again and felt immediately at home again. Since then, the 25-year-old is looking forward to when she can welcome her her Omani friends to Germany. She is currently doing her Master's degree in Physical Geography in Frankfurt and works as a freelance science journalist.

Bruno Kaiser, Co-Autor von „Reisen im Oman – Aufbruch im Morgenland" (with Natascha Plankermann, ab 22).

Bruno Kaiser, Co-author of 'Exploring Oman – Dawn of the Orient' (with Natascha Plankermann, from 22).

Bruno Kaiser ist langjähriger Präsident der Deutsch-Omanischen Gesellschaft.

Bruno Kaiser was President of the German-Omani Association for many years.

Corinna Kuhs, Autorin von "Im Paradies der Taucher" (ab 44)

Corinna Kuhs, Author of 'A Diver's Paradise' (from 44).

Corinna Kuhs lebt und arbeitet als freie Journalistin mit Schwerpunkt Reise und Tauchthemen in Düsseldorf. Zudem ist sie Tauchlehrerin und kennt die Unterwasserwelt des Oman: Mehrere Monate lang lebte sie in Qantab. Ihre Lieblingstauchplätze sind das Wrack Al Munassir und Jissah Point.

Corinna Kuhs lives in Dusseldorf and works as a freelance journalist. She specialises in travel and diving topics. She is also a diving instructor and knows the underwater world of Oman well after living in Qantab for several months. Her favorite dive sites are the Al Munassir wreck and Jissah Point.

Autoren/Fotos Authors/Photos

Georg Popp, Autor von „Juma Al Maskari und Georg Popp: Freunde fürs Leben" (ab 186) und Toleranz, Verständnis und Koexistenz: Omans Botschaft des Islam (ab 132). Der Künstler und Fotograf Georg Popp beschäftigt sich seit über 25 Jahren auf sehr intensive und persönliche Weise mit dem Sultanat Oman und seinen Menschen.

Georg Popp, Author of 'Juma Al Maskari and Grog Popp: Friends for Life'(from 186) and ‚Tolerance, Understanding and Coexistence: Oman's message of Islam' (from 132). The artist and photographer Georg Popp has work closely with the Sultanate of Oman and its people for over 25 years.

Viele Fotos haben die Herausgeberinnen auf ihren Reisen gemacht. Weitere Bildquellen:
Many photos were taken by the editors on their travels. Additional picture sources:

Arab Adventures (28, 50, 53, 54, 57, U4); Khalid Alfahdi (Titelmotiv, 206, 209); Lubna Abdullah Al Balushi (120); GaPa Tourismus_Emanuel Nöhmeier (197), OakHill (66, 69, 70, 72/73); GUTech (26/27); Rebecca Hahn (178, 181, 182/183, 185 IATI: 154, 159); ITHRAA (76, 8); Bruno Kaiser (20); Friedrich Klütsch (90, 93, 94, 96, 97, 98, 99); Manfred Klupsch (2, 100, 103, 104, 106/107, 108, 111); Corinna Kuhs (44, 47, 49); Verena Kyselka (126, 129, 130); Dr. Jörg Lux (170, 175); Ralph Matzerath (62, 63); Olms Verlag (140); Times of Oman (30, 34, 36, 40, 42/43; Graphiken 112, 115, 118); Oxea (58, 64); Georg Popp / Arabia Felix (135, 136, 139, 186, 189); Florian Schröder (147, 150, 153); Dr. Conrad Schmidt (167); Uwe Sengele (198/199); Eva und Pius Schmidt (144, 149), Titel: Adobe Stock #272499478 © Zamurovic

---

Tipp zum Weiterlesen
Den umgekehrten Weg wie die Herausgeberinnen dieses Buchs schlug Salme, die Tochter des Sultans von Oman und Sansibar und einer tscherkessischen Sklavin, im Jahr 1866 ein: Sie verließ seinerzeit heimlich die Insel Sansibar, um den Hamburger Kaufmann Heinrich Ruete zu heiraten, dem sie in seine Heimat folgte. Als 1886 ihre Memoiren erschienen, erregte das Buch große Aufmerksamkeit und wurde sogleich in mehrere Sprachen übersetzt. Salme erzählt vom exotischen und turbulenten Alltag in Sultanspalast und Harem im 19. Jahrhundert.

Tip for further reading
In 1866, Salme, the daughter of the Sultan of Oman and Zanzibar and a Circassian slave, took the opposite path: she secretly left the island of Zanzibar to marry the Hamburg merchant Heinrich Ruete, whom she followed to his homeland. When her memoirs were published in 1886, the book attracted great attention and was immediately translated into several languages. Salme writes of the exotic and turbulent everyday life in the Sultan's Palace and harem in the 19th century.

Emily Ruete, geb. Prinzessin Salme von Oman und Sansibar: Leben im Sultanspalast: Memoiren aus dem 19. Jahrhundert Verlag, Cep Europäische Verlagsanstalt, ISBN-10: 3863930436, 24,90 Euro.

Special thanks to...

Basem Hannouneh, Arabic translator
Peter Love, English translator
Birgit Woitke, graphic design (k2g.de)
Nina Plankermann, graphic design / Cover
Dr. Mohammed Al Hassan, Ministry of Foreign Affairs of the Sultanate of Oman
Hind Al Barwani, International relations, Ministry of Foreign Affairs of the Sultanate of Oman
Saif Al Jahwari, Counselor, Embassy of the Sultanate of Oman

Hans-Christian Freiherr von Reibnitz,
German Ambassador in the Sultanate of Oman until 2017
Etihad Airways
Abdul
Amur
Tarzan
... and to all who supported us